21 DAYS IN SWANSEA

Andy Botterill

APS Books
Yorkshire

Also By Andy Botterill

An Appointment With God

At Heart A Romantic

Miscellaneous Thoughts

Sick Note & Scrapbook

Welcome Lonely Hearts

Years Spinning By Out Of Control

APS Books,

The Stables Field Lane, Aberford, West Yorkshire, LS25 3AE

APS Books is a subsidiary of the APS Publications imprint

www.andrewsparke.com

First published worldwide by APS Books in 2025

A catalogue record for this book is available from the British Library

Day One (Monday)

Edward Chapman was on his way to Swansea, by train. He'd picked up his connection from London at Didcot Parkway, having made the short journey from Oxford, where he lived. In fact, he lived in a small village just outside Oxford, but you don't need to know the name of that. It isn't especially relevant at this point, if indeed it's relevant at all. What is perhaps relevant is he owned a big house with his wife and was quite well-known in the village where they lived. He was a man of some substance, recently retired and financially comfortably placed. He'd done very well for himself. He wasn't short of money. They didn't go without. But now unusually he was on a train to Swansea. It wasn't unusual for him to travel by train, but generally in the opposite direction, into London, where he'd worked in *The City* as a financial trader and speculator or investment banker, as he called it. He'd played the markets, invested cleverly, and been rewarded amply in return. He'd promised himself he'd retire at sixty and he'd done exactly that. He'd retired shortly after his sixtieth birthday, just a month or two earlier, even though the money was still coming in, both during the good times and the bad ones. He'd earned enough never to be short for the rest of his life. He'd live out his days in relative wealth. There was no point being greedy, however. It was time to kick back a little, to put his feet up and relax. That at least had been the idea just a month or so before, when he'd left his place of work for the last time. Now, on a kind of whim, he was travelling west towards South Wales. But more of that in a bit.

Edward had done all the usual things that he would have done when travelling to London. He'd got himself a coffee and a newspaper at Didcot Parkway station. He'd sipped his coffee, whilst he sat waiting on the platform. Only this time he carried a small travel bag with him. The train had been on time, at least within a minute or two. He'd waited patiently to get on. He wore a white shirt, brown trousers, black shoes, and a lightweight raincoat. He wasn't so very differently attired to his working days, except he had no tie, and his sports jacket was folded neatly away in his bag. Edward was of medium height and build. He was slightly overweight, like most middle-aged men, and kept his hair cut short, as he'd noticed it begin to slowly recede and thin once he'd hit his fifties. It had been thick and strong once as a young man and he'd worn it long accordingly, but those days were well and truly gone.

Edward found himself a seat by the window. He sat down and let out a barely audible sigh of relief. The train wasn't especially busy. Why would it be? It was the middle of the day. He laid out his coffee and newspaper on the table in front of him, and placed a book beside them, which he might read at some point if he got bored on the journey. It would be good to get away, he thought. He needed it. It had been a while, too long in truth. He was still thinking about that once in a lifetime, post-retirement trip somewhere hot and exotic, but hadn't got round to planning it yet. He'd intended to take such a break with his wife in the coming summer. It might never happen now. Instead, he was taking an impromptu trip to Swansea, the city of his old university, where he'd been an undergraduate some forty years or so years earlier. Now he was going back for the first time since he couldn't remember when. He'd gone back from time to time after first graduating, but the visits had gradually become less frequent, until eventually they'd stopped altogether. How long it had been now, he wasn't quite sure. It must have been around thirty years and perhaps longer.

Edward wondered what Swansea would be like. He wondered whether he would recognise it, even though it had once been his home, for three years. It was bound to have changed in the years since. How could it not have done? Just as he'd changed too. He was a very different person to the confident, some might say arrogant, young man who'd graduated at the age of twenty-one. Even then, he'd somehow known he would get on. He couldn't wait to get back to the Home Counties, where he'd come from, and make his way to London. He'd gone into investment banking. It wasn't necessarily his chosen path. It was a career that chose him. In part, he was bowing to parental pressure to have a lucrative job, and everything that came with it, including the security, material possessions and home comforts it provided. Edward had a flair for investment from the very start. He was an economics graduate after all. What else was he going to do? He was very successful at what he did. Still part of him, an unfulfilled part, had always yearned to be something else; perhaps an academic, a museum curator, a writer, or an artist, perhaps a gallery owner. He'd just never had the chance. He couldn't complain, however. Life had been very good to him. It had treated him well, better than most.

In short, his job had made him quite rich. Now, he had the leisure time to enjoy it if he so wished to do so.

The train sped along the tracks. It was a fine spring day outside. The sky was blue, with barely a cloud to spoil it. Edward knew that was likely to change as they neared Wales, where the weather was prone to change quickly from sunshine to rain. As they reached the outskirts of Bristol, it grew a little darker overhead. Edward was unconcerned. The weather didn't really matter to him. He had other, more pressing things on his mind. At the Severn Tunnel, the train slowed momentarily almost to a halt, to let another train ahead of it pass through first. It took around five minutes to travel the four and a half miles under the waters of the River Severn. It was part of the journey Edward remembered well, from his many trips back and forth along the same line as a student. When the train emerged on the other side, Edward was finally in Wales.

The countryside was just as he remembered it. To his surprise, he could even remember the Welsh names of the cities and towns the train passed through, Newport, Cardiff, Bridgend, Port Talbot, Neath and finally Swansea. It all came flooding back to him with an unerring familiarity, as if he'd never been away. He was particularly familiar with the section of the line from Cardiff to Swansea. Cardiff had been the destination for many a Saturday afternoon shopping visit in his student days. He'd taken great pleasure in the boutique shops of the legendary, historic arcades there. Even that was history to him now. It had been a while since he'd been to that great city either.

You might wonder why Edward was going to Swansea. He'd left in a relative hurry earlier that morning, not long after his younger wife, Alice, had headed out for work at her Oxford publisher's office, where she was a PA, just as she always did. Edward hadn't told her he was going. In fact, he'd decided on impulse after she'd gone. He'd just left a note on the kitchen table, which she'd read no doubt when she got home. The note had simply said not to worry and that he'd be in touch in due course. Afterwards, Edward had quickly packed a few belongings together and calmly walked out the front door. He'd got a taxi to the station and now he was on a train. His fellow passengers were entirely oblivious to his concerns and his reasons for being there, just as he was to theirs.

Alice was actually Edward's second wife. He'd been married before. His first wife had died of cancer. Her name was Angela. She'd only been forty-five. They'd had two children together, Victoria and Henry, now both grown up. Angela's death had been hard to take. It had affected him deeply. They'd been very much in love. After that, Edward had retreated into himself, in quiet, dignified mourning. He'd gone into his shell and had found it difficult to come out again. He'd been on his own for five years, being a father to Victoria and Henry, as they slowly evolved from young teenagers to adults. Eventually, he'd met Alice. They'd been introduced by friends at a dinner party and had been together ever since. They hadn't had more children. Edward wouldn't have minded, but Alice didn't want them. She was too career-minded for that, she said. Besides, he had two already. Wasn't that enough? She was too busy for kids of her own, she claimed. Too selfish might have been more accurate, Edward thought.

He realised Alice had married him for his money and his standing in society, not his looks or personality. She was ten years younger than him. He could give her everything she'd ever wanted, a big house, expensive new cars, luxury clothes and jewellery, holidays abroad, whenever they liked. Oh, it was a fine lifestyle indeed. Why wouldn't she grab it with both hands when she had the chance? She'd done exactly that of course, and who could blame her? Edward was a highly respected pillar of the local community. He and his wife were guests of honour at just about everything going. The freebies were just too good to turn down. Alice loved them. Now sadly, in the blink of an eye, it had all turned sour.

The weekend had started well enough and as it usually did. The couple had enjoyed a gentle game of doubles at their local tennis club in the morning. They'd been playing another pair, who were not only fellow members but friends as well. After the game, they'd all gone for a pub lunch and taken a leisurely river walk, before retiring to their respective houses for a quiet evening of television. Edward had got up late on the Sunday morning, mowed the lawn, before heading to watch a local, early-season cricket match on his own. It was afterwards that things had started to unravel and go wrong. Edward had been travelling back from the ground and taken a different route to the one he normally did. That was when he spotted them, hand in hand. He'd done a double-take at first. He'd even had to stop the car to look back, just to make sure. There was no doubt. It was Alice, with a young, handsome work colleague he knew to be called Paul. They were emerging from a restaurant. They didn't notice Edward driving past. They were too immersed in each other. They looked like they didn't have a care in the world.

Edward was in a state of shock. He felt like his whole life and everything in it had fallen apart in an instant. It had crumbled before his very eyes. He considered following the couple and having it out with them, but his thoughts were too jumbled and confused. Besides, what good would it do? Instead, he drove home slowly in silence. He'd long since forgotten the score of the match he'd just seen. Unusually, his team had won for once. He no longer cared. It no longer seemed important. It seemed trivial by comparison. In the comparative safety of his study, he poured himself a large whisky. He would have lit a cigarette if he had one, but he'd given up smoking years ago. There was nothing for it but just to sit and await Alice's return. He confronted her of course. The worst thing was she didn't even deny it once he started pressing her for the sordid details.

'You're late,' he commented curtly when she finally walked through the door.

'Yes, I was a bit held up,' she replied, walking straight past him.

'What were you doing?' he asked.

'Nothing special, just a bit of shopping,' she said.

'Look, I saw you Alice, with Paul from your office,' Edward said, accusingly.

'Indeed,' Alice responded, deciding perhaps it was time to pour herself a drink too. 'Well, you were bound to find out eventually, I suppose,' she added, with a resigned tone in her voice.

'I suppose I was,' Edward agreed.

'It can hardly come as a complete surprise,' she continued. 'What did you expect? You were away at work a lot,' she pointed out.

It was true. It wasn't a total shock to him, yet it was a shock to him at the same time. How could he have been so oblivious? How could he have been so imperceptive? How could he have been so naïve and stupid? It all made perfect sense now. It was so obvious in retrospect, her working late in the office, the occasional weekends away for book launches and promotions, the unexplained absences, and other things he'd chosen to overlook. He guessed he hadn't wanted to know the truth. He'd turned a blind eye to the small hints and clues, that could have led to suspicion and further interrogation.

'Then there's the age gap, Edward. It's become more apparent of late. I'm still a comparatively young woman. You've not been well. Yet, I still have needs you've been ignoring,' Alice said.

Edward nodded. That was also true. He'd had minor health niggles that had hastened his retirement, or at least confirmed to him he was doing the right thing in stopping at sixty. An excessive fondness for a scotch and soda after work or a large red wine with an over-indulgent lunch had led to mild heart arrythmia. It wasn't fatal, more an inconvenience and irritation in truth. Besides, he was feeling rather better now, since receiving treatment and giving up work. He'd been able to return to exercise and gentle sport, but he perhaps hadn't shown Alice as much attention as he should have. He was regretting that now. Why wouldn't younger men like Paul be interested in her? She was an attractive woman. And it wasn't hard to see what Alice saw in him. He was young and handsome and was gaining a growing reputation as a creative designer in the art department where Alice worked.

'Are you planning to leave me for him?' Edward asked, with more composure than he actually felt.

'I really don't know what's going to happen,' Alice said. 'Perhaps I'll have to move out, now you've found out about Paul.'

'Hadn't you better decide which one of us you want first?' Edward suggested.

'It isn't as easy as that,' Alice said. 'Besides, let's not have a scene, darling. We're both too tired tonight.'

With that, she'd retired to their bedroom and Edward to his study, where he'd continued to sip whisky, alone in his thoughts and in quiet contemplation, trying to make some sense of the sudden revelation that had quite simply overwhelmed him. He'd slept in one of the spare rooms that night. In the morning, Alice had got up and gone to work as if nothing had happened. She'd said very little at breakfast. She hadn't even mentioned it. That was when Edward had formulated his plan. He needed to get out. He needed to escape. He needed to get away, to sort his thoughts out and decide what to do next. What better then, than a short break in the city of his former university for some time to reflect.

As soon as she'd gone, he'd phoned a little guesthouse he remembered on the Oystermouth Road, overlooking the bay and beach. He'd walked past it many times, walking from the university campus to the city shopping centre. It was out of season, and they had no trouble accommodating him. He could stay more or less as long as he liked. Of course, he could have booked himself into a five-star hotel. He could have afforded to, but he didn't want that experience. He wanted something more rustic and authentic. This was only forty pounds a night, including breakfast. It could hardly have been cheaper. Some of the hotels he stayed at in London cost hundreds a night. This would be very different. It was exactly what he needed.

As the train approached Swansea, the stops became more frequent. From his carriage window, he observed the ruins of Newport Castle, standing on the muddy banks of the River Usk, with the shopping precinct behind. As the train left Cardiff Central Station, his eye was drawn to the imposing landmarks of the Principality Stadium on one side of the track and the Cardiff City Stadium on the other. On either side of Bridgend were some miles of lush, green, Welsh, rolling countryside, which the train tore through at an impressive speed. Edward knew they'd reached Port Talbot when he caught sight of the steelworks and its myriad of chimneys, pumping a thick cloud of industrial pollution into the atmosphere. Yet to his left the town was overlooked by a succession of steep, unblemished hills, that could have formed part of the Brecon Beacons and wouldn't have been out of place there. On glimpsing the outline of Neath Castle, Edward knew he was nearing his final destination. He was only minutes away now.

Whilst distinct, separate geographical entities in legality and tradition, Neath and Swansea effectively ran into each other, to form one sprawling urban conurbation, inhabited by thousands of small, terraced houses, that had filled the valley of the River Tawe since the days of coal mining and copper smelting, providing homes for the workers of the industrial revolution to live in. What struck Edward most was the signs of that industrialisation still so evident in his day had largely vanished. The scarred landscape had predominantly been healed. The trees planted to cover Swansea's industrial past had now grown to maturity to form a forest of green vegetation. There was no sign of the brown colour of copper that had continued to stain the earth long after the smelting had ceased. The waters of the River Tawe looked clear and clean and were running freely. That was a miracle in itself.

The train drew to a halt and Edward and his fellow passengers alighted on the platform. It was the final stop for this particular service, though no doubt some would be continuing their journeys west or inland. As Edward emerged from Swansea Station, light rain was falling. He was neither surprised nor particularly concerned, despite the fact he'd left in glorious sunshine. He was used to it raining in Swansea and he was glad he'd worn his raincoat as a natural precaution. Wet was how he remembered Swansea best, usually during the days of autumn and winter, when the days were darker and shorter. It was no different now, even though it was spring. Edward had checked the forecast before he left. The rain was meant to clear later, and brighter weather was expected over the coming days. He didn't really care. It made no great difference to him. In some ways, rain reflected his grey mood.

Edward wandered down the High Street towards the city centre, once considered one of the most rundown High Streets in the United Kingdom. Edward was pleased to observe the much-needed renovation had finally begun, and some of the derelict, empty buildings had been replaced by independent cafés and interesting-looking, boutique businesses. It was a definite improvement from the last occasion he'd walked down the same street. Edward reached the ruins of Swansea Castle, a notable historic monument in the city centre. He was glad to see it was still standing, although a nearby shop specialising in the sale of Welsh gifts to tourists had now gone, he noticed. Edward paused for a moment, to take a photograph on his phone of the castle's silhouette against the grey skyline. Duly satisfied, he moved on.

Edward continued by foot down Oxford Street, towards Swansea Indoor Market. He was glad to find they hadn't redeveloped that, and it was much as it had been some forty years earlier. It was still busy and the veteran sellers of cockles, laverbread and Welsh cakes, mainly ladies. were still much in evidence and doing brisk business. Edward looked at his watch. It was afternoon and he realised he still hadn't eaten. He found a small coffee shop just outside the market, where he sat down and ordered a pot of tea, a pasty, and a cake. It was just what he needed. He decided he'd return another day. It would be a good place to start each day, with a relaxing coffee and an opportunity to read his book and collect his thoughts, without being bothered by anyone else.

Edward felt reinvigorated by his simple meal. He passed Swansea Grand Theatre, before turning left and heading towards the beach and Oystermouth Road, where he was staying. The Civic Centre was on one side of him, Swansea Prison on the other. He took the more attractive beach path. Once he passed the municipal buildings, he was treated to the view he'd been half waiting for. Despite it still being overcast, he could see the entire length of Swansea Bay stretching out ahead of him, from Port Talbot and further to the east, to The Mumbles and Gower Peninsula to the west. It was a view he'd seen many times on his daily trek from his digs on the edge of Sandfields, where he'd lived in his final year, to the university campus.

It was about a fifteen-minute walk along the Oystermouth Road to the guesthouse where he was staying. He'd deliberately chosen one parallel and almost directly behind the road in which he'd once lived. At the guesthouse, he was greeted by the owners, an Alan and Gwen Evans. He remembered their names from his telephone conversation with them. They were a middle-aged couple, probably only a year or two younger than he was himself. Edward completed the formalities of signing himself in. He'd paid for several days in advance and would pay for more as required. Mr Evans gave him the key to his room and showed him where it was located. As he climbed the stairs, Edward noticed there was a small bar in the adjacent breakfast room, with basic spirit optics and a few bottles of wine and beer neatly lined up, waiting to be opened. It was likely he'd make good use of that in the coming days, he thought to himself.

Once inside his room with the door closed, Edward collapsed on the bed. The room was only small, but it suited his needs perfectly. He had a bed, a bedside table, a chair, a chest of drawers, a mini wardrobe, a television set, a sink, a shower, and a toilet. What else did he need? What was more, from his bedroom window he had a perfect view of the whole of Swansea

Bay. Perched above the main road, he could see the sand extending out all the way to the water's edge. Edward closed his eyes and went to sleep. For a minute he wanted to forget all about Alice. He wondered if she was home yet and had read his note. Probably not, he decided. He'd text her later to say he'd arrived safely and would then switch his phone off for the next day or two at least, until he had actual need of it. He wanted minimum contact. So far, he'd received no messages from her. She obviously felt no great guilt over her affair with Paul. He'd expected an apology at least. He hadn't even really had that the previous night. He doubted he'd get one now in truth.

When Edward woke up, he made himself a coffee. He was pleased to see the rain had stopped. It was still grey outside, but the skies had lightened. There was even a touch of blue in the distance over Mumbles Pier. The weather changed quickly in these parts, as the sea breeze blew rain and cloud in, only to blow them over again. Edward sipped his coffee and opened his book. He'd brought several with him. This was a short one – *Notes from The Underground* by Fyodor Dostoevsky. Edward had read it many years ago as a student but had largely forgotten its contents. It would be good to reread it. He recalled it was about a loner and an outcast, how appropriate considering the rather strange circumstances of his visit. Edward read a few pages and then stopped. He could see from his window the weather had continued to improve. Perhaps it was time to take another walk and get a little more much-needed fresh air in his lungs.

Edward stepped outside and could feel the sea breeze on his face. Fine particles of sand were blown against his ageing skin. He didn't mind. It reminded him he was no longer in Oxford or London. He was in Wales, and he was by the seaside. Edward walked further down the Oystermouth Road, before turning inland at Victoria Park and walking past the notable Brangwyn Hall. The second-hand shops on St Helen's Road, where he used to search for rare vinyl records, had mainly been replaced by a countless array of late-night eateries, he observed. The city centre itself had changed less, although most of the famous, old department stores had now closed their doors for good, including *David Evans*.

Edward made his way to Wind Street. It had once been home to Swansea's banks and commerce. Now it was celebrated for its pubs, café-bars, and nightlife. Edward hoped to find somewhere to eat there. It was only early evening, and the shops were still just closing. A few young men and women were heading for their nights out. Judging by the short skirts most of the women wore, Edward realised this road or *Wine Street* as it was known locally, wasn't really for him. It made him feel old and oddly out of place. He continued hurriedly along, until he came to a little wine bar that was more to his liking. It was pleasingly quiet, and he could enjoy a glass of wine and a pleasant meal there in the sanctity of his own company.

Edward walked back along the refurbished Swansea Marina, that had still been docklands and decaying industry in his day. He passed the old premises of the *South Wales Evening Post*, which appeared to have been converted into a hotel. The striking, stone building that housed the Dylan Thomas Centre, opened since his graduation, stood before him and he made a mental note to visit it. None of this had existed during his time in the city, not the yachts and pleasure craft that filled the waters of the marina or the luxury apartments and cafes that adorned the sides of the manmade harbour, that now made up the *Maritime Quarter*, home of the National Maritime Museum. No doubt Edward would return to this area, to enjoy all it had to offer over the coming days. For now, he was content to wander slowly back to the guesthouse where he was staying. Once inside he made another cup of coffee, read his book for a bit, watched a little television, before slipping into bed.

It was only then he remembered he still hadn't contacted Alice or indeed heard from her. He'd expected a string of worried messages and phone calls by now. None had been forthcoming. It was good of her to be so concerned about his welfare, he reflected, dryly. That in itself said as much as any words could. Neither he nor the years they'd spent together meant very much to her, it appeared. Edward started composing a text to her. It was almost the same as he'd written in his note, before setting out. There wasn't very much more to be said. *Have arrived safely. No need to worry. I'll be in touch when I'm ready. Just need time to think,* it read simply. With that he pressed send, turned over and fell asleep.

Day Two (Tuesday)

Edward woke early. He'd deliberately left his curtains slightly ajar, so the morning light of outside would act as a kind of natural alarm clock. He woke to a perfect view of Swansea Bay, bathed in glorious sunshine. Clear, blue skies were overhead, and the clouds of the previous day had vanished from sight. To Edward, it looked simply perfect. It gave him a feeling of renewed encouragement and optimism, after the weekend's shock to his system. He switched on the television at the end of his bed, so he could listen to the news. He liked to keep abreast of current affairs and the financial markets, even when he was away. It was a habit from his working days. Old habits were hard to break, he found. He checked his phone, to see he had indeed turned it off as he intended. There would be no messages from Alice, as least none that he'd open or acknowledge if he could help it. He'd maintain radio silence for a while. He'd let her stew in the mess of her own making. Although perhaps he too was in part to blame. He should have seen in coming. He was too focussed on making plans for his impending retirement. He'd been keen to tie up all the loose ends and leave nothing unattended. Perhaps he'd neglected Alice a little as a result. Perhaps he'd unwittingly encouraged her into Paul's eager arms. It was too late to change that now.

Edward took a leisurely shower. The water was warm but not quite as hot as he'd have liked. Still, what could he expect for forty pounds a night? It was agreeable but it wasn't *The Waldorf* or *The Savoy* or *The Dorchester*. He didn't want it to be, although he had stayed at all those places in the past. Not lately, however. He no longer felt the need for pretension and to be something he wasn't. He preferred simplicity and to keep things basic. He'd left his old extravagant lifestyle behind him. He had no great wish to return to it. He'd leave that to others, to a new generation of investors and bankers. In his pomp, showing off had been part of the game and the path to success. Now, he saw through all that for what it was. It was superficial and fake. It didn't really matter how many new cars and luxury holidays he had. It hadn't stopped his first wife dying or his second wife leaving him.

Edward looked at his watch. It was ten to eight. Breakfast was served between eight and nine. He put his clothes on and brushed his teeth. He guessed he'd be one of the first ones down. He descended the stairs carefully. He was starting to feel every one of his sixty years, although he hoped the holiday would breathe new life into him.

Mr and Mrs Evans stood at the bottom of the stairs, ready to greet him with a friendly smile. 'Good morning, I hope you slept well,' Mr Evans said.

'Yes, very well, thank you,' Edward replied.

He had indeed slept well. He hadn't even had to get up for his customary pee in the middle of the night. That in itself was highly unusual and proof that he'd been spark out to the world. Mr Evans showed him to a seat by the window. He was indeed the first down, as he'd half expected to be.

'This is the breakfast menu,' Mr Evans said, handing him a laminated copy of what was on offer to staying guests. 'Can I get you a fruit juice? Orange or apple?' Mr Evans asked.

'Orange would be lovely,' Edward said.

'Tea or coffee?'

'Tea, I think,' Edward said.

'Would you like cereal?' Mr Evans continued.

'No, I don't think so,' Edward answered, as he casually perused the menu. 'I think I'll just have the full, cooked breakfast and some toast,' he said.

There were other choices on offer – hot porridge, scrambled eggs, poached eggs, beans on toast. Perhaps he'd try some of these on future days, but he was content to be filled by a full, cooked breakfast on this, his first day.

'Sausage, bacon, beans, mushrooms, tomatoes. Anything you don't want?' Mr Evans enquired.

'A little bit of everything will be fine,' Edward confirmed.

Mr Evans left the room, presumably to take the order to his wife, who Edward imagined was given the full reins of the kitchen. That was her domain. A few minutes later, Mr Evans emerged with a pot of steaming tea and a small jug of milk.

'Do you take sugar?' Mr Evans asked.

'No, thanks,' Edward said.

He'd tried to give it up, in his unsuccessful attempts to lose weight. Too many business lunches and dinners had caused him to pile on the pounds, which he'd found difficulty shifting, even when he'd ceased to attend so many. Once the weight was on, it was on. That was the problem. Edward poured himself a cup of tea and took a sip. It felt warm and refreshing on his lips and tongue. Meanwhile, another guest, a young woman, possibly an international student, had come in and was shown to a table. Edward didn't have long to wait, before his cooked breakfast and toast were brought out and placed in front of him.

'Is there anything else I can get you?' Mr Evans wondered.

'No, this will be plenty for me,' Edward said.

'So, what brings you here? Business or pleasure?' Mr Evans asked, deciding the formalities were over and it was time to engage Edward in real conversation.

'A bit of both,' Edward replied, rather cryptically. 'But mainly pleasure, I suppose,' he added.

'Have you been here before?' Mr Evans enquired.

'In the very distant past. I was a student here more years ago than I care to remember,' Edward explained.

'Oh,' Mr Evans said, suddenly looking up, indicating Edward had now fully captured his interest. 'Where did you live? Were you nearby?'

'I lived in various places,' Edward said. 'I was on campus in halls of residence in my first year, then in Brynmill and the Uplands. In my final year, I was very nearby, in Sandfields, in a road just behind here. In fact, that was why I chose this guesthouse. I used to walk past it when I walked this way to the shopping centre, though I doubt you were the owners then.'

‘Oh no, we didn’t have the guesthouse then. We were cockle pickers in those days. I collected them and Gwen sold them in Swansea Market. It wasn’t a bad living, but I’d had enough by the time I was fifty, so the last few years we’ve been doing this instead.’ Mr Evans said.

‘I saw the cockle and laverbread sellers are still in the market,’ Edward commented.

‘They’ll always be there, whilst there’s a market,’ Mr Evans said. ‘Mind, I wasn’t that keen on laverbread myself. Gwen likes it though.’

It was an acquired taste for sure. Edward had taken some home for his family once. Only his dad, who had Cardiff connections, had claimed to like it, probably out of loyalty for his home country more than anything. Edward had found it distasteful in the extreme, although he could eat a cockle or two if he was forced to. He just didn’t like the gritty taste of sand that came with them. He'd never make a proper Welshman, he reflected to himself.

‘Maybe if I stay long enough, I’ll get to like it too,’ Edward said, diplomatically.

‘Any special plans for the day?’ Mr Evans asked.

‘I thought I might visit a couple of museums,’ Edward replied.

That was indeed his intention. He wanted to visit the old City Museum he knew well from his student days, as well as visiting the more recently opened National Maritime Museum. After finishing his breakfast, Edward returned to his room. He spent a little longer getting ready and then headed out. The museums didn’t open until 10am, so he had a little time to kill first. He made straight for the small coffee shop by the market, where he’d had his lunch the previous day. He thought he could enjoy a coffee and read his book for a little while, whilst he waited for the museums to open. When he walked in, the lady serving at the counter looked up.

‘Weren’t you in yesterday?’ she enquired.

‘Indeed, I was,’ Edward said, feeling slightly embarrassed to be recognised.

He was surprised she remembered him. He wasn't an especially noticeable person, not these days at least. Perhaps once in his youth, but those times had long since passed.

'What can I get you?' she asked.

'Just a coffee and one of your delicious cakes,' Edward replied, holding out his bank card to pay.

'Take a seat and I'll bring them across,' he was told.

Edward made himself comfortable and got out his book. It wasn't long before his coffee and cake were brought to him.

'A good book, is it?' the lady enquired.

'Well, yes, I suppose it is,' Edward answered, slightly taken back by her enquiry. 'It's considered a classic of European literature if you like that kind of thing. It's not for everyone though.'

'Me, I like a good thriller or detective story,' the lady said.

'Dostoevsky did write about crime too, in a way at least,' Edward said.

'I should have said; I'm Meredith, by the way. What's your name?' the lady asked.

'I'm Edward.'

'Well, enjoy your coffee and cake, Edward,' Meredith said.

'I'm sure I will,' Edward responded.

With that she left him in peace to his book. When he'd finished, he quietly got up.

'Perhaps we'll see you again tomorrow?' Meredith wondered, as Edward moved towards the door.

'More than likely,' he replied, cheerfully.

He could already see how quickly he could slip into a routine here. In many ways, it really was like coming home. Edward wandered up towards the ruins of Swansea Castle and back down Wind Street, in the direction of the Maritime Quarter, where the city's two main museums were located. He stood outside Swansea Museum. It looked exactly the same as it had forty years before. It had hardly changed at all. He went inside. That had hardly changed either. There were three rooms and a short corridor of exhibits downstairs and two rooms of exhibits upstairs, as well as a small garden outside. Three of the rooms were exactly as he remembered them. The room dedicated to natural history had always caught his imagination as a student. He was less enamoured with the ceramics and pottery room. He never had been as a young man. There were also rooms featuring both costume and Neolithic artefacts. The centrepiece of the collection remained the room dedicated to Welsh social and industrial history, notably the rural, Welsh, cottage kitchen, with its elderly resident, resplendent in traditional red and black Welsh dress. For some reason, that single image had remained in Edward's head through all the years since. Another, a painting of a storm in Swansea Bay, he could no longer find. Perhaps it had been carefully put away for posterity since his last visit.

Edward had been a regular visitor to the museum as a student. His fairly relaxed economics timetable had usually allowed him to go to the shopping centre several times a week. On at least one of those occasions, he normally made the additional walk to the museum. It was generally quiet. He welcomed the peace. It provided a much-needed break from the hectic nature of the campus and student life. His fellow undergraduates thought him a little odd. He didn't care. He'd do what he wanted, whatever anyone else thought. He'd always been his own man, pretty much anyway, although perhaps not in his choice of job. There, he'd bowed to parental pressure to an extent. He wondered what life might have been like if he'd followed his heart and a different course. Part of him had been in broad agreement with his parents. Like them, he'd thought money and security important at the time. They seemed less so now, although that was easy to say, as he finally had as much money as he could ever possibly want or need.

Edward had met his first wife, Angela, at Swansea. She'd been a mathematics undergraduate. They'd met at a dance at a pub and dancehall by the Clyne Halls of Residence on the Mumbles Road. He could no longer recall its name. It had probably long since closed anyway. It had been unusual for Edward to go the Clyne Halls site. He generally resided on campus, in town, or in the student pubs in the Brynmill and Uplands area of the city. Quite often, they ventured all the way into The Mumbles, but rarely stopped halfway. He was glad he did. If he hadn't, he wouldn't have met Angela. She'd come from Hampshire. Edward had dated a couple of girls casually earlier in his first year, but nothing serious. He knew straight away Angela was the one. Pretty soon, they became inseparable. Edward lost his virginity to her. Indeed, she'd remained the only woman he'd slept with until her tragic, premature death. Even afterwards, there was only Alice.

After graduating, Edward and Angela had moved to Oxford, where they'd remained within a few miles ever since. She'd become a successful accountant, counting Oxford University among her distinguished clients, whilst he'd commuted to his financial job in London. Eventually, they'd got married and had children. They'd never considered staying in Swansea, despite both enjoying their time there. They'd both been in an almighty hurry to get back to England and get on with their lives. They imagined there weren't the same opportunities for them in South Wales. Perhaps they'd been wrong. Perhaps in retrospect they could have both become academics at the university. They could have got a little house in Blackpill or West Cross, overlooking the bay. It might have been a less stressful life for Angela. It might have enabled her to live longer.

Leaving the old museum behind him, Edward headed towards the marina and the National Maritime Museum. The short walk only took him a few minutes. The National Maritime Museum was a large and imposing building from the outside. It stood on the northern side of the marina. An impressive display of historic vessels were moored in the waters on the quayside immediately in front of it. Despite noting the changes and developments the day before, Edward remained giddily in awe of the major transformation since the days he'd known this part of the city. The mouth of the River Tawe had largely been an area to be avoided. That was no longer the case. Now, it was a haven for visitors and a desirable place to live for the affluent middle-class like himself.

Edward paused at the entrance, where his eye was caught by a selection of stunning vintage vehicles, lovingly restored to their original, gleaming factory condition. The natural route around the museum took him upstairs first. The main gallery there was a celebration of Swansea's maritime past, including small displays to the side on Welsh social history. It struck Edward that the Welsh celebrated their history and culture so much better than the English did, and in a way the English struggled to match. The English on the whole weren't all that interested in how their ancestors had lived. The Welsh by comparison were very much interested. They were proud of coming from humble and hard-working roots. The difference was palpable.

The main gallery downstairs was dedicated to the industrial heritage of Wales, including the coal, steel, and copper industries. Most of that was gone but the memories lived on in the artefacts and records on display. Edward was blown away that such a museum should exist that wasn't even there in his day. At the end of his tour, he decided to stop in the museum's café for a late lunch. He looked at his watch. It was nearer two o'clock than one. How time had flown. He checked his phone. It was still off, as he intended. He wondered if Alice had tried to call or text. Probably not, he reflected. She was glad no doubt that he was gone, and she was temporarily rid of him at least. She of course was happy with Paul, he presumed. She didn't need him, Edward, in her life, not anymore. He was surprised too how little he was thinking of her. It was as he'd already accepted it was over and he wasn't willing to fight for her anymore. Instead, he thought of Angela, his deceased, first wife.

Finishing at the museum, Edward began to slowly meander his way back along the Oystermouth Road, in the direction of the guesthouse where he was staying. Once he reached the sandy beaches of the bay, he could see the Mumbles headland clearly in the distance. He paused around halfway back, to sit on a bench and get his book out. It was still warm and sunny. No rain so far today, although light rain showers were forecast for the evening. It wouldn't matter then. Edward sat back with a feeling of relaxation and contentment. He should have felt more anxious than he did. Alice was about to leave him for a younger man. He'd circumvented that by leaving himself and taking himself out of the equation. Already, all that unseemly bother seemed far away, almost as if it had never happened. It was true everything remained unresolved and up in the air, but it could wait. Edward was certain it would all work itself out one way or another in due course. He didn't really want to think about it too much. It didn't really bear thinking about. It had come as too much of a shock at first. Now, he'd started to come to terms with it. Instead, he was content to reflect on the past and his days as a student in Swansea with Angela all those years ago. Years that had long since passed and he could never have back. He was trying, however, to relive them as best as he could. In some ways, they seemed much more relevant than the present.

Back at the guesthouse, Edward took a much-needed nap. He didn't have the stamina he'd once had in his prime and at the height of his working powers. The mild heart arrythmia, whilst under control, sapped his energies a little. He was slowly learning to live more healthily. He no longer drank as he once did. Normally a glass or two of wine or beer was enough. Of course, Alice's revelation had driven him to drink rather more whisky than he normally did. Now he was away from her, he didn't feel quite the same need. He could continue the good habits he'd tried to instal since retirement. He wanted to be healthier. He wanted to be more active. Hence the gradual return to tennis and walking further.

After his nap, Edward found a quiet pub on Brynmor Road, where he enjoyed a pint with his evening meal. It was a pub he'd frequented as a student. Edward took the scenic route back, down King Edward's Road towards the St Helen's Rugby and Cricket Ground, where Edward had watched many a first-class rugby match back in the day, when Swansea had entertained the likes of Neath, Llanelli, Pontypool and Cardiff, just as he'd been a frequent visitor to the Vetch Field, to watch Swansea City. That ground had since made way for a proposed housing development, as both the city's main football and rugby teams, Swansea City and *The Ospreys*, now played in a new purpose-built stadium out of town at Landore. St Helen's remained open, but only for Swansea's cricketers and amateur rugby team. That wasn't the only thing that had changed, Edward observed. Most of the pubs that had served visitors to the ground had also vanished. Pubs where he'd misspent many hours when he should have been attending lectures or revising. It had simply been too tempting and too easy not to. That was the life of the student after all.

It was about seven when Edward returned to the guesthouse. He found Alan and Gwen Evans sitting alone in the breakfast room, which doubled as a guest lounge in the evening, watching the television. The small bar in the corner of the room remained ominously unused. If no other guest wanted to take advantage of it, Edward might as well do, he decided.

'Mind if I join you?' he asked.

'Not at all, be our guest. Indeed, you are our guest,' Mr Evans said.

'That's a clever pun,' Edward noted, with a flicker of mild amusement.

'So, how are you getting on? Have you settled in all right?' Mrs Evans enquired.

'Very well, thanks,' Edward replied.

'Is your room to your satisfaction? Have you got everything you need?' Mrs Evans continued.

'It's very nice. No complaints at all,' Edward assured her.

'Can I get you a drink?' Mr Evans asked.

'A whisky and soda would be perfect,' Edward said. 'Do you want me to pay for it now?'

'No, we can just add it to your bill when you leave, and any more you have,' Mr Evans said, getting up to pour Edward his drink.

'So, how long do you plan to stay with us, Mr Chapman?' Mrs Evans asked.

There was something about Edward's dignified demeanour that he always tended to be addressed in that manner and not by his Christian name.

'Please call me Edward. No need to be formal. I'm on holiday,' he said.

'Then call us Gwen and Alan,' Gwen said.

'I'll certainly do that,' Edward agreed. 'In answer to your question, I don't really know how long I'll be staying. Maybe a few days, maybe a week, maybe longer. I have a few things to sort out. I'll just see how it goes, but I'll be sure to keep you informed.'

'Well, you can stay as long as you like, as far as we're concerned,' Alan reiterated.

'Alan says you were at university here,' Gwen commented.

'I was, a very long time ago,' Edward confirmed. 'You could say this is a nostalgia trip for me, a revisiting of my past, if you like.'

'I notice you're travelling alone,' Gwen remarked, trying not to be too prying, but nonetheless providing Edward with a convenient opportunity to provide further explanation if he wished to.

'Indeed I am. My wife, Alice, has work to attend. We live near Oxford. She works for a publisher there. I, on the other hand, am recently retired and time is largely my own,' Edward explained, taking a lingering sip of his whisky.

'Do you have any children, Edward?' Gwen asked.

'Yes, two, Victoria and Henry. They're both grown up. Victoria works for an advertising agency. Henry is more of a free spirit. He travels a lot, through Europe, Asia, and Australia, picking up work where he can find it. Sometimes I'm quite envious of him and wish I'd been more like that. He's younger than Victoria. Hopefully, one day his wanderings will cease, and he'll settle down somewhere. I'm not too concerned if he doesn't. He's living his own life at least.'

'Like you, we have two children too, a boy and a girl also, as it happens. Like yours, they've both flown the nest now,' Alan said. 'One is local, the other lives in Cardiff. They're near enough that we still see quite a lot of them. There's always a bed here for them if they need it. They know that which is good.'

'Alice is actually my second wife,' Edward resumed, suddenly deciding to reveal a little bit more about himself.

Alan and Gwen seemed like nice people. Why shouldn't he open up to them? What did he have to lose? Why should his life be a closely guarded secret? In the past, he might have been reticent. There was no need for that, he realised. It didn't really matter who knew what. He wasn't yet ready to tell them about Alice's affair, however. That still struck too much of a nerve within him for the time being to tell anyone else, even if he was slowly coming to terms with it himself. He was still too proud to admit such a thing had happened to him, a person of his standing and position. It was positively shameful to lose his wife to another man if nothing else.

'Victoria and Henry are the children of my first wife, Angela. We met in Swansea. That's part of my reason for being here,' Edward continued, at last.

'How lovely,' Gwen commented.

'Well, not entirely. Angela died,' Edward said, almost having to choke back a tear he hadn't expected. Instead, he took another generous gulp of his drink, to hide his momentary emotional discomfort.

'I'm very sorry to hear that,' Gwen said, trying to console him, even though she barely knew him.

'It's OK. It's been a while now. It was breast cancer. She was only forty-five. But I still have the children and the memories of her, particularly here. I'll never lose them,' Edward said.

'That's something, I suppose,' Gwen said.

'Indeed, it is,' Edward agreed,' suddenly composing himself and forcing himself to be jolly and cheerful again.

He was here to reflect, but not to be sad. He preferred to remember the good times he and Angela had shared.

'Can I get you another drink?' Alan asked, noticing Edward had finished his first.

'No, I think I'm all right. It's time for me to head to bed,' Edward said.

With that, he took himself off towards the stairs and up to his room.

'Goodnight,' he said, as he departed.

'Goodnight,' Alan and Gwen replied, in unison.

Day Three (Wednesday)

It was his third day in Swansea. They were passing quickly. Edward woke up feeling suitably refreshed after his museum visits the previous day. In his head, he'd already worked out a new itinerary for the day ahead. He was an organised man. He'd had to be in his work. He'd never lose that trait now, he realised. It would be with him always. Every day should have meaning and purpose. Time shouldn't be wasted. He didn't like to take things as they came, even on holiday. He liked to have a clear plan, even if to others it might seem merely like aimless drifting. It wasn't to him. There were places he wanted to visit. Slowly, one by one, he'd get to them. At least that was his intention. He'd do his very best to achieve his aims.

Edward got up a little later than he had done the previous morning. He didn't rush down to breakfast. He didn't need to after all. He was in no particular hurry. He'd get it all done in his own good time. He found Alan Evans waiting for him, just as he had been the day before. Some of the guests were already seated and eating. Edward found a different table on this occasion. His preferred one by the window was already taken. That was the price to be paid for coming down later. It was a modest one though. Edward didn't really care where he was sat. It made no huge difference to him.

'Would you like the same as you had yesterday, or something different?' Alan asked.

'The same would be perfect,' Edward answered.

He imagined he'd have the same breakfast every day for as long as he stayed. Perhaps he should have scrambled or poached eggs once, just to be different. He was a man of routine, however, and routines were hard to break. If he stayed long enough, he would have something different one day, he told himself firmly. He was on holiday after all. There were no rules, and if there were, he was allowed to break them. Besides, he made the rules. They were his to do what he wanted with.

After breakfast, Edward pottered about in his room for a bit, before heading out. He still hadn't contacted Alice. He wasn't ready to yet. He wondered if she was spending her nights alone in the big house, or did she have Paul for company? Perhaps she'd already moved into his place? Perhaps Edward would get back to find all her stuff had gone and she with it? He wasn't going to worry about that now. What would be would be. He and Alice had enjoyed a relatively happy ten years together. Perhaps that was enough.

Edward went out wearing his raincoat. There was cloud overhead, and knowing Swansea as he did, it would probably rain at some point. It wouldn't matter all that much. He planned to spend much of the day inside. As on his other days in the city, he headed first towards the small coffee shop by the market. He hoped the friendly face of Meredith would be there to greet him. She was a cheerful, salt of the earth type, well-built and proud of it. He guessed she was in her mid to late thirties. She was of mixed ethnicity, but her accent was 100 per cent South Wales, an accent that always took him back to his days as a student.

'What can I get you today, Edward?' Meredith asked, when he walked in.

He was one of the first customers of the morning, although there were a couple of others outside, huddled round coffees and smoking. Inside, it was virtually empty.

'You remember my name. I'm impressed,' Edward commented.

'Do you remember mine?' Meredith asked.

'Indeed, I do. It's Meredith,' Edward announced, proudly.

He'd made a point in business of always remembering people's names. It was one of the tricks of the trade, to put potential clients at their ease.

'Very good,' Meredith complimented him. 'So, what will it be?'

'I'll have a coffee, and do you know what, I think I fancy a donut today,' Edward announced, offering his payment.

'A wise choice. The donuts are excellent, even if I say so myself. You take a seat and I'll bring them over,' Meredith said.

Edward made himself comfortable and as on other days got his book out. It was only a short novel, and he was well on the way to finishing it. He'd have to start another one soon. He'd brought a couple more books with him. That might not be sufficient. He'd keep his eye open for a bookshop or two on his wanderings that day, he decided. He hoped he'd find one. He loved browsing old bookshops at his leisure and occasionally finding something interesting. There were usually plenty of bookshops for him to choose from. So far, he hadn't seen many in Swansea. The one or two he remembered appeared to have closed.

'Are you here on holiday?' Meredith asked, when she brought him his coffee and donut.

'Sort of,' Edward nodded. 'It's a mini break if you like.'

'Got anything exciting planned for today?' Meredith enquired.

'I'll take a look at the gallery and perhaps pop in the Dylan Thomas Centre. I haven't been there yet. Later, I might wander down to the old university campus. I was a student there many years ago,' Edward explained.

'Oh, really. So, you know Swansea quite well,' Meredith commented.

'I did. This was back in the late 1970s, early 1980s. It's changed a bit since then,' Edward admitted.

'I wasn't even born then,' Meredith laughed.

'Exactly. It was more of a provincial town in those days, I'd say. It has more the feel of a city now,' Edward reflected.

'I like living here,' Meredith said. 'It's got shops, pubs and cafés, and the beach and the Gower Peninsula aren't far away.'

'I like it too,' Edward agreed.

With that, Meredith left him to his coffee and book, as another customer had wandered in, to attract her attention.

'Many thanks,' Edward said, when he'd finished, taking his empty cup and plate back. 'I'm sure I'll be in again later in the week,' he added.

'I'll be here, I expect. I don't have a day off until Saturday this week,' Meredith said.

Edward only had days off now. That was the good thing about being retired. After leaving the coffee shop, he headed towards his first destination, the Glynn Vivian Art Gallery. It was located on Alexandra Road, near the railway station and opposite Swansea College of Art. Edward used to visit it sometimes as a student when he'd had pretensions of being an artist himself. Ultimately, he'd put those dreams behind him to make money instead. He'd got lucky. His timing had been perfect. He'd managed to jump on the bandwagon of Margaret Thatcher's mid-1980s, mini financial boom. He'd done well then, although he wasn't really a political animal himself. He still partly saw himself as someone with an artistic temperament. It had just gone largely untapped and to waste. He liked art and literature. He might return to those inclinations one day in retirement, he thought, when he had nothing else to do with his time. He had no grandchildren as yet. Neither Victoria nor Henry appeared to be in any great hurry to provide them. He'd need something else to keep him occupied.

To reach the gallery, Edward headed up onto the Kingsway. It was one of the main roads through the centre of Swansea. Once it's side streets had been filled with popular if slightly seedy nightclubs. On Friday and Saturday nights, there had been long queues outside them, as they'd filled with eager clubbers, who'd descended from the valley communities. As far as Edward could see, all that had vanished. It reflected a general decline in city nightlife everywhere. Clubbing wasn't as popular as in his day. Young people were far too busy with their phones, making posts on social media. Edward had no interest in that. It was all nonsense, as far as he was concerned. He'd leave that to the younger generations. It was too late for him to get started with that foolishness now, although his work had required that he had a passing understanding of the internet and its applications, even if he personally chose not to avail himself of them greatly.

It wasn't just the nightclubs that had largely closed, Edward noticed. Swansea had once been a mecca for small, working men's pubs and clubs. There had been one or more on every street corner and in every residential road across the whole of the city. Some were tiny, little more than a front room in a terraced house. It appeared the majority were no more, victims of changing tastes and habits. Once, they'd provided an after-work haven for the hard-working men of the local industries, but those industries had been in terminal decline for years, until they'd more or less ceased to operate altogether. So too had the pubs now, as a kind of inevitable by-product of the industrial closures. One departure was a knock-on effect of the other. That was progress if it could be called that. Of course, the old pubs weren't for the likes of English students like Edward had been. They were pubs for the people of the local communities. Edward and his fellow undergraduates wouldn't have been welcomed in any of them. Even at the time, Edward understood and respected that fact. He and his friends mainly stuck to the student pubs in the vicinity of the main university campus.

From the outside, the Glynn Vivian Art Gallery was an impressive historic building in its own right. It always had been. Edward recalled that about it. Inside, it had clearly been refurbished since his last visit. It looked clean, modern, and new. A visitor's café now stood to the left of the entrance desk. There were ten rooms in all to be perused. Edward started downstairs in the main entrance hall, where there was a visiting exhibition. To the sides, there were rooms filled with more of the gallery's permanent collection. It was bigger than he remembered it. He dutifully looked at every exhibit in turn, taking in what he could about them.

Upstairs, there were delicate, ornamental ceramics on view and a gallery he could look down from onto the exhibits he'd already seen. Edward concentrated most attention on the main exhibition of fine art. This was the biggest and to his mind most impressive room. It had several sections. The paintings which struck a special chord with Edward were the ones of the Welsh coal miners and steel workers, staring sullenly out from huge pieces of painted canvas. The brush strokes were precise and well-executed by the artists concerned. The faces they'd captured were grimy, sad, and unhappy. These people hadn't been content in their work, it was obvious. They'd been grudgingly accepting at best, hostile at worst. The images remained in Edward's head for some days afterwards. Nothing else he saw there could quite match the way these paintings had moved him. Their beauty contrasted sharply with the daily horror of the ordinary, working, Welsh men's lives they portrayed. It was a fitting homage to them and the lives they'd lived.

Edward sat in the café afterwards, quietly reflecting, over a pot of tea. When he was ready, he left the gallery and walked down the High Street and on towards Wind Street, in the direction of the Dylan Thomas Centre. Edward had vague memories of a pedestrian tunnel under the main road. But if it had been there once and he hadn't just imagined it, it wasn't there any longer. Edward had to wait for the traffic lights to change and the stream of fast-moving cars to stop, before crossing in safety. Once on Somerset Place, he made his way to the Dylan Thomas Centre. He hadn't been there before. He was immediately impressed. There was an exhibition and shop downstairs and a restaurant upstairs. It was a fitting commemoration of the great man and giant of Welsh literature. Edward was no Dylan Thomas expert, but he was familiar with some of his work. He'd read *Portrait of the Artist as a Young Dog* as a young man and had seen *Under Milk Wood* performed. He knew some of the poems like *Do Not Go Gentle into That Good Night*, *And Death Shall Have No Dominion*, as well as *Fern Hill* of course. He liked them, though Dylan wasn't a personal favourite. Edward principally considered himself an admirer of English authors George Orwell and JG Ballard, as well as the American surrealist Kurt Vonnegut.

Even so, Edward hoped to find inspiration in the words and images of Dylan. He hoped they might provide an answer and solution to his own problems and issues. Looking round at the memorabilia and photographs on display, it was hard not to be moved by Dylan's short life and the literary impact he'd made, from a relatively humble upbringing in Swansea's middle-class Uplands, to publication at an early age, a life in London, before eventually returning to Wales. A successful BBC radio career had followed and sell-out tours of America. He wasn't even forty when he died, a life cut short by drink and chronic bad health, that he'd been afflicted with since childhood. In those thirty-nine years, Dylan had crammed in more than most did in a lifetime. He'd done much more than Edward had done. Although in his lifetime at least, Edward was probably the richer man, he reflected with a touch of irony. Until the later years, when the radio performances and the American lectures became a success, Dylan had struggled to make enough money as a writer to live on. No doubt since, when it was too late, there would have been ample royalties from his estate to provide a generous income.

After taking in the exhibition, Edward sat in the café-bar upstairs and ordered lunch. Unusually for this time of day, he chose a pint of Welsh bitter to wash it down with. Perhaps it was in honour of Dylan, a keen imbiber of the local brews himself. Edward's only concern was the beer might make him drowsy afterwards. It wasn't a huge problem. He could always stop at the guesthouse for a brief nap on his way to his next port of call. This he did. He lay down on his bed for half an hour or so to recharge his batteries. It was early afternoon and it had started raining lightly, just as he reached the cover of the guesthouse. Luckily, it had largely stopped by the time he woke up and got ready to go out again. He continued on his way round the bay, towards the old university campus. He was aware a new purpose-built Bay Campus had now been opened on the Port Talbot side of the River Tawe, but the old Singleton Park site would always be the home of Swansea University to him. He knew nothing of the other, except that it existed. He didn't even plan to visit it. Only because it held no memories for him, and memories were his business and a major reason for his being there.

It did make him realise, however, that modern-day Swansea was quite different to the one he'd known forty years earlier. It had grown and developed in his absence. It was a more cosmopolitan, multicultural, metropolitan city to the one he'd left. The many department stores may have closed their doors, but they'd been replaced by shiny, new, out of town, drive-in, retail parks. Swansea and the rest of the world had changed and moved on. Edward wasn't sure he'd changed with it. He was still stuck in the past. It was where he felt he belonged. Now he was heading back to that past and the campus that had been his home from the ages of eighteen to twenty-one.

As Edward passed the St Helen's Rugby and Cricket Ground, the clouds above him darkened again. He felt a large drop of rain on his cheek, then another, which ran down onto his shirt collar. Within moments, it was raining heavily. He was getting soaked to the skin. He looked around for cover, but he knew from battling the elements along this stretch of the road many times in the past, there was little or none to be found. The strong breeze coming off the waters of the bay only made it worse. Edward decided to postpone his visit to the campus until the following day, when he hoped the weather would improve. Instead, he turned back and took a deter down King Edward's Road, where he'd be slightly less exposed to the wind and rain. He meandered his way through the narrow, back streets and off one he noticed a small, second-hand bookshop, where he decided to take momentary shelter, until the rain subsided.

He opened the door and went inside. Just being out of the wet for a moment made him feel instantly better. He shook some of the surface water from himself, before proceeding further into the shop. It was a funny little place, a bit dingy and not particularly well-organised by the look of things. Nonetheless, it was the kind of quaint, old, second-hand bookshop where he liked to poke about. If he was lucky, some rare book or bargain might jump out at him. That was his hope at least. If not, it wasn't time wasted. By the time he left, perhaps the rain would have stopped. That in itself would have made it well worth the effort of interrupting his journey to go in. He started to browse the shelves of poetry and literature. Those were the areas that interested him most, together with history, ecology, and geography.

He'd been there a while, before a middle-aged lady, perhaps just a few years younger than he was himself, let her head emerge from what he presumed to be a back office, to address him. She peered over her glasses, to take him in first, before speaking. Perhaps she was assessing whether he was a serious customer, intent on a purchase, or had just made a temporary escape from the inclement weather, as was indeed the case. Edward noticed a Golden Retriever, or some similar breed of dog, lay contentedly asleep at her feet, in a basket by her desk. Edward was no expert on dogs. He'd never been particularly taken by the beasts, but he knew an animal of that colour was a Retriever or perhaps a Labrador. It was more likely the latter, he realised, on closer inspection.

'Can I help you?' the bookseller enquired, politely. She had a gentle, courteous tone to her voice, as if her question was genuinely meant, and she wasn't just trying to get rid of him.

'I'm only browsing, to be honest with you,' Edward admitted.

He felt a little embarrassed by the admission, but there was no point lying. He didn't want to raise her hopes of a sale, though he wouldn't hesitate to make a purchase, if he spotted anything there that he wanted. He was always on the look out for a good book.

'Well, if there is anything particular that you're looking for, just ask,' she said. 'I might have it somewhere.'

'I'm always after vintage editions of anything by JG Ballard or Kurt Vonnegut,' Edward said. 'I also collect 1970s *Fontana* editions of the thriller writer, Eric Ambler.'

'Is there anything on the shelves?' the bookseller asked.

'I haven't seen anything yet,' Edward replied, as he continued to browse.

He was still looking. There was much to go through. He'd only really scratched the surface.

'The thing is, not everything I have is out. There are loads I haven't had time to properly go through yet and price up,' the bookseller explained.

Edward had noticed that. There were mountains of books piled up on the floor, that hadn't yet found their allotted spaces on the shelves. All kinds of gems could be hidden there, among the many which clearly weren't gems, at least not in Edward's eyes.

'The problem is I'm here on my own,' the bookseller continued. 'I could do with a bit of help really, but it's not so easy to find, not the right kind of help anyway. Sometimes I can't even open, if I have an appointment or have to go out for some reason. I have to close for a bit just to take the dog for a walk.'

'That's all right. I can see it's difficult,' Edward sympathised, getting a sense of the lady's predicament.

'I tell you what, if you can come back in a day or two, I'll see what I can dig out for you. How does that sound?' she suggested.

'That would be perfect, but you needn't go to all that bother for me,' Edward said.

'It's really no bother,' the bookseller said. 'That's what I'm here for.'

'Well, it really is most generous of you,' Edward enthused. 'I hope I'm not just wasting your time.'

'You won't be. I have to do it anyway,' she said.

'Well, thank you again,' Edward repeated, as he began to make his way towards the door.

'By the way what's your name, love? Just in case I find anything,' the bookseller called out, as Edward prepared to leave.

'Edward,' he said.

‘OK Edward, I’m Jill and I’ll see you on Friday, if that works for you? I should have a chance to go through a few more of the new books by then,’ she said.

‘I’m staying just round the corner, so Friday will be fine,’ Edward said. ‘To be honest, I can pop in anytime whilst I’m here,’ he added.

‘How long will that be for?’ Jill asked.

‘I’m not quite sure, but a while longer,’ Edward told her.

He realised he still didn’t know the answer to that question himself. With that, he excused himself and went back outside. The rain had eased a bit, but it made little difference to Edward, as he was already soaked. When he got back to his room, he took all his wet clothes off. He laid them neatly on the back of a chair and hoped they’d dry by the following day. At this point, Edward realised he hadn’t come prepared for an extended stay. He’d left in a hurry, with little idea how long he’d be staying for. He hadn’t really thought that part through properly. He only knew that he needed to get away. He only really had one change of clothes with him. He realised now that wasn’t enough. He might have to pick up a few more, to keep him going.

Edward got in the shower. He wanted to wash off the rainwater. As before, it wasn’t quite as hot as he’d have liked. He wanted it piping hot. It was far from that. It was tepid, though it was probably better for the planet and helping to keep energy costs down, he reflected. Edward still emerged feeling somewhat refreshed and better than he had. Even with his raincoat on, his shirt had been virtually stuck to his back. He’d been glad to get it off. Now he was back in warm, clean, dry clothes again. It was spring, not long until summer, in fact. He hadn’t thought he’d need much in the way of outer garments. He’d been wrong. It didn’t take much wind and rain to feel cold, whatever the season.

Edward chose to have his evening meal at another old haunt on the Brynmor Road, washed down with large glass of red wine, not perhaps the fine vintage he might have enjoyed at his favourite wine bar in Oxford or the West End, but nonetheless, it hit the spot. Again, Edward went early, before the pub became busy. He’d didn’t want to sit around and wait for the noisy football patrons to arrive, although he had nothing against the game. He enjoyed it in the privacy of his own home. He just didn't want it to impinge now on his moments of quiet reflection.

Edward was back at the guesthouse by 7.30pm. He looked in on Alan and Gwen in the breakfast room that doubled as a lounge or living room in the evening. Or was it vice versa? Was it a lounge that doubled as a breakfast room in the morning? Edward wasn't sure. It didn't really matter. Again, the couple were alone. Edward's fellow guests evidently weren't big drinkers. He liked a tipple but was no longer a big drinker himself. The heart arrythmia had put a stop to that, and other pleasures on top. Now, Edward was committed to looking after himself and living out his retirement in reasonable health, or as good as he could manage.

'Will you join us?' Alan asked.

'Why not? Just for a quick one,' Edward replied.

'Whisky and soda again?' Alan anticipated.

'Yes, please,' Edward said.

He'd just have the one, before going up to his room. He then sat down to recount some of his day's adventures to Alan and Gwen, before heading upstairs, where he read and watched television for a while, before going to bed. He still hadn't told them what had happened concerning his wife, Alice. He wasn't sure if he ever would. For the time being, it remained his secret. He hadn't told anyone else yet. He still didn't like to admit it, even to himself. He was both too ashamed and too hurt that such a thing had taken place, to him of all people. It had made him realise one thing. Alice had never meant as much to him as Angela had. Indeed, she never could. That was one thing he was happy to admit now. Being back in Swansea had reminded him of that fact once and for all. There was no question. Angela not Alice was the single most significant love of his whole life.

Day Four (Thursday)

After his usual breakfast, Edward went out quite early. The weather had returned to how it had been on his second day. The skies were blue, and the sun was out. It was how the bay looked at its best, although it had a kind of rugged beauty even in the wind and rain. He hoped the rain would hold off, at least until he'd visited the university campus. The open walk along Oystermouth Road and then Mumbles Road left the walker heavily exposed to the elements. There was little protection, as the rain blew off the beach and sand dunes. As often as not, it seemed to blow into the face of the walker heading in the Mumbles direction. Edward had no such worries today. It was warm and there was only a very gentle breeze. He could barely feel it on his skin.

As had become his custom on such days, Edward sat on a bench looking out onto the bay for a few minutes, soaking up the sunshine, before setting out. The tide was always high in the early morning and the water's edge was only metres away. Later in the day, it would probably be a mile or so out, as the beach at this point was so flat. Edward felt strangely content, considering events of the last week. He loved to just sit and look at the bay, from the ugly outline of Port Talbot Steelworks in the east, to the comparative beauty of Mumbles Pier and lighthouse in the west. The lighthouse was located on a jagged outcrop of rock, the last point visible to the naked eye before the coastline turned inwards to Langland and Caswell Bays. Edward made a mental to visit at least some parts of the Gower Peninsula before returning to Oxford. Perhaps he'd get a bus out there at the weekend, if he was still here, if thoughts of Alice and Paul together hadn't dragged him homewards, to confront them in their twisted deceit and their shoddy affair.

The occasional dog walker or runner out on their early morning run passed Edward, as he sat alone in his thoughts. He said *good morning* to those who happened to catch his eye and smile at him. He'd landed on his feet with the guesthouse where he was staying, he reflected. He'd been lucky to find Alan and Gwen. They seemed a nice, genuine couple. They certainly weren't in it for the money, with the rates they were charging. He couldn't complain about that. He'd be sure to stay with them another time if he ever came to the city again. He thought he almost definitely would return. It felt wonderful to be back.

Edward kept his eyes focussed firmly on the beach. He and his friends had drunkenly played about on it many times, after pubs had kicked out in the nights of the spring or summer months, or they'd had too many beers at lunch in the college bar and decided to take the afternoon off. What better than to play in the dunes that led to the soft, smooth sand. Edward seemed to remember there had been many more pubs on the Oystermouth Road forty years earlier. There were still a number of guesthouses and hotels, but very few pubs to be seen. Edward recalled doing pub crawls from one end to the other as a student. *The Bay View* still stood proudly on the western corner. It was where Edward and his now long deceased father had eaten on their first visit to Swansea, when Edward had come for interview all those years ago. He'd no idea he'd end up at Swansea then. It hadn't been his first choice, but he'd come on a fine day like this. He'd been impressed by the bay, the campus on the seafront, the shops, and the cultural heritage. Swansea had leapfrogged some of his other choices in England and he'd ended up there. Wales wasn't so unfamiliar to him. He had relatives in South Wales on his father's side. They used to come to Cardiff, Penarth, Barry Island and Porthcawl when Edward was a child. He had fond memories of his times there, particularly the fun fairs, which had been a delight and something special to look forward to for himself and his sister.

Before he knew it, Edward had let a whole hour pass. It was nearly ten o'clock. There would be no coffee in town today. It would mean going in the wrong direction first and then coming back. Edward didn't have the energy for that. He was already planning quite a long walk ahead front of him, without adding to it further. Meredith would no doubt miss with him, with his predictable order of coffee and cake. See, he was already breaking his newfound routine. Perhaps he wasn't quite as set in his ways as he thought he was. Perhaps Swansea was changing him.

Edward walked on the beach side, where he could retain a view of Mumbles in the distance. He could see St Helen's Rugby and Cricket Ground on the opposite side of the road to where he was walking. Some groundsmen were busy working on the pitch. The rugby season was just ending and the cricket one was just beginning. Edward was surprised to pass a swanky new café-bar on the beach side. There had been nothing like that in his day. Café-bars of the type so favoured in modern times didn't exist then. There were old fashioned pubs, greasy, local cafés, and expensive restaurants to choose from only. There was none of this casual dining. Eating out was either a practical thing or a rare treat. There was nothing much in-between, not like today, when any town or city of moderate size was overwhelmed with them.

Edward reached the bottom entrance to Singleton Park and continued walking. He actually walked straight past the main university entrance. He wanted to walk the whole length of the campus, before heading back inside. He walked as far as the traffic lights at the bottom of Sketty Lane, where he stopped. The athletic ground and football pitches he played on as a student still stood on the western side, just as he remembered them. Singleton Park Boating Lake still stood on the other. Edward had once fallen into its mirky waters, during an afternoon of high jinks in his final year. One too many lunchtime beers had led to the suggestion of a group of them going boating, with the inevitable consequences that followed.

Edward took the scenic route into the university grounds through the park. He stood in front of the main College House. It had changed very little. It was pretty much exactly as he remembered it. Halls of residence, including the one where he'd resided in his first year, towered over the rear. Geography and social sciences departments still lay to the left of him as he looked, or at least the buildings where they'd been housed, and humanities and the main library to the right. It was Edward's understanding that engineering and some of the more scientific and mathematical departments had now moved out to the new Swansea Bay Campus. Having graduated almost forty years earlier, he had little idea what the exact division was based on. He would only glean a little more information as he wandered about for himself.

What did strike Edward was whilst all the buildings from his day still stood proudly in place, a myriad of other unsightly buildings had popped up in every available space between. It created an odd, incongruous sprawl. The buildings looked mismatched and unplanned, at least to him. The original buildings had enjoyed a similar look and feel to them. The new ones were all different. They created a mishmash effect. Edward wasn't overly impressed. He didn't like it all that much, he realised. That was progress for you though, he reflected. More students needed more buildings. Naturally, the numbers of undergraduates there had increased massively since his day. No doubt, they'd only continue to increase. It was just the way of things.

It was strange really, walking round and taking everything in. Whilst the campus had changed in many ways, in others it hadn't changed at all. Edward found it both comforting and disconcerting. Everywhere, new buildings had sprung up among the old. It made it hard for him to get his bearings and know exactly where he was. He decided to make his way to the old college bar in Union House. He assumed that would still be there. Some students still liked to drink. On his way, he noticed the main college refectory was still in its original location. He was almost surprised. It hadn't changed as much as he'd expected. He'd half anticipated it would have been turned into one of those fashionable new eateries, operated by one of the popular casual dining chains. Whilst it was being run as a concession, at least it appeared to be an independent one.

The college bar was there too, just as it had always been. It was here Edward would have his morning coffee, though inside it had changed out of all recognition. It had a trendy new name, designed to appeal to students. It had been given a modern makeover. It still served alcohol, but it was less of a bar, more a chic, barista-style coffee house. It wasn't at all as he remembered it. It bore little resemblance to the place that he, Angela, and their friends had started many a misspent evening with a few pints. Edward ordered himself a coffee and a flapjack. He chose a *flat white* from the list on offer, although in truth he didn't really know what that was. What made it different from a *latte* or an *Americano*? He had no idea. A coffee had been a coffee in his day. It still was in his mind.

Edward sat with his coffee and flapjack and took in his surroundings. Students were scattered at the tables round him, all with laptops, tablets, or phones in front of them. They'd had none of these electronic devices when he'd been an undergraduate. They'd had pen and paper or an old, manual typewriter if they were lucky. How times had changed. It really was another world. Edward got out his book and read a few more pages. He'd almost finished it. He'd have to start another the following day.

Forty years earlier, Edward had felt very comfortable here. It had been his second home. He no longer felt comfortable, he realised. He was too old. Too many years had passed. These young people had no place in his life and memories, nor he in theirs. His thoughts were inhabited instead by the ghosts of forty years earlier, who'd all moved on. Edward had been young once, just as these students were. He'd had his life in front of him. Now, he'd lived it. He'd selected his chosen path. It had worked out pretty much as he'd hoped and according to plan. He still had regrets. He remembered the carefree faces of some of his friends doing English, drama, and history degrees. They'd had even fewer lectures than he had and many less than the likes of Angela. Sometimes, he'd been envious of their free time and lazy lifestyles, which had been even greater than his own. Of course, the majority hadn't gone on to earn as much money as he'd done. That didn't mean, however, that they didn't have happy lives. No doubt, they did, most of them.

Edward's dreams had been different once. Inspired by the creative individuals round him, he'd briefly dreamt of being a poet, a writer, or an artist. Now, he was surrounded by a new generation of youthful, hopeful, eager faces, with their own aspirations. Some would be successes, others wouldn't be. It was just the way of the world. Who was to know what would befall each one and what lay ahead of them? Edward had no clue. He couldn't judge by looks alone. Of course, it was a much more cosmopolitan, multicultural place than it was in his day, as it should be. It had been largely dominated by Welsh students then, with a generous percentage of English thrown in. Now it was very diverse, reflecting the changes in society in the time that had passed, since he himself was studying for a degree.

Edward finished his coffee and flapjack and left through the main College House entrance. He headed towards Singleton Abbey and Singleton Park. He wanted to view the whole campus, though he realised he wouldn't return on this particular visit to Wales. He felt out of place there. There had just been too much water under the bridge to spend too long here. It was a young person's institution, quite rightly, not for old men like him. Edward recalled the faces of the lecturers who'd taught him. Most would be dead now, or very elderly, he realised. Many hadn't been young then. They'd be in their eighties or nineties now if still alive. He hoped the younger ones at least would still be living. They'd be in their late sixties at best or seventies now, he imagined. He presumed all would be long retired. He doubted he knew a single soul there now. Once, he'd known hundreds to say hello to and greet by name, not anymore.

It was time for Edward to leave. He'd seen what he'd come for. He walked past Singleton Abbey and out into the wide, green expanses of Singleton Park. Once, he'd have crossed straight over to the Byrnmill and Uplands areas. This time he was going a different way round. He wanted to see the whole park in all its glory for a change. He remembered playing football and rugby there with friends as a student. He was too old and a tad too rotund for such games now. That had been mainly at weekends or in the easy weeks after summer exams, when time had been their own, to do with as they wished. Sometimes, they'd gone for a quick game after lectures. More often than not, they'd gone to the pub. He dreaded to think how many pints of beer he'd drunk as a student. It had been a lot.

It was a good job he'd cut back in recent times, before it was too late, and his bodily organs suffered serious, long-term damage. Largely for health reasons, he now mainly restricted himself to a wine or beer at mealtimes, or a scotch and soda before bed. He couldn't imagine giving up altogether. Alcohol had been too big a part of his life for too long. Not only as a student, drink had been practically compulsory during his working days. It was a way he and his fellow financial whizzes coped with the stress of their jobs. Liquid lunches and a few after work were the norm. Edward had been happy to go along with it. He'd always enjoyed a tipple. He thought little of the consequences, until he'd received the diagnosis of heart arrythmia. That had probably been caused by a combination of excessive drinking and work pressures. The damaging mix of both had in all likelihood played its part. It didn't really matter which had been the biggest contributory factor. It was just something Edward had to learn to live with now. He'd need more complicated medical procedures if he ever wanted it cured completely.

Edward took a circular route round Singleton Park, so he wouldn't miss any part. He meandered his way through the ornamental gardens on the southern edge. He remembered taking occasional romantic walks with Angela there on quiet Sunday mornings forty years before. He wondered why they hadn't come more often. Their priorities had probably been elsewhere. The prospect of a lazy lie-in or a pub lunch no doubt seemed more appealing at the time. Occasionally of course there were essays to be written at weekends, or assignments and mathematical problems to be solved in Angela's case. Generally, she seemed to carry a higher burden of work than he did. Edward was expected to undertake a lot of extracurricular reading. Most of the time he didn't bother. He considered attending the majority of his lectures, seminars and tutorials to be sufficient. Ultimately, that had got him through.

It was this area of the park which Edward had come to most often during his final exams. It had provided a welcome break from revising. The quiet stillness and the gentle sound of birdsong had provided a calming distraction. It had helped to relax and revive him and keep him sane. He'd built regular coffee breaks and quiet walks into his revision routine throughout those last months. Some students had cracked under the pressure of finals. They'd found it too much. Edward had not been one of them. He'd always done the minimum to keep his head above water. That had stood him in good stead. Others had reached their final exams with the sudden painful realisation they'd done absolutely nothing for three years. They'd left themselves too much to catch up on. Edward had been sensible and practical enough to ensure his work was mainly up to date. That had proved a blessing and both he and Angela had left with creditable degrees.

A little further on, Edward passed the beautifully constructed, highly ornate, 19th century, wooden, Swiss cottage, with its bold, carmine red panels and pale blue and cream decorative frontage. It was the park's most famous landmark and he remembered it well. There was now a mobile coffee shop outside. That hadn't been there in Edward's day. People hadn't felt the same need for constant takeaway coffees when he'd been a young man. Now, for most working office folk, it was a daily routine they couldn't survive without.

Edward took one or two photos on his phone as he went. He had done on the day of his arrival when he'd taken some of the ruins of Swansea Castle. He'd turned his phone off after that, to avoid any unwanted calls or messages from Alice. He'd since relented and turned it back on again, so he could at least have some of the benefits it provided. He'd deliberately left it on silent and not checked his phone calls or texts. He didn't want to hear from Alice, though he could tell from his screen notifications she had now texted and tried to ring. He would have been a bit surprised if she hadn't at some point. No doubt, she wondered where he was and what he was doing. He just wasn't ready yet to listen to what she had to say. He would do eventually in his own good time.

It would be a shame, however, not to keep some visual record of his trip, he decided. For that reason alone, he'd turned his phone back on. A few pictures would just be something to enjoy when he got home, he reasoned. It would be a small memento and reminder of the places he'd been to and visited. They were just snapshots he was taking, not works of art. They weren't intended to be that, but they'd provide a few pleasant memories of what he'd done he could look through and treasure at some later date in the future.

At the northern edge of the park, Edward encountered a small stone circle he had no recollection of. He could see the arrangement wasn't historically authentic but a more modern reproduction. A quick *Google* check revealed it had been erected to celebrate the 1925 Welsh Eisteddfod. It was almost a hundred years old, unlike the neolithic ones he and Angela had observed on a walking holiday on Dartmoor they'd once enjoyed in their young, energetic days of early marriage, before Victoria and Henry had been born. In some ways, the recollections of that holiday now seemed even more distant to Edward than the days he spent at Swansea. Swansea and his time as a student suddenly seemed comparatively recent and no longer a thing of the distant past, now he was back visiting the locations he'd formerly considered to be home.

At the top end of the park, where the entrance there continued into the residential area of Sketty, Edward took a left turn towards Swansea Botanical Gardens. These were something of a hidden treasure of the city and a feature Edward had little recollection of as student, though he may well have visited at some point. He'd read of the gardens since and had always been keen to visit. Now, he was finally doing that. As he walked past the neatly landscaped and well-maintained flower beds and formal, floral arrangements on display, they stirred no memories in Edward. He suspected he'd never visited them before, although he couldn't be absolutely certain. He was only guessing that, as the gardens were slightly concealed from view and not on an obvious way through the park. From at least one of his student houses, the park had been a natural route to the campus. Edward didn't recall ever taking this particular path, though he might well have done. If he had, he'd forgotten.

Edward was impressed by the park and took a few more photographs. He was fortunate he'd come on a fine day. As well as the outside flowerbeds, there were greenhouses housing exotic and tropical plants.

These would die exposed to the elements, but were flourishing in the warm, humid air behind glass. Edward thought he was the only visitor enjoying the delights the garden had to offer, but once outside he encountered a retired couple also making the most of the floral beauty on display. He guessed they were in their late sixties, early seventies, a decade or so older than he was himself. They stopped him and asked if he'd mind awfully taking a picture of them.

'Of course not,' Edward replied. 'It would be my pleasure.'

'I used to come here as a child,' the lady explained, handing Edward her phone. 'I lived just around the corner. We still come here when we can. It hasn't really changed in all that time.'

'I was at the university, but I don't think I've been before,' Edward admitted. 'I didn't realise it was here.'

'It is well hidden,' the lady agreed. 'Lots of people who've lived here for years don't know about it.'

'I wonder, would you be so good as to take a photograph of me too,' Edward asked, after taking a couple of pictures of the couple. 'I'm by myself, you see,' he explained.

It would be good to have at least one photograph of himself on holiday, he thought.

'We'd be delighted,' the gentleman spoke, returning the favour and taking Edward's phone from him, to take his picture.

'Well, enjoy the rest of your day,' Edward said, after he'd posed for his own photograph.

'You too,' the couple said. 'Enjoy your time in Swansea.'

Eventually, Edward left the Botanical Gardens and re-joined the main park. It was time for him to move on. He departed by the top gates and meandered his way through Sketty and into the middle-class Uplands neighbourhood. He passed pubs, shops, and cafés he remembered visiting as a student. In his second year, he'd lived very nearby. He could have walked past the house he used to live in, but he decided to do that another day. It would require a minor diversion; one he'd make another time. Instead, he continued past the shops towards town. He passed the road where Dylan Thomas had lived as a boy. Again, Edward didn't stop. His long walk had made him hungry. He was ready to get back to the city centre and to eat. The time he normally ate lunch had elapsed some time earlier.

Edward could have found his way into town with his eyes closed. He hadn't done it for years, but he'd done it so many times in the past, it remained ridiculously familiar to him. It was engrained on his mind. He was almost surprised by the familiarity of the buildings he passed. Although a few had changed purpose, in general this particular area of Swansea had barely changed at all. It was much less changed than some parts of the city centre and the marina area for example. By comparison, the road into town from the Uplands was little altered, though there were more elegant café-bars and eateries than there had been, Edward observed. Regarded as the affluent part of Swansea, there had been a number even then.

Eventually, he dropped back down onto the Kingsway and made his way to a café on the side of Swansea's Grand Theatre, that had caught his eye on a previous stroll. He passed Meredith's coffee shop. He wouldn't be in today. She'd wonder where he was, he reflected. At the theatre café, he found a table and enjoyed a leisurely late lunch in the elegant surroundings. He'd always been fascinated by old theatres and cinemas. He could picture himself on the stage or working as a theatre director or manager. Perhaps in another life, one he hadn't lived. He'd always been keen on films, even as a student. He'd been less of a theatregoer. To his shame, he hadn't been a regular at either of Swansea's main theatres as a student. Some of his more artistic friends had gone from time to time. He hadn't usually joined them. He'd been more dedicated to Angela and to drinking. He partly regretted that now. They could have gone together. Neither one of them had suggested it at the time.

Of course, they'd been many times since, in and around Oxford. Subsequently, he'd gone with Alice after Angela's death. Theatre hadn't meant that much to them as undergraduates. Neither had eating out. They'd saved most of their money for alcohol. They'd occasionally gone for a fry-up in a local café or a curry in a late-night Indian restaurant. In those days, some stayed open very late in Swansea, so they could be open for drinkers after the pubs had kicked out. It was one way of getting round the more rigid licensing laws of forty years ago. Once or twice, he and Angela dined out as a couple somewhere nice, but those occasions had been rare. It was hard to imagine, but eating out wasn't such a thing then, not as it has since become.

By the time Edward left the café, it was gone 3pm. He decided to go to one or two shops before returning to the guesthouse. In *Marks & Spencer*, he bought some functional clothes, to add to those he'd brought with him in his travel bag. Alice liked him to buy expensive, designer labels. He considered it a waste of money. She wasn't with him now. He was happy to settle for the kind of practical, timeless quality he knew *Marks & Spencer* would provide him. Edward bought socks, underwear, several shirts, and a pair of trousers. He anticipated they'd see him through a small extension to his planned stay. If he stayed longer, he might need another jacket too. That could wait at present. Edward was unconcerned if he couldn't carry all the new clothes back to Oxford with him. Any he couldn't carry he'd leave behind with Alan and Gwen or give to charity. Alternatively, he might buy another bag to carry them in. He wasn't worried either way. The money didn't matter to him. He had plenty to live on. A few pounds spent on clothes was of no great consequence. Neither was the forty pounds he was spending every night on bed and breakfast. He could stay as long as he liked, forever if he wanted.

Edward didn't dine out that night. Instead, he popped to a Chinese takeaway he'd noticed when walking past the Brangwyn Hall. He ordered a selection of savoury dishes that he knew he'd enjoy but would be no good for his waistline. He then took them back to his room to eat alone. He didn't go down for a drink that night. He decided to leave Alan and Gwen in peace. He'd join them again another night at the weekend. After he finished eating, Edward read for a bit. He finally finished his book. He'd start another one the next day. Edward found himself identifying a little with Dostoevsky's protagonist, though he wasn't quite so introverted, paranoid, and reclusive. Edward was happy in his own company, as he was now, but could be a social creature when he needed to be. That was the big difference. Edward knew how to play the game. That skill had served him well in the world of work. It had made him a rich man. It didn't stop him being alone now. With that thought in his head, Edward rolled over and fell asleep.

Day Five (Friday)

After breakfast, Edward relaxed in his room for a while, watching television. He checked the weather forecast before setting out. It was mainly fine, with just the occasional light shower expected. Looking out of his bedroom window across the bay, Edward could see it was clear and relatively cloudless at present. He hoped it would stay that way, perhaps long enough anyway for him to get out and back again. Edward tried on some of his new clothes. They felt a little stiff, as was only to be expected, having just been pulled from their cellophane packaging. No doubt, they'd soften as he wore them. They fitted him quite nicely, which was the main thing.

Edward took the bay route into the shopping centre, along the Oystermouth Road. That seemed to be his preference in the daylight hours. At night, he generally favoured the route which took him along St Helen's Road and then along Oxford Street. As he had done on most other mornings since his arrival, Edward made his way first to the coffee shop by the market he'd chosen as his daily starting point for virtually anything he was doing. He hadn't visited the previous day, as he'd been heading in the opposite direction, to the university campus. Today, he was back where he felt relaxed and comfortable and in what was now a new home from home for him. Meredith was there to welcome him with a friendly smile. Her warm, easy-going demeanour was infectious. It made Edward feel cheerful, even when circumstances could possibly have made him feel otherwise.

'Good morning,' he said confidently, as he walked in. 'And what a lovely day it is, I should say.'

'We missed you yesterday,' Meredith told him.

'I'm sorry I didn't call by. I wasn't really heading this way. I had to go the university campus, the Singleton Park one,' Edward explained.

'It would have been a bit out of your way, coming here first,' Meredith acknowledged.

'That was what I thought, sadly,' Edward agreed.

'Anyway, what can I get you today?' Meredith asked.

'A coffee naturally, and do you have a Bakewell tart? If not, anything you think is nice will be perfect,' Edward said, happy to bow to her better judgement.

'I do have a Bakewell,' Meredith said.

'You know I shouldn't really. I had a cooked breakfast only an hour or two earlier. I'm having one every day at the moment. It won't be good for my girth. Oh well, I am on holiday,' Edward laughed. 'I bought some new clothes yesterday. I'll have to go back and get some bigger ones if I start expanding, thanks to your lovely cakes.'

'Everyone deserves a treat now and then,' Meredith said.

'They do, but I have them every day,' Edward admitted guiltily, as he paid for his order.

'I'll bring them over shortly,' Meredith said.

Edward went to find a table and sat down. He pulled out a book. It was a new one. It was *The Rum Diary* by Hunter S Thompson. He'd read *Fear and Loathing in Las Vegas* and greatly enjoyed it. He'd then tried *Hell's Angels* and hadn't enjoyed it so much. He'd got bogged down in too much detail and lack of any real plot. It really was a factual history of the early years of the Hell's Angels movement, who Hunter S Thompson had ridden with, and an exposé of their often-controversial activities. A friend had recommended *The Rum Diary* as a good one. Edward had picked it up among a small pile he'd shoved in his travel bag virtually as he was walking out the door. What he had with him was little more than potluck or luck of the draw. There was absolutely no planning or logic to his choices. It had just been a matter of grabbing what was nearest to hand. *The Rum Diary* was one of those.

It concerned a young journalist of dubious moral backbone travelling to San Juan in Puerto Rico, to take up a post at a struggling newspaper. There, he becomes embroiled in a complicated love triangle and other sorts of shady dealings, all fuelled by consummate quantities of rum of course. He sounded like the kind of anti-hero Edward liked reading about. Edward had always been too conventional and too sensible deep down to be like that himself. It didn't stop him enjoying reading about such characters. He felt he could have been more daring and spontaneous in another life, if only given the chance. Both Angela and Alice might have liked him to be. Perhaps he was a little too formal for his own good. It was time to change all that and let his hair down a little, at least what he had left of it.

'I see you finished your book then,' Meredith remarked, as she placed Edward's coffee and Bakewell tart down.

'Yes, last night. It was rewarding in its own way,' Edward said. 'I'm just starting a new one. I've been told it's entertaining and I'll like it.'

'I have to admit it's not one I've ever heard of,' Meredith said. 'You do read some odd books.'

'They're not to everyone's tastes,' Edward acknowledged. 'But I normally enjoy them. If not, I can usually find some interest in them. I hate to start a book and not finish it.'

That was a point of pride with Edward, however hard going he found a book. One of two he'd found very difficult to get to the end of. *Visions of Cody* by Jack Kerouac and *Ulysses* by James Joyce were two that immediately sprung to mind. Edward generally focussed on modern classics. By that he meant anything from the mid-19th century. Most he found pleasure reading. There were one or two writers he considered somewhat overrated, including James Joyce, who he'd been delving into a little of late. Edward could appreciate being of an Irish, Catholic background would certainly assist in the appreciation of Joyce's work. The books which Edward had read hadn't resonated greatly with him. *Dubliners* and *Portrait of the Artist as a Young man* had been adequate but no more. Of course, Edward wouldn't have expressed that opinion to a proud Irishman. He'd be more than likely lynched. It would be like dismissing Dylan Thomas in Wales. Edward didn't dislike Joyce. He just wasn't entirely convinced his books were as significant as they were considered to be by critics of literature. Edward imagined *The Rum Diary* would just be a drunken rollercoaster ride of excess, fun and the inevitable shame that followed. That would suit Edward well. Highbrow literature wasn't required on this occasion, though Hunter S Thompson was an accomplished enough writer of his genre and in his own right.

'I don't finish them if they're boring,' Meredith said.

She had a point. Why persevere with something he wasn't enjoying? It made no sense, even though he'd done it many times in the past. Great literature was sometimes something to be endured and persisted with, a bit like opera, or the greens and vegetables that came with an otherwise enjoyable meal. That was how Edward viewed it. He didn't like to surrender to the slow pace and dullness. He liked to get to the end, even if the journey hadn't been entirely satisfactory. He was confident there would be no such issues with *The Rum Diary*. Even if he didn't like the book, at least he'd enjoy his cake and coffee, he reflected. Books weren't always easy. Sometimes they were hard work. Perhaps ultimately that was part of the appeal.

'You're probably wise,' Edward replied.

For all his supposed education and worldly wisdom, Meredith's practical sense was probably far greater than his. He continued to live within the constraints of middle-class narrowmindedness. It was time to break free of those shackles too. Alice wouldn't have allowed him to stay in a guesthouse like the one Alan and Gwen were running. It had to be four or five-star at least. She wouldn't have allowed him to come to Meredith's coffee shop every morning. She'd have considered such places beneath them. She'd have settled for nothing less than morning coffee or afternoon tea at *The Ivy* or somewhere equally exclusive, not that Edward considered there was anything wrong with such places either. They had their own place in the order of things. Alice would have been concerned about wagging tongues in the village where they lived if they were seen anywhere less sophisticated. Stuff all that pompous nonsense, Edward told himself proudly. He wanted to get back to basics and mix with honest, decent, working people, like he was unwittingly or perhaps deliberately surrounding himself with in Wales. This was real life, not that pretence and fakery back in his Oxfordshire village.

'Enjoy your cake. I made it myself,' Meredith said.

'I'm sure I will,' Edward assured her.

She then left him to his coffee and cake and his new book. When he'd finished, Edward placed his bookmark at the point he'd broken off and closed his book. He said his goodbyes and stepped back out into the fresh air. It was still sunny with little cloud overhead. Edward hadn't forgotten he'd promised to visit the bookshop again. It had been raining then. It would be fine this time. Edward walked down the whole length off Oxford Street. At the end, he turned onto St Helen's Avenue towards King Edward's Road and the small side street where the bookshop was located. Edward found it without too much difficulty. As soon as he walked in, Jill, the bookshop owner, remembered him immediately.

'I wondered if you'd be back,' she greeted him, affably.

'I said I would and I'm a man of my word,' Edward asserted. 'Did you think I wouldn't be?' he added.

'I never doubted you,' Jill said. 'You look the reliable sort.'

'I like to think so,' Edward said.

'I'm sure you are,' Jill replied.

He noticed her dog was sleeping quietly in its basket, in what Edward presumed to be its customary place of daytime rest. It was very well behaved. It appeared to be no trouble at all. Edward had to acknowledge that, even though he himself was no great lover of dogs. There had been a bad experience with Victoria in a park when she was a child. A dog off its lead had bitten her on the hand when she'd reached out to stroke it. She'd been fearful of them after that. She'd sought to avoid dogs at all costs afterwards. By default, Edward had avoided them too. He didn't want to see his daughter upset or worried. This one seemed all right, however, and unlikely to bite or bark at anybody.

'So, did you find anything for me?' Edward asked, at last.

'As a matter of fact, I did,' Jill replied. 'I found a couple of things that might be of interest.'

She then retreated to her back office to fetch them. She came back with two books in her hand. One was a 1968 *Panther Books* edition of JG Ballard's *The Crystal World*. Edward recognised it by its cover. It was Edward's favourite of Ballard's early novels from his so-called science fiction period, though Edward didn't really consider Ballard to be a science fiction writer. He was far too innovative, ground-breaking, and unique to be categorised by one genre of writing alone. He broke the boundaries and defied literary generalisation. He had his own style and like one of Edward's other great favourites, Kurt Vonnegut, pretty much created his own genre, that was unlike that of any other writer. More importantly, whilst Edward had a copy of the book, he didn't have this particular edition of it.

The other book was a beautiful 1970s *Fontana* edition of Eric Ambler's *The Mask of Dimitrios*, one of only a couple Edward didn't have in that particular imprint. Jill had done very well. Some considered the garish 1970s book covers like the Eric Ambler ones to be crude and vulgar, with their bright colours and mildly sexist images. Edward had loved them as an adolescent. He still loved them now. So what if they were products of their time and like Ian Fleming's *James Bond* series would no longer be considered politically correct. What did it matter? To Edward, they looked great then and they looked great still. What was more, now he'd have almost all of them in his collection.

'I'll have them both,' Edward said, immediately. 'How much for the pair?'

'Does ten pounds seem a fair price?' Jill asked.

'Very fair indeed,' Edward said, opening his wallet and passing the money across to her.

'So, you're a collector of books,' she said, looking him quizzically up and down.

'I wouldn't quite say a collector, but I do like books,' Edward admitted.

'Who's your favourite author?' Jill asked.

She made the question sound like she was testing him.

'I'm not sure I have a favourite. I do like JG Ballard and Kurt Vonnegut. But if I had to pick just one, it would probably be George Orwell,' Edward said. '*Nineteen Eighty-Four* is my very favourite novel. *Keep the Aspidistra Flying* is another.'

'*Animal Farm*?' Jill asked.

'Strangely it's not a personal favourite,' Edward said. 'Although I know a lot of people love it.'

'I had a first edition of that. It went for a thousand pounds. It would have gone for a lot more if it had been in better condition,' Jill said.

'Who's your favourite author?' Edward enquired.

'Do you really need to ask?' Jill chuckled. 'Why, Dylan Thomas, of course. I'm Welsh. I live in Swansea, and I own a bookshop. Who else could it really be?'

'Who else indeed,' Edward agreed. 'I like him well enough, but I'm not that familiar with his work.'

'Well, you should become more so, whilst you're here in Swansea,' Jill told him. 'It's a nice day. Why don't you head down to The Mumbles and check out some of his old haunts? A lot of them have gone, but there still one or two left, and it's lovely there on a day like today,' Jill said.

'You know, that's a very good idea, and I may just do that,' Edward said.

He'd been planning to take a bus round the bay and walk to Mumbles Pier. Why not today? Today was as good a day as any.

'Do come back again though. I might have more books for you. I'm still going through them,' Jill said.

'I'll certainly do that,' Edward promised. 'I have to say your dog is very well behaved. Is it a Labrador?' Edward asked.

'She certainly is. She's called Beti, with the Welsh spelling,' Jill said. 'She's getting on a bit, but she still enjoys a walk. Perhaps you'd like to take her out one day?' Jill suggested.

Edward suddenly fidgeted rather awkwardly. He couldn't do that, could he? Then he thought, why not? He was embracing new experiences. Why couldn't he take a dog for a walk?

'Does she walk far?' Edward enquired.

'She's not the quickest, but she'll walk as far as you want to take her,' Jill answered.

'Sounds a bit like me,' Edward said. 'I'm not as quick as I once was.'

‘Would you like to take her?’ Jill asked.

‘Of course, I’ll take her,’ Edward said, with an assured tone in his voice, even if he didn’t feel totally assured underneath.

Why shouldn’t he do this poor lady working on her own a favour? It would be at no cost to him.

‘That’s very kind,’ Jill said.

‘Will you be here on Monday?’ Edward wondered. ‘Perhaps I can do it then if I haven’t gone home before. I don’t think I will have done.’

‘Monday will be perfect, as I can walk her myself at weekends,’ Jill said.

‘I’ll see you on Monday then,’ Edward said.

‘I’ll be here,’ Jill said. ‘So will Beti, waiting for you.’

‘And thank you for finding the books,’ Edward added, as he was leaving.

‘My pleasure,’ Jill said,

‘I think I’ll take your advice. I think I’ll head down to The Mumbles. I’ll get some lunch there and have a little look around,’ Edward confirmed,

‘Have fun and see you on Monday,’ Jill said, as she showed him out of the bookshop.

He waved back, as he walked off down the road. What a polite man, she thought to herself, wondering also why he was holidaying alone by himself in Swansea of all places. Meanwhile, Edward headed back onto the Oystermouth Road, where he went in search of a bus stop. He remembered from his student days there was a regular service round the bay into Mumbles and further on to the Gower Peninsula for those with destinations there. Edward would do that another day, perhaps even at the weekend if the weather remained good. There was no point going up onto the Gower in the rain. He’d done that on one occasion with Angela as students. It hadn’t been their best idea. They’d only got off the bus briefly once that day at Rhossili. That was enough. Faced with a fierce wind and beating rain in their faces, despite the fact it was June, they’d almost immediately got back on a bus again and returned to Swansea bus station not a moment too soon.

Edward waited patiently for a bus to come. He was in no particular hurry, though he'd be ready to eat once he got there. It wasn't long before a bus arrived. It was full of retired folk just like himself, he noted, though most a few years older than he was, in their seventies and even eighties at a guess. Edward paid his money and got on. He would have been entitled to a free bus pass if he lived in Wales, he realised. He wasn't yet where he resided in England. He didn't mind paying. He didn't consider the return fare a lot to pay. He might even walk back if he had the energy, or some part of the way. He'd decide that later. In the meantime, he simply sat back to enjoy the pleasant bus ride around the bay. He looked out for familiar sights he hadn't seen in years as he went.

The bus let Edward out opposite the impressive local landmark that was Oystermouth Castle. Edward found a modern, barista-type coffee house in an arcade off Newton Road to have his lunch. As luck would have it, a light shower of rain fell whilst Edward was eating. When Edward emerged back in the daylight, he did so in glorious sunshine. He wouldn't have known if had rained at all but for some dampness on the pavement that was quickly drying. Mumbles had more shops than Edward recollected. Many were quite interesting, boutique ones, tailored towards the tastes of Edward's generation. Back in the day, the shops had held little interest for Edward and his friends. They'd only been interested in the pubs, or the *Mumbles Mile* as it was known to them. Of course, they'd mainly come in the night-time then and done one end to the other, finishing up on Mumbles Pier, where there was a student nightclub when Edward was an undergraduate. Now as an older man, Edward could appreciate the shops had an appeal too and were well worth a visit by themselves. That had been lost on him at the time, but not anymore, as he casually browsed as he walked along.

He decided to start at Oystermouth Castle. He'd only viewed it from a distance in the past. He'd never taken the trouble to enter its extensive, meadowed grounds. He was most impressed. In fact, he was a little horrified he'd allowed such a gem to pass him by. He couldn't even claim it was hidden, as he could Swansea's Botanical Gardens. The castle dominated the skyline. He'd just never previously bothered to make the short walk up the hill to see it properly. Now he was there, Edward walked the full circuit of the grounds, pausing occasionally to sit on a bench and enjoy the lush greenery he was surrounded with. He took a couple of pictures of the castle entrance and walls, standing nobly and proudly against a background of clear, blue sky. He didn't venture inside. This was just the beginning of his journey. Other destinations nearby awaited him.

At the bottom of the hill, Edward turned right and continued his gradual if meandering progress in the direction of the pier and lighthouse and what was effectively the end point of the bay before it wove back inland on itself. Edward tried to work out roughly in his head where the almost continual succession of pubs had formerly started. They'd once lined the northern side of the bay road one after another. Jill was right. Almost all had vanished, to be replaced by exclusive apartments, more boutique shops, and the occasional café-bar. Dylan would have been horrified. Of course, he might have been a man of the times and moved with them. Somehow, Edward doubted it. He'd have been dismayed at the closure of his favourite, rustic watering holes, just as Edward was himself. Edward could hardly believe his eyes. He wouldn't have recognised the place. He'd have thought he was somewhere else if he hadn't known better. Edward continued to walk the length of the *Mumbles Mile*. Only a couple of the pubs he'd frequented as a student and that he was aware had once been popular with Dylan Thomas remained. It was a major change indeed, and perhaps reflected changes in people's everyday drinking habits. It was still a lovely place. It just wasn't the Mumbles Edward remembered.

Edward took the opportunity to take a few pictures on his phone of the bay, looking back towards Swansea and Port Talbot, and of Mumbles Pier and the lighthouse. The nightclub that had been so popular in his student days was now a café and ice-cream parlour, with an amusements arcade attached to the back. Edward wouldn't have known it was the same venue he'd enjoyed so many a drunken evening during his misspent youth. He only knew it had to be, as there was simply nowhere else where it could have been. Oh, how being there now took Edward back to another place and another time. He'd kissed many a girl there before he'd met Angela, he reflected. Afterwards, they used to go together religiously almost every week throughout their three years at university. The weekly trip had always remained a highlight and one of the main nights out in their hectic, student social calendar. Edward recalled the frequent occasions they'd missed the bus back and had been forced to walk the four a half miles home to where they lived. Going to bed in the small hours, they then had to get up early the next morning and attend lectures nursing tired, nagging hangovers. Those really were the days, Edward considered, with a note of nostalgia. He realised he was surrounded by others enjoying the scenery and leisurely walks in the sunshine. He was so lost in his own wistful thoughts, he barely noticed them.

On the way back, Edward stopped in one of the few original pubs that still stood where it had not only forty years before but when Dylan Thomas had drunk there as a young newspaper reporter and aspiring poet in the 1930s. There, Edward ordered a pint of locally brewed ale, which he raised and drank in Dylan's honour. Edward hoped it would fortify him for the long journey ahead. Edward stayed on the coastal path, overlooking the sandy bay, where there was room for both pedestrians and cyclists to proceed safely in unison. The path now extended all the way to Swansea and beyond to Port Talbot and perhaps even further. Edward didn't remember it going that far unbroken in his day, but it possibly had done. Generally, they'd been forced to keep to the main road, to avoid walking back in pitch blackness and perhaps ending up in the sea in their state of almost inevitable drunkenness. Edward could recall that happening to more than one student back in the day. Those who'd ended up in the sea were generally too drunk to either care or remember.

By the time he'd reached Blackpill, Edward had walked several miles and found he was beginning to tire. He decided to stop there, to rest his weary legs and wait for a bus to pass. He still had his return ticket. It wasn't long before one came along. As Edward got off at the nearest bus stop to the guesthouse where he was staying, another light rain shower began to fall. Perhaps it was as well he was returning when he was. He spent a pleasant hour or two in his room, waiting for the rain to pass, before popping out to get something to eat. On his return, he sat in the lounge for a while, enjoying a drink with Alan and Gwen. He told them about his day. He explained he was particularly struck that so many of the Mumbles' pubs of yesteryear had gone.

'It's very different these days,' Gwen commented.

'It's still nice but it's not what it was,' Alan confirmed. 'It's catering for a different sort of visitor than in the past.'

'I'm a bit of a traditionalist, I'm afraid,' Edward said. 'I like things to stay the same and remain as they were.'

With that, he finished his drink and started to head off towards bed.

'I think we'd both agree with you there,' Alan nodded, as Edward said goodnight.

Day Six (Saturday)

Edward enjoyed what he realised was his sixth cooked breakfast in a row. He'd already decided to have something else the following day. He would at least once a week for as long as he was there, although he still had no idea how long that might be. He was undecided. Whilst he was enjoying himself and doing different and diverse things, he'd remain in Swansea. One morning, he'd probably wake up and decide to get the train back to Oxford in the same spontaneous, casual manner he'd decided to come in the first place. An almost childish whim had brought him here. Something similar would probably take him back again. He'd spent all his life planning for every eventuality. He was done with that. He was only really planning one day at a time, the one he was in. The days after would he imagined take care of themselves.

It was the weekend, and the breakfast room was a little busier. The tables were largely taken with pre-season holidaymakers, no doubt anxious to enjoy their breaks before the schools broke up for half-term and then the summer. Most of the week, Edward had found himself in the company of lone, travelling businessmen and students from abroad, visiting the nearby university campus. There was a noticeably different atmosphere at the weekend. It had been very quiet on the weekday mornings. Alan had made most of the conversation. Now, there was a little more chatter among the holidaying retired couples and one young family with two children. Edward imagined they were just enjoying a weekend getaway to the Gower Peninsula, which he planned to visit today possibly. By Monday, they'd probably be gone and back where they'd come from. Once again, he'd be breakfasting virtually on his own. Having eaten, Edward gave his thanks to Alan and Gwen and said he'd see them later.

'Any plans for the weekend?' Alan asked, in his usual warm and enthusiastic manner.

'I thought I might head out onto the Gower if the weather stays fine,' Edward replied. 'If I don't make the most of the sunshine, it's sure to change.'

'Yes, indeed. Make hay whilst the sun shines,' Alan agreed.

Edward smiled back. He'd made a good choice with this guesthouse, if a lucky one. Alan and Gwen were cheerful and welcoming. He'd certainly landed on his feet here. In his head, he was already making plans to return should the chance arise. He was determined to try and make it happen if he could. He wouldn't leave coming to Swansea so long again. Perhaps he'd make it an annual pilgrimage. He'd always intended to return regularly after graduating. Angela had planned too as well. They had at first. Then the kids had come along, and real life had taken over. They could have brought Victoria and Henry to the Gower more. Edward wasn't quite sure why they hadn't. The children weren't all that interested in their parents' Welsh past in truth. There were places nearer to home they liked to visit.

Edward sat on his usual bench, looking out over the bay for a few moments, before taking the coastal road to the bus station. He had little doubt he could pick up a bus on the Oystermouth Road, but he preferred to go the main bus station by the Quadrant Shopping Centre. He could enquire there what his best options were for visiting the Gower, and perhaps pick up some bus timetables. It didn't really matter if he spent the whole day meandering from one bay to the next, as long as the rain held off. Edward decided not to visit Meredith's coffee shop. He recalled Saturday was her day off that week. He'd no doubt see her again the following week, when he returned for another one of her delicious cakes.

Edward made his enquiries at the information desk. He was advised to get a rover ticket, which would allow to hop on and off any bus that passed. That seemed ideal for his needs. As it happened, the first one that he got on was the same one he'd used the previous day to reach The Mumbles. Again, it was very busy and there was hardly a seat left free on it. It made good progress down the Oystermouth Road, which it joined at the junction just past the guesthouse where Edward was staying. It passed the St Helen's Rugby and Cricket Ground and the lower entrance to Singleton Park. Then it passed the entrance to the main university campus, where several students got on and off, despite the fact it was the weekend. After that, they passed Singleton Hospital and the boating lake and the sports field and complex, where Edward had played many a match in his youth.

He'd been good at football, rugby, and tennis among other sports, but he'd never considered himself part of the Athletic Union's cliques. Each sports had its own, but Edward had never quite managed to become a member of the inner circle of any, despite his relative sporting prowess. At a big university, there was of course always someone better, no matter how good you were at any given sport. If you were good at rugby or football, someone else was an international. Indeed, several notable Welsh internationals had been at Swansea when Edward was there. It had made him feel a little ordinary and he'd turned his attentions instead to other interests, just playing sport purely for pleasure.

The bus continued into Blackpill and past the entrance to the picturesque expanses of Clyne Gardens. It was another scenic location Edward wished to visit before his return home. It had been popular place of solace for Edward and Angela when they first met, and she was still a resident of Clyne Halls. They'd gone there much less after their first year, when they'd taken rooms in a shared house in the Uplands, but it had retained happy memories for them.

After Blackpill, the bus passed through the small community of West Cross. Edward had always been grateful for a local, convenience store there, where he could buy a drink and a snack, when he occasionally chose to take an afternoon stroll from Swansea to Mumbles and back again. Of course, he'd been young and fit then. It had been no great undertaking at the time. It would be too much for him now. The small stretch of the route he'd walked the previous day had been enough. The bus passed Oystermouth Castle where Edward had previously got off. This time he stayed on for another couple of stops, eventually getting out at the Langland Bay car park.

It was a beautiful late spring day in May, when Edward alighted in pleasant sunshine with blue skies above him. He could feel the warmth of the sun on his skin. Langland and it's the adjacent bay of Caswell had been regular destinations for Edward and his friends in the summer term, when exams had finished, and they were yet to return home. There, they'd frolicked happily and playfully on the sands before retiring to a local hostelry. Strangely, they had rarely ventured further onto the Gower, though one or two of their fellow undergraduates had rented accommodation at Bishopston and Gowerton, normally those privileged few with cars. Very few students had owned cars in Edward's days. It was common to now, Edward observed.

Edward hadn't been to Langland for forty years or more, but the view and the beach at least seemed quite familiar to him. It appeared relatively unchanged and untouched, which was always a good thing in Edward's mind, although the number of buildings seemed to have expanded since Edward's day or how he remembered it. He recalled it being quieter. Perhaps it was a little busier simply because it was a nice day. Edward and his friends had probably gone on a weekday not at the weekend. It was no matter. Edward would be lost and absorbed in his own silent thoughts, regardless of how many others were enjoying the same walk.

This was the start of Edward's journey proper for the day. This was one of the reasons he'd come. He wouldn't be spending time on the sand, as he had as an undergraduate. There would be no opportunity for that. He had to press on. He'd be taking the coastal path round to Caswell Bay. He'd done so in his student days and would now do so again. He was sure he and Angela had done the walk together at least once. It was less than two miles, and it was easily negotiated, even for a man of his advancing years. He'd even googled it to check. It was considered one of the easiest and most gentle walks to take on the Gower. That suited Edward to a tee.

Edward wasn't a huge fan of heights, but this was just about tolerable to him. He didn't have to walk too near any edges. Instead, he could just enjoy the views onto the two bays and the sight and sounds of waves crashing against rocky outcrops below. There were parts of the Gower that were far steeper and harder to traverse. Edward would certainly avoid those. The cliffs here were relatively gentle in comparison and for much of the walk a handy handrail provided protection from falling.

As he walked, Edward's thoughts turned inevitably to Alice. He'd managed to push her to the perimeters of his mind for the last day or two and not think about her too much. Now, she was back again with a vengeance. It was probably because it was the weekend. Edward wondered where she was. Was she at home? Was she with Paul at his place? Worse still, was she with Paul in Edward's house? Perhaps she'd gone to stay with her mother or a friend whilst the dust settled. Perhaps she was packing her suitcases and preparing to move out at that very moment. Perhaps Paul was on his way over in the car to fetch her. Perhaps none of these possible scenarios was the correct one. Perhaps she was simply carrying on as if nothing had happened and was now waiting patiently for Edward's return. He had no means of knowing which was the case. All this was idle speculation on his part.

He really must phone her at some point, he reflected. At the very least, he should check her messages and perhaps text her himself. He just couldn't quite bring himself to. The betrayal had been enormous. The shock had been great. Whilst he wasn't as angry as he could have been, he still felt humiliated and was finding it very difficult to forgive her. It hadn't been a total surprise of course. She was young and attractive. Paul was handsome too. They probably made a fine couple. They were no doubt perfect for each other. Edward's looks on the other hand were on the wane and slowly fading. He wouldn't get any better-looking now. That was certain. He'd been a fool. He'd been taken advantage of. He was partly at fault. He had to shoulder a degree of the blame. He should have seen it coming. He should have put two and two together before. He'd been painfully slow to catch on.

Even as he thought about Alice, the natural beauty he was seeing slowly began to push her out of his mind. The air was clean and fresh. It was a joy to breathe it in. The views were quite breathtaking. He could see for miles all around him. Seabirds of all sorts flew to and from the rocky ledges below and above him. As he walked, he took a number of photographs for posterity. At one point, he was fortunate enough to see the head of what he took to be a grey seal break the foamy surface of the blue-green seawater. Edward stood and watched it in wonder for a while. He could see its sleek, streamlined shape, gliding gracefully through the waves. It was perfectly suited and adapted to a marine life. Eventually, Edward lost sight of the seal, as it plunged to greater depths. It had been a brief, exquisite moment. He'd witnessed nature in its natural element first-hand. The memory would remain with him for a long time.

It wasn't much further before Caswell Bay came into full view, as he gradually descended down onto it. It actually seemed even more familiar to him than Langland had. Perhaps it was his imagination, but it seemed even less changed. It really was unspoiled beach and rocks, just as he remembered visiting as a student. Then he, Angela and their friends would have headed straight for the clear, blue waters to swim and splash about. Some families with children were doing just that. Edward would leave them to it. His swimming in the sea days were a thing of the past and long behind him. He'd come prepared for walking not paddling and getting wet. He was happy to see others enjoying the beach and cool waters, however.

At the Caswell Bay car park, Edward waited for a bus to take him on the next leg of his Gower journey. He bought himself an ice cream to enjoy, while he waited. It would replace his usual morning coffee. It felt like summer anyway. It was so pleasant Edward didn't mind waiting the thirty or more minutes it took for a bus to come. He happily got on, as the bus meandered its way round the bay towards Bishopston. As it crossed the delightful, rugged Gower countryside, he could see the scenic outline of Three Cliffs Bay emerging in the distance. He wouldn't stop on this occasion, although part of him would like to have done. It wasn't somewhere they often went as students. He'd perhaps only been there once on a field trip. Oxwich Bay Beach and Port Eynon followed similarly shortly after, then Mewslade Bay Beach. Edward only got out again when the bus stopped at Rhossili. Rhossili Bay Beach was Edward's furthest planned destination.

He recalled the last time he'd been here he'd been battered by high winds and rain, despite it being June. It was very different today. There was just a light breeze, and the seas were calm and blue. The skies above were almost cloudless. It was like chalk and cheese. Edward preferred it like this. Who wouldn't? Only a sadist. Edward definitely wasn't one of those. He was now a retired man who enjoyed his creature comforts and disliked discomfort. He'd spent most of his working life in an office. He wasn't a hardy, outdoor type by nature, although he was happy with this. Sitting on a bench and looking at the sands that extended long into the distance, he felt content. It would take a lot of this to upset him, he thought.

Edward found a charming café by the National Trust Visitor Centre, where he could have his lunch. In fact, he found two and couldn't decide which to go into. He was so undecided, he ended up having his lunch in one and a dessert in the other. It seemed the only fair thing to do in the circumstances. Something of a self-made man himself, Edward was always keen to support and do his bit for local businesses. Having finished eating, Edward found another pleasant spot from which to observe the beach and read his book. There, he was happy to spend an hour or two relaxing in the agreeable and gently warming sunshine.

It was late afternoon when Edward finally rose to his feet. He could have walked further along the bay, but it was hot, and he found he couldn't be bothered. Instead, he slowly ambled his way back to the bus stop. There, he got the inland bus that took him straight back into Swansea, although he could still enjoy views of the coastline and sea for most of the way. It had been a lovely day, one of the best. They all had since his arrival, each as good if not better than the day before. He was very glad he'd come away. He was thankful for the time he was spending in Wales, with his memories. It was exactly what he needed. It was helping him get his head straight and come to terms with events of the last week. They didn't seem quite so important now. Part of him was starting to view it as relatively trivial in the grander scheme of things. After all, Angela had always been the one. It was never Alice he was coming to realise.

Edward slumped on his bed and dozed for a while when he got back to his room. When he eventually woke up, he switched the television on and made himself a cup of coffee. He then read for a bit, before jumping in the lukewarm shower. It hadn't got any warmer since his day of arrival. It was keeping the guesthouse's running costs down. Perhaps that helped to make it so cheap. Edward emerged feeling refreshed. Once dry, he put on another of his clean, new shirts. It was Saturday night and he'd already decided he was going out. He'd hit the town, in a manner of speaking. He wouldn't have his evening meals at one of the local pubs tonight. He'd make his way into the city centre and find somewhere there. He was to all intents and purposes a single man now. Alice had Paul, or at least had been with him. Perhaps Edward might get lucky and meet some eligible divorcee he could have a conversation with. He knew he was only kidding himself. He wasn't ready to meet anyone else, even if he could. He'd need to properly resolve the situation of his marriage one way or another first and let a certain amount of time pass to heal. Only then could he think of the possibility of letting someone else into his life. Even so, the thought that he was going out like the old days brought a glimmer of a smile to Edward's face.

It was nearly seven o-clock when Edward set out. He took the St Helen's Road route. The centre was busy of course. It was a Saturday night. It was hardly surprising. Young men and women were heading out in their droves for the evening. There were people of all ages, but the majority were in their twenties and thirties. That was one change that had taken place since Edward's day. Back then, anyone over twenty-five going to a nightclub would have felt practically geriatric. People got married, settled down and had children earlier in life. Now, these things were often left to their later years. People continued pubbing and clubbing into their forties and even fifties. They often resumed after painful divorces. That would never have happened when Edward was a young man. Now, anyone could go out if they wanted to, although the majority naturally remained young or younger than Edward. He of course was beyond even the most upper limit of what would have been deemed acceptable to go to a nightclub. He wouldn't be doing that even if he could. He fully intended to be back at the guesthouse not long after nine o'clock.

Edward found a pleasant café-bar on what had once been the site of the *David Evans* department store, in which to eat. It was quite busy, but not unacceptably so. Edward chose a table in a quiet corner where he could eat in private relaxation. The lighting was dimmed, so Edward didn't feel too conspicuous alone. He was probably the only diner eating by himself. It didn't overly concern him. He was used to it. He'd had to many times during his working days. It had been normal then, though he'd often dined with work colleagues too. Alice wouldn't have been able to do it. She'd have felt too awkward, wandering into a crowded café or bar without someone to accompany her. That was the good thing about being happy in your own company and own skin, as Edward was. He didn't feel he required anyone. He was happy if they wanted to tag along, but he didn't need them. He was yet to feel homesick. He was very content pottering about as he was.

Edward enjoyed a large glass of *Malbec* with his meal. As it was a Saturday night, he decided he'd also have a pint of ale before heading back. He walked past the pedestrian area that was known as Castle Square and turned down into Wind Street by the ruins of Swansea Castle. It had once been a scene of trouble on Saturday nights in the past, but a lot of the pubs had been replaced by trendy, modern eating houses, so it wasn't quite as rowdy these days. It was still lively, but most of the vocal groups of tipsy young men and women weren't interested in an old man like Edward. They let him be and walk past them unmolested, for which he was grateful. Although he felt a bit like a fish out of water, he was interested in observing what young people got up to in the modern world. He'd been so long married or looking after children growing up, he really had little idea. He hadn't really socialised properly since he was about thirty, except for work and related events, and the kind of more sophisticated social gatherings the older, middle-class folk of Oxford enjoyed. These included things like dinner parties, exhibition openings and book launches. Through his own contacts and Alice's, and his status as a rich, local dignitary, he was invited to more than his fair share of such things, it had to be said. What Edward was witnessing now was very different indeed.

Edward passed an Irish pub of one side of the street and a *Wetherspoon's* on the other. He also passed one where he could see scantily clad females cavorting on the tables for the benefit of the punters. That definitely wasn't Edward's kind of place. It hadn't been when he was a young man. It certainly wasn't now. It was something he'd had have more expected to encounter on the streets of London's Soho than in Swansea, although he did remember seeing one or two strippers at nightclubs in the city centre back in the day. He'd never seen any in Oxford, though there was probably a place somewhere nearby if you wanted that kind of thing.

Eventually, Edward found a bar that was a little more salubrious, at the bottom end of Wind Street near the Maritime Quarter, where he sat and enjoyed a pint of strong, locally brewed beer. When Edward left, he looked at his watch. It was nine o'clock. It was time to head back. Wind Street was distinctly busier and noisier now. Swaying members of several hen parties were cackling loudly. There was drunken shouting. A group of homeless people were having some minor altercation. Edward had seen enough. It was time to leave and make good his escape. He'd only returned here as it was Saturday night. He slipped almost unnoticed through the gathering scenes of alcohol-fuelled mayhem. He walked past the market, the Quadrant and the Grand Theatre and headed downwards to take the coastal path back. It was still only twilight. He'd welcome the peace and quiet of the waters of the sandy bay, after the clamour and commotion of the city centre.

Back in the welcome familiarity of the guesthouse, Edward pushed his front door key into the lock. He wasn't surprised to find Alan and Gwen still up and sitting in the lounge. Both had a small glass in front of them, which they were sipping from, as they relaxed watching the television. Edward would have one with them before heading up, he decided. It was the weekend, and it was too early to go to bed.

'Mind if I join you?' he asked.

'Of course not,' Gwen replied, the first to speak. 'We only wish more of our guests took advantage of our little bar. Hardly any do. I'm not sure they realise it's here.'

Edward had in fact been staying a few days before he found a folder, detailing all the guesthouse's facilities and amenities, tucked away in a drawer, some he had no idea about.

'Will it be a scotch and soda?' Alan enquired, quickly rising to his feet in response to Edward's sudden appearance.

'It will indeed if you have one,' Edward replied.

'So, how was your day?' Gwen asked. 'The weather stayed nice, and we managed to get out for a walk round the bay ourselves.'

'Did you make it up onto the Gower?' Alan wondered.

'I did,' Edward said. 'It was lovely there today, not all that different from how I remembered it, though one or two new things to see of course.'

'The National Trust looks after large parts of it, so it stays relatively unspoiled,' Alan said.

'I'm sure that's a good thing,' Edward commented. 'You wouldn't want buildings popping up all over it.'

'Definitely not,' Gwen agreed.

'Have you had any more thoughts about how long you'll be staying with us?' Alan enquired.

'Not really,' Edward answered, truthfully. 'But I think it will be another week. By the way, when the weekend's over, let me pay you for everything I've had so far.'

'You can settle up at the end of your stay,' Alan said.

'No, I insist. I wouldn't want to take advantage of your hospitality. One good thing about a life in finance is that I'm not short of a bob or two now,' Edward said.

'Well, if you're happy to,' Alan said.

After three drinks, Edward decided perhaps it was time he opened up a little to Alan and Gwen about his real reasons for being in Swansea.

'This is a kind of holiday for me, but it wasn't planned,' he started to explain. 'I'd been meaning to come for some while but was always too busy with work. Just recently I retired, so it became a realistic possibility. Time suddenly is more or less my own, to do with as I will, probably for the first time since my long summer holidays as a student. As I mentioned, I was an undergraduate here and it's where I met my first wife, Angela. It holds many memories for me.'

Edward paused for a moment and took a sip of his drink. He wondered if he should go on, and then he thought what the hell! They seemed like nice people.

'What actually prompted me to come away this week is that I saw my second wife, Alice, with another man, a work colleague called Paul,' Edward disclosed.

Gwen let out a little gasp of shock.

'Oh no,' she said.

'Are they having an affair?' Alan asked.

'Well, I confronted her and that appears to be the case,' Edward confirmed. 'Alice is younger than I am and an attractive woman. Paul is very handsome. I shouldn't be surprised really. It just knocked me for six and I decided to come here to get my head straight and decide what I should do about it,' Edward said.

'Well, stay as long as you like to do that,' Alan said, looking concerned for his guest.

'Thank you, I will,' Edward responded, trying to remain dignified in difficult circumstances.

'Marriages can recover from these things, if you both try to work through your problems,' Gwen said, trying to be helpful in an awkward situation.

'I know they can,' Edward agreed. 'I'm just not sure it's what I want. I can see now perhaps Alice was with me for the wrong reasons. My first wife, Angela, was my true soulmate. I tried my best to pretend it was the same with Alice, but it wasn't really. That's why I need time to think. I haven't been in touch with her yet or checked or answered her messages. I'll have to at some point. I may well get back to find she's gone anyway. Perhaps that's what part of me wants. Then, I won't be left with any difficult decisions to make. It will all be decided for me. It will be a fait accompli.'

'I hope things all work out,' Gwen said, smiling sympathetically at Edward.

'I'm sure they will,' he said, finishing his drink and getting up. 'Time for me to get to bed, I think. I've said more than enough for one evening. Goodnight, see you in the morning.'

'Will you want your usual breakfast?' Alan asked.

'No, I think I'll have something different tomorrow,' Edward said. 'Poached eggs would be nice.'

Day Seven (Sunday)

Edward got up slightly later than he had on other mornings since arriving. It was Sunday after all. He would have had a small lie-in at home, though not a long one. He didn't believe in wasted time. As a child, he recalled his father staying in bed until midday or after on a Sunday, reading the Sunday newspapers, normally *The Telegraph* and *The Times*. His father was usually shattered after a hectic week in a busy office and needed to recuperate. Edward didn't like to do that. He was usually up by nine at the latest. Often, he'd be off to play tennis or for a planned walk or there was tending to be done in the garden. Sometimes, he had office work to catch upon before Monday morning.

Today, Edward didn't rush down to breakfast. He'd noted in the information folder, breakfast continued until ten on a Sunday morning. It finished at nine on other mornings, unless by special arrangement. Being a punctual person, Edward had always gone down between eight and half past. He felt it was the polite thing to do. No doubt, Alan and Gwen had other things to get on with and it was better for them to get breakfast done and dusted as soon as they could. He imagined stragglers and latecomers would be mildly annoying. Edward would never be like that. It wasn't in his nature to put people out. He tried his best to fit in and not be an inconvenience. As an older man, he really preferred not to be noticed. Of course, he'd been louder and more confident in his youth. He'd had some of the *look at me* attitude then. He'd wanted to stand out once. He'd wanted to make his mark in the world of work, and he had. All that had slowly dissipated over the years. Now, he was content to come and go barely making any impression at all.

Edward looked out of his bedroom window across the bay. Being a Sunday morning there were a fair few runners and dog walkers, more than on other days. The sun had retreated, and it was cloudy above. Edward couldn't really complain. Coming at this time of year, he'd been pretty lucky with the weather so far. It had been mostly fine. He'd only been caught in a few showers. You had to expect some in Swansea. It was South Wales. It had a tendency to be a bit wet, ever since he'd known it as a small child, coming to visit grandparents and members of his extended family in and around Cardiff.

No, Edward didn't rush down for breakfast. For once, even he'd take advantage of the extended time he had to take it in. Instead, he made himself a coffee and switched on the television. *Countryfile* or some similar programme was on. He liked programmes about the countryside and the natural world, particularly on God's supposed day of rest. Such inoffensive viewing would suit him perfectly. Edward turned on the shower and jumped in. It was still only lukewarm. He really should mention it to Alan. He was sure Alan would endeavour to fix it, but it seemed petty to do so. It was better to suffer in silence. It was the British thing to do. He was only paying forty pounds a night, he reminded himself. He was probably lucky to have his own shower and toilet at all. Besides, it wasn't actually cold. It just wasn't as hot as he'd have liked it, and how he had it at home.

Eventually, around 9.15am, Edward wandered down to the breakfast room. As on the previous morning, it was busier than it had been on weekdays and there were fewer tables to choose from. He still had no trouble finding one, tucked away in a corner. It just wasn't his favourite one by the window. He'd only get that when it was quiet and if he came down early, he realised. He was unconcerned. He didn't really care where he sat. It was only breakfast. One seat was pretty much as good as another. Edward wasn't by nature a narrow-minded man, given to being over fussy about small details. It had never really been in his interest to be so. That hadn't been the key to business success and making money. He'd always needed to keep abreast of the bigger picture. It had been the same in personal affairs. That was why he wasn't quite as upset by Alice's underhanded actions and infidelity as he might have been.

Edward was pleased that Alan and Gwen had remembered he was departing from his usual full, cooked breakfast and had opted for poached eggs on toast instead. It would make a less filling change, as he planned to have Sunday lunch out today, if he could find a nearby pub serving it. He'd noticed one or two on Byrnmor Road that probably did a traditional roast. Edward would look at least. If they weren't serving Sunday lunch, he'd just settle for something else. He wasn't too bothered.

As on other days, Edward forewent cereal. Even as a child, he'd never been fond of it. He found something distasteful about the sogginess of it, soaked in cold milk as it was. Instead, he just settled for an orange juice and some toast with marmalade, as he waited for his eggs to be brought out. Alan also presented him with a pot of steaming tea. If only the shower was as hot, Edward chuckled merrily to himself. Even perhaps the lukewarm water of the shower was a small blessing. It served to wake him up each day.

Edward wasn't solely a tea or coffee man. He varied it. He liked both. Generally, he ordered tea with his breakfast. On a couple of mornings, he'd chosen coffee instead, when he felt in need of a pick-me-up. More often than not, he made coffee in his room, though sometimes tea. His mid-morning preference was usually for coffee and had been lately when he'd been taking it at Meredith's coffee house. He usually opted for a pot of tea if he stopped anywhere in the afternoon. On returning to his room in the early evening, it was normally coffee, but then tea just before bed. All in all, he varied back and forth between the two quite a lot, depending on the time of day and his mood. As the day wore on, he generally switched to decaffeinated over caffeine, as it was better for his heart. It was a good reason to modify his intake of sugar and alcohol too, though he didn't always do that quite as well as he should. He liked a glass of wine or a beer, as well as a cake.

Edward decided to have a quieter, lazier day, as it was Sunday, just as his father and his father before him would have done. After breakfast, he pottered in his room for a while. He then made him way past the Brangwyn Hall and down St Helen's Road in search of a local shop. There were a few he recalled that he'd passed on his way in and out of the city centre. He didn't have any difficulty locating one. He bought a newspaper, *The Observer*, some chocolate, and a carrier bag to put them in. He'd didn't want them to get wet if it started raining. He didn't return immediately to his room. Instead, he took the scenic route back, continuing to the end of St Helen's Road and then right onto Dilwyn Street and West Way. This took him back down onto the Oystermouth Road, allowing him to walk back with bay, sand and sea views to enjoy. He was passed by a number of runners as he strolled. Even a few of the dog walkers were quicker than he was and overtook him.

Back in his room, Edward whiled away several hours reading his newspaper and then his book. He realised he'd barely heard the news that week and had rather lost touch with the world and what was happening in it. Back at home, he often had *Radio Four* on in the background or the *BBC News Channel* playing. Even if he wasn't sat down closely following it, he inevitably took some in. He'd left all that behind him since coming away and had almost actively avoided the news, although he'd caught a few snippets in passing when it had been on. He had seen the news once or twice, but in nothing like the detail and depth he'd usually have done. Perhaps he feared Alice's face coming on, with an item on *Wife seeking lost husband.* Now that would be embarrassing.

Around twelve-thirty, Edward slipped out. Again, he passed the Brangwyn Hall, as he did so often on his strolls. He was still yet to go in. One day, he would if he remembered to. Edward stopped at a hotel bar on the corner of Brynmor Road he thought might be serving Sunday lunch. He'd had his evening meal there one evening earlier in the week and it had been quite nice. The bar was an occasional haunt from his student days, not a regular one but one they used to go in from time to time. Edward was lucky. They were serving Sunday lunch. He ordered roast beef with all the trimmings and a glass of red wine, *Shiraz*, to go with it.

Edward got himself a seat, whilst he waited for his meal to arrive. He wondered if Alice was doing the same. Perhaps they were sat in a pub somewhere back in Oxford, enjoying Sunday lunch together. Perhaps he was cooking it for her. Perhaps she was cooking it for him, in Edward's home. Perhaps they weren't together at all. Perhaps they'd decided not to continue their affair, after being discovered, after being found out for the cheats they were.

All the same, Edward couldn't help wondering what Alice was doing. He got out his phone and stared at it. He could see from the call record Alice had rung him three or four times and had left several messages. She'd also texted a number of times. Perhaps he should ring her back. A week had now passed since her revelation. Perhaps it was time. Edward didn't really want to. He wasn't quite sure what he wanted to say to her. He still didn't know if he wanted to stay with her or if indeed it was time to part ways. He hadn't made his mind up. The correct course of action remained unclear to him. That was why he was here. That was why he'd escaped to Swansea and still hadn't returned home.

Eventually, with a degree of reluctance, Edward glanced at one of the texts. *Where are you, Edward?* it read. *What are you doing? Have you lost your mind? Have you gone mad? What will the neighbours say?* Who cared what they had to say? Bugger them and their opinions! No doubt they'd have a few choice words to say about Alice and Paul if they knew the whole truth. There was little concern in Alice's tone for Edward's welfare. Her only thought was how it might reflect on her. That was enough for Edward. He didn't really need to read any more. He deleted the rest without reading them. He would get in touch with her at some point. It would just be when he was ready and on his terms not hers. He wouldn't be hurried. It was she after all who'd committed the adultery.

Edward imagined Alice wanted the best of both worlds. She wanted to have her cake and eat it. She wanted to remain in the big house with Edward, enjoying the lifestyle she was accustomed to, whilst keeping her lover on the side. Edward wouldn't give her that. She'd have to choose Paul or him. She couldn't have both. It simply wasn't on, not in Edward's world. Things weren't as simple as that. They were more complicated. Some older men might have accepted their younger, glamorous wife taking a lover. Edward wasn't one of them. He had too much pride for that. She should count herself lucky that he'd gone away and allowed her to stay there instead. He could have just kicked her out on the spot and had the locks changed. It was his house after all, the same one he and Angela had bought together. It was in his name. He'd never had Alice added. Why would he have done? He'd paid off the mortgage outright and covered all the bills on it after all. It was his place and always would be, even if he had to pay Alice off in some messy divorce settlement. Although after what had happened, maybe he wouldn't want to go back there. Maybe he'd need to get a new place and start afresh. Perhaps Alice and Paul had been carrying on under his roof. There was a lot to sort out.

Edward's Sunday lunch arrived. He forced himself to put all that to the back of his find as he tucked into his roast beef with relish. He was lucky in some respects. He'd only been in Wales a week and already he'd made new friends. There was Alan and Gwen at the guesthouse, Meredith at the coffee shop and Jill at the bookshop. That was the good thing about being a man of relative routine. He saw the same faces on an almost daily basis. Very quickly, he remembered them, and they remembered him. He fully expected to see Meredith and Jill a number of times in the coming week. He hadn't forgotten he'd promised to take Jill's dog, Beti, out for a walk. He wasn't all that good with dogs but was sure he could manage it. It couldn't be that hard. Millions of people had dogs in this country alone. They were everywhere. If others could walk them, surely, he could too. Beti seemed a peaceful and compliant beast. Perhaps Edward might even bond with her given long enough.

Edward couldn't help wondering why Jill didn't arrange a dog sitter or a dog walker to take Beti out. It didn't seem quite fair keeping Beti cooped up in the shop all day, although she seemed content. She wasn't a young dog. She was getting on a bit in dog years. She spent most of the day asleep. Perhaps she was happy like that. Jill seemed a very likeable lady, but maybe not the most organised. She had so many books she was yet to go through and price. She didn't know all her stock and what she had, even though she had some good ones amongst the chaff. She didn't keep regular hours. She seemed to open as and when she wanted. If she had to go out or wanted a day off, she'd just shut.

It would be very different if it was Edward's shop, he decided. He'd open and close on the dot, according to whatever hours were advertised on the shop's front. He wouldn't come and go as he pleased. If he needed help, he'd just hire someone else to be there when he couldn't be. Perhaps he'd do that anyway. He'd have a manager to look after the day to day running of the shop. He, meanwhile, would be the owner and would go out to source the stock or sit at home or in the back office, quietly doing the books and other things. He had it all worked out in his head. It would run like clockwork. Every book would be catalogued. He'd even go online, so he could sell books there. It would all run smoothly and efficiently, not in the haphazard way Jill was running it. Oh well, it was her shop. She could run it as she liked. Edward would just run it very differently if it was his place. It would never be that. He was retired. He was too old to start again, although a small part of him found the notion appealing. It did make Edward realise he missed Jill. He'd be very happy to see her again the following day.

After lunch, Edward wandered the short distance down to Victoria Park, where he sat for a while to let his food go down. He took out his latest book from his raincoat pocket. He'd already made pretty good progress with *The Rum Diary*. It didn't take many pages to realise it was a thinly disguised account of Hunter S Thompson's early journalistic life. The main character, one Paul Kemp, lived an easy, carefree existence. He had no ties and no commitments. He could rock up virtually anywhere and ply his trade on some failing, English-speaking newspaper, where he could come and go more or less as he pleased, spending more time in the local bars than the office, whilst pursuing any attractive, young woman who happened to cross his path. It sounded very appealing.

Edward supposed it reminded him a little of his life as a student before he'd met Angela. He'd been young and carefree once. Part of him had harboured pretensions of maintaining a lifestyle like that, even after graduating. Of course, he'd been far too responsible for such nonsense. He'd had Angela to consider for a start. They wanted to build a future together, get married and have children. That wouldn't happen with Edward failing to put down roots. What kind of life would they have had if he'd been an international globe-trotter, flitting from job to job and country to country? It didn't bear thinking of. There were parental pressures on top. They couldn't just be ignored.

No, Edward had done the right thing. He'd gone straight from university into a good job, then another one. He'd taken every promotion that had come along. Now, he wondered if he'd done the right thing. Perhaps he and Angela could have allowed themselves a year off to travel the world and see some of its delights. Angela had only lived to forty-five. She'd crammed a lot into those years, but much of it had been work or work-related. Perhaps in retrospect they should have allowed themselves more relaxation, more downtime and enjoyment. Perhaps they could have taken a small leaf out of Paul Kemp's book, or Hunter S Thompson's, and let their hair down a little for a short while. Of course, Hunter S Thompson had led an entire life of drunken debauchery. Edward wasn't advocating that, but a little fun and aimless wandering, as his own son Henry was enjoying, had its place in life.

Edward had begun his university study just as most robust young men of eighteen did. He liked sport. He liked music. He liked drinking. He liked women. He didn't mind a modicum of studying. He was keen to do enough to get by. He wasn't anxious to do much more than that. Then he met Angela and he became more dedicated and serious in all aspects of his life. He still drunk with her and their mutual friends. They still went to nightclubs. They still nursed hangovers, but the relationship gave his life more direction, and more purpose to his being there. He knew what he had to do. He could have his share of fun, but ultimately, he needed to leave with a good degree and get a good job afterwards. He did just that. So did Angela.

The person who graduated at twenty-one was a more sensible, rounded, mature individual than the one who'd arrived as a brash, over-confident eighteen-year-old, still wet behind the ears and inexperienced in the real ways of the world. The lessons of university had stood Edward in good stead for the rest of his working life. It had moulded him into a man he was. It had helped make him very well-off. So why did he harbour some regrets? He shook his head. He couldn't quite fathom it himself. Why did he view habitual losers such as the inadequate *fictional* journalist Paul Kemp with a degree of envy? He guessed it was largely because he and Angela's life together had been cut short. Perhaps they hadn't got the balance quite right. They'd dedicated too much of their time to work. They could have taken more holidays and given more of their attention to other things, including their children, even if there was never any doubt of their love for them.

It was too late now. Edward was just an old stiff, who enjoyed a glass of red wine with his lunch, a game of tennis on a Saturday or Sunday morning, the occasional round of golf with old work colleagues, a walk to the pub for a pint of real ale, watching a game of football, rugby, or cricket, when he could catch one, reading a book or newspaper, a scotch and soda before bed. He was set in his ways and liked routine, perhaps a little too much. He had done this, however. That had taken a degree of courage on his part. He'd come away. He'd taken himself out of his comfort zone, without a clue how long he planned to stay, without speaking to Alice, and more importantly without running back to her straight away, with his tail between his legs.

Victoria Park was only a little one, but charming of its kind, with its views of the sandy bay. After breaking off from his book, Edward made sure to traverse it several times, so he'd seen every nook and cranny. Sunday had always been a slow day at university. He'd never greatly liked the weekends when he'd been in halls of residence and lived on campus. They'd never felt quite right and had a slight pervading sense of mild gloom, unlike the weekdays which had always been buzzing with much going on. A lot of students had returned to their hometowns at weekends, particularly the Welsh ones, who lived quite nearby. Edward returned home himself a few times each term. Some went more than others. Some went home most weekends, perhaps to see boyfriends and girlfriends. Others hardly returned home at all, not even in the holidays. Perhaps they had something to stay away from. It varied an awful lot. Individual patterns and habits were very different.

It had been better when Edward had moved out into a shared house. He had Angela then. Sometimes, everyone in the house gathered to do a communal roast, washed down with a few beers. Those occasions had been fun. They'd enjoyed a shared spirit of camaraderie, mutual liking, and respect. Edward missed those days. He'd never have them back. They'd all enjoyed such mighty plans and ambitions, only some of which had come to fruition. Edward hoped to be a best-selling author. He was yet to write anything of any note. He feared now it was too late. He'd made more money than perhaps in his wildest dreams, but somehow it didn't quite satisfy him. It left him with a slight feeling of emptiness and longing. He didn't know why. He was just being silly, he told himself. Really, he'd been a great success. It wasn't like he could look at any of his fellows from those days and say anyone had done markedly better. They hadn't. He was probably the richest by far. If they googled his name, they'd find he had a *Wikipedia* mention and had been bestowed with all kinds of financial honours. The problem was it didn't really mean anything to him. He'd rather have been Paul Kemp, getting drunk in some Puerto Rican bar, eyeing up the women. No, he didn't really want that. He'd always been faithful to the women in his life. He did want something. He just wasn't sure what it was.

Edward left the park and for no special reason decided to meander aimlessly back towards the city centre. He stopped at another pub; one he didn't know from memory. It wasn't one he recalled going in as a student. It was one of those more modern sports bars, with multiple television screens and pool tables etcetera. Edward wasn't sure it had even been there in his day. If it had, it had changed out of all recognition. Edward settled down to watch some rugby union that was screening. It was mid-May, and the football season was just about done and the cricket one had just begun. There were only football league play-offs and European finals still to be concluded. Some had already taken place. Because he'd been away, Edward had largely lost touch with the results and what was going on in the sport. It didn't worry him too much. He was just as content watching rugby union, where the season continued until the end of the month and indeed into June, whilst he supped his pint. Edward liked both sports. He'd also come to appreciate cricket as an older man and enjoy its gentler pace, although it wasn't his favourite game.

Of football and rugby union, Edward didn't really have a strong preference. He was unusual in that. In football, he followed Arsenal. In rugby union, he supported Harlequins. He'd been an occasional visitor to both the old Highbury ground and latterly the Emirates Stadium, when working in London, to see Arsenal, as well as to the Twickenham Stoop to watch Harlequins. Edward was of course a keen follower of Oxford United and went to see some of their home games. He'd even taken both Angela and Alice once or twice in the past, although neither had been especially smitten with the matches they'd seen. They'd both made a token effort to get into it for Edward's sake, but it hadn't really been their thing. After letting them try it out, Edward had usually gone alone, although he'd taken the kids from time to time when they were younger. Henry didn't mind it. Victoria wasn't a huge fan. Naturally, Edward always kept abreast of the results of Swansea's football and rugby teams too. It had been a habit since his student days. It was too late to change now.

The game wasn't quite over when Edward continued on his way. It was after four o'clock. On a total whim, Edward wandered into a cinema he happened to pass. It was partly because it had begun to rain. Edward had no idea at all what was playing. He just bought a ticket and went in. It turned out it was one of those modern, fast-paced remakes of a film from his youth. That itself was based on a book that Edward had read as a young man, so he knew the plot well. He could easily pick it up, even though the film had just started, and he'd missed the first few minutes. It didn't really matter. It wasn't so different from the original in storyline at least and he could immediately find where he was in proceedings. He soon began to lose himself completely in the story. It was pure escapism on Edward's part, and it was something Edward had done as a student many times. He'd often taken himself off to the local cinemas, frequently alone, to catch the new releases, as many as he could. He'd been a bit of a film buff. Angela had come with him sometimes, though she hadn't been as keen as he was. His interest in films had even extended to film scores and soundtracks. John Barry and Ennio Morricone had always been his two favourites and had remained so of the genre throughout his life. The university had hosted a very active film society, of which Edward was an avid member, which had allowed him to watch all the classics of yesteryear, as well as latest ones to hit the screens. He'd never lost his interest in cinema. He retained it to this day.

When Edward emerged from the cinema, he looked at his watch. It was gone six-thirty. There was no point going back to the guesthouse, before heading out again for his evening meal. He might as well have something now he was out. He noticed there was another *Wetherspoon's* just round the corner from the cinema. It wasn't fine dining, but it was cheap, cheerful, quick, and easy. Such places served their purpose and would suit Edward's needs well. There, he ordered a curry and a pint. It would be his last alcoholic drink of the day. He wouldn't join Alan and Gwen for a nightcap, not tonight, he decided. He'd had two or three drinks, perhaps more, already. It was enough. There were things to be done the next day. He had to keep a clear head.

He also had to think of his heart. Too many drinks made it beat fast, and could make it jumpy, just as too much sugar and tea and coffee could. He kept mainly to decaffeinated after the first few of the day. Indeed, he'd bought his own jar of coffee and teabags with him, which he kept in his room for that very purpose. He could drink as much of those as he liked and generally switched to them later in the day, except when he was out and about. Shame it wasn't the same with alcohol and he could drink as much of that as he liked too. Of course, he could have chosen non-alcoholic beer, but he saw no point in that. Still, he enjoyed the alcoholic drinks he had. The curry was very nice too. When he finished, he wandered back in the gradually receding twilight, feeling full and content. He was ready for bed.

Day Eight (Monday)

'Good morning and what would you like for breakfast today?' Alan asked cheerfully when Edward appeared in the breakfast room shortly before 8.30am. 'Would you like poached eggs or is it back to your usual?'

'It's a weekday, so back to a full, cooked breakfast, I think,' Edward replied. 'Perhaps I'll try the scrambled eggs another day.'

'A full, cooked breakfast it is,' Alan confirmed. 'A good choice, and would you like tea or coffee to drink?'

'Tea would be nice,' Edward said.

He'd have his daily coffee hit later that morning at Meredith's. Edward was able to take his favourite window seat. Most of the weekend vacationers had returned home. It was quiet again. Just one other middle-aged man sat at another table. He had the appearance of a serious-looking businessman, about to conduct some important bit of business, but presumably not anxious to spend too much on his accommodation. If he had been, there were all kinds of state-of-the-art, high-rise, luxury hotels by the marina, which hadn't been there in Edward's day. It wasn't what Edward wanted anyway. He'd had enough of those places, staying over in London in his working days. Where he was staying was simple and basic and much more to Edward's taste. He didn't greatly envy whatever meetings and deals the businessman had lined up in front of him that day to conduct. Edward was glad to have put all that behind him. To his surprise, he barely missed it at all.

After breakfast, Edward paid Alan everything he owed to date, before taking his usual early-morning stroll along the seafront, walking on the beach side of the Oystermouth Road, towards the shopping centre. It was grey overhead, so he'd taken his raincoat with him, and there was a slight chill in the air for May. He hoped the rain would hold off. It had most days so far. He'd just been caught in a few showers. Careful timing had enabled him to miss the worst of most of them. Rain had in part led him to see a highly entertaining film the previous day. He couldn't really complain about the weather so far on his stay. He had to anticipate a bit of rain in South Wales, he reminded himself. It wouldn't be Swansea with constant blue skies and no precipitation.

Edward made his way to Meredith's coffee shop. He liked to start his day there when he could. He liked to have a routine. It was part of his plan for coming away. It was an idea in his head. For a short time, he wanted to establish and act out a sort of alternative life. It was more than just a holiday to him or a brief getaway. He wanted to get a flavour of what it would be like to live in another city again, one he'd once known well. Hence, he was renting a small room in a locally-run, private guesthouse not a suite at the Swansea Marriott Hotel. He could have stayed there. He had no doubt it was very pleasant. He just didn't want to. He wanted something more akin to how his student life had been in a shared house. Of course, he could have rented a self-contained flat or a holiday let. It had just been a bit short notice for that. No, what he'd done was ideal. It was in fact perfect for his needs.

'Good morning,' Edward greeted Meredith cheerily, just as Alan had done to him first thing.

Perhaps Edward just wished to pass on a bit of that good humour and joviality. It was after all good to be alive, at least at his age. He was in his sixties now, no spring chicken. Some he'd known in his working life weren't alive. Some of his colleagues hadn't made retirement. Some had succumbed in their fifties. Stress of the job and other factors had led to cancer, heart disease and other ailments. The working hours they endured had also proved costly to marriages and relationships, as it had perhaps to his own. It had driven some of his colleagues to drink, heavy smoking, excessive eating, which had ultimately caused untimely death. He was one of the lucky ones who'd made it relatively unscathed. He should celebrate that fact, he realised.

'How are you? Did you have a good weekend?' Meredith asked, returning his sense of cheerfulness. She was a naturally good-natured person, it was obvious.

'I did, and I hope you did too,' Edward said.

'As a matter of fact, I did. It was very nice just to have some time off,' Meredith admitted.

'So, what do you recommend today?' Edward asked, getting down to business.

'The chocolate brownies are very nice and only just come out of the oven,' Meredith said.

'Do you make them all yourself?' Edward asked.

'Not all, we get a few in, but I try to make what I can. I aim to make a few fresh ones every day. People seem to like the traditional ones best here. The Welsh cakes always sell well, of course. I think I'll be making Eccles cakes tomorrow,' Meredith explained.

'I'll be sure to have one if I'm in,' Edward promised. 'A chocolate brownie would be lovely for now and my usual latte,' he added.

He generally had a latte. He liked its milkier quality and smoother texture, although he occasionally asked for a cappuccino or Americano. In general, he didn't really mind, and he was happy to have any kind of coffee with milk brought to him, however they chose to make it. He wasn't an aficionado of the barista-style coffees sold by *Costa* and *Starbucks* and other similar outlets. He didn't really know what most of those were. It had just been a black or white coffee in his day. Generally, Edward was happy with that. He didn't see the point of all this choice, and it was largely lost on him.

Edward returned to *The Rum Diary*. He pulled it out of his pocket and began to read. He wondered what mess, Paul Kemp, aka Hunter S Thompson, would get in today. Would he be at risk of being fired for turning up drunk again, or worse still not turning up at all? Would he miss the deadline for filing his story and spend his day instead drinking rum in the nearest bar? Would he make moves on his friend and colleague's attractive girlfriend? If only Edward could have been so impulsive and irresponsible. Perhaps in a parallel lifetime. He hadn't been in the one he actually lived. He'd been a responsible and respected man. He'd even valued his position as a pillar of the local community. Many times, he'd been asked to run for office or become a councillor. His neighbours naturally assumed he was a supporter of The Conservative Party, because of his big house and his wealth and how he'd made his money. In fact, he leaned more to The Labour Party, though he wasn't really a political beast. He saw beyond all that. It had always been prudent to keep his political inclinations to himself where he worked. Most of his colleagues were keen *Conservatives*. They were after all the party of commerce and business. Edward had just manipulated all that to his own personal advantage, and that of his family's. They were his responsibility after all.

After he'd finished his coffee and cake, Edward headed out of the shopping centre and down St Helen's Road, towards the second-hand bookshop. He hadn't forgotten he'd promised to call by and even take Jill's dog, Beti, out for a walk. He wasn't quite sure where he was going to take her, probably along the bay, perhaps down to the marina, and back again. Edward could get a spot of lunch there. He'd noticed there were a lot of quayside cafes, where he could sit outside with the dog, as long as the rain held off. If it started raining, it might be a quick walk. He assumed dogs didn't like getting wet any more than humans did, although he wasn't really sure. He didn't know too much about them in truth.

'I said I'd come, and I didn't want to let you down,' Edward announced, as he entered the bookshop.

'So, I see,' Jill said, looking up and peering over her reading glasses at him. 'It's good to see you again,' she added, with the intention of making him feel relaxed and welcome.

'Have you found any more books for me?' Edward asked, with a hint of hopeful expectation in his voice.

'I've been rather busy I must admit. I haven't had a chance to look,' Jill confessed. 'You know, if you really want, you can come in and look through the unpriced ones yourself one day when you have the time. You might find something else interesting in there somewhere.'

'I'm sure I will, and I might just do that,' Edward said.

'I've been meaning to ask, what brings you to Swansea, Edward?' Jill enquired, getting straight to the point. 'Are you here on holiday?'

'Kind of,' Edward answered. 'You could say I'm having a short break here. I'm staying at a local guesthouse. I'm recently retired and now time is more or less my own. I can spend it how I like.'

'Sounds nice,' Jill said. 'Why Swansea of all places?'

'I was a student at the university, a long time ago. Forty years to be more precise. I met my first wife here,' Edward explained.

'First wife?' Jill asked, wishing to learn more.

'She was called Angela. She died. She was only forty-five. Breast cancer, which eventually spread. She fought it valiantly, for the children's sake as much as mine, but eventually there was nothing more the doctors could do,' Edward said, with sadness. 'I still miss her though.'

'I lost my husband to cancer too, of the liver,' Jill announced. 'He was older, early sixties. His name was John. He liked a beer, but he was educated and a good man.'

'I'm sorry to hear that. We have something in common then,' Edward remarked.

'I guess we do, though I doubt we have much else in common,' Jill laughed. 'I'm a vegan for a start.'

'I'm definitely not that. I'm a confirmed meat eater,' Edward said. 'I can't imagine becoming vegetarian or vegan now at my age.'

'It's not so hard, if you put your mind to it and stay committed,' Jill said. 'Besides, it's never too late to change, Edward.'

'I suppose not,' Edward conceded.

She was right, of course. It wasn't too late to embrace new ideas and give up old, entrenched ones.

'I'm not much of a drinker either,' Jill continued. 'Or I haven't been since John died. I'll have a glass of wine if someone's offering.'

'I drink, or least I did,' Edward admitted. 'Aren't you missing out on all the fun things in life then?

'Not really, I don't see it like that. I believe it helps keep me a more balanced and happier person, and a healthier one,' Jill suggested.

'Fair enough. It makes sense if it works for you,' Edward acknowledged.

'It does,' Jill confirmed.

'Any children yourself?' Edward asked.

'I have one daughter, Megan. She's grown up. She's an artist. She works with ceramics, which she sells to tourists from a little studio in West Wales,' Jill said.

'Sounds a nice life. I have two offspring, Victoria, and Henry, both grown up also,' Edward expounded.

'Are you remarried, Edward?' Jill asked.

'I am, but it's complicated,' Edward accepted.

'Oh, how's that?' Jill pressed.

Edward had opened up a little to Alan and Gwen. Why shouldn't he to Jill as well? Did it really matter if he exposed his shame to her?

'It's one of the reasons I'm here actually,' Edward confessed, sadly. 'I found out my second wife, who is a decade younger than I am, is having an affair. I needed to get away to think things through.'

'That's very sad to hear,' Jill said. 'I hope you manage to work things out.'

'What will be will be,' Edward said, philosophically. 'Have you remarried, Jill?'

'Oh no, I'm very much single. I don't have time for relationships, what with Beti and this place. Do you think the shop would be the state it is if I had someone to help me? Jill laughed.

'I suppose not,' Edward agreed, looking around at the piles of unsorted books. 'I can see it's a lot for one person.'

'It definitely is,' Jill confirmed. 'So, are you taking Beti out for a walk for me?

'That's what I'm here for?' Edward nodded.

'She's an older dog, so you can just keep her on her lead,' Jill said. 'She'll be happy to trot along behind you.'

'I was planning to take her down to the marina, where I may get a spot of lunch, and then back again.' Edward said.

'That should be fine,' Jill concurred, attaching Beti's lead to her collar and passing it to Edward.

'Come on then, Beti. Time for your walk,' Edward said, not totally confident of his ability to perform the basic task that lay ahead.

'Here, take some of these treats with you and give her a few. She likes them,' Jill said, handing Edward a small packet.

'I'll do that then. I'll turn to bribery if she won't go where I want her to,' Edward joked, and then set off.

'Bye, see you later and thank you,' Jill said, closing the door.

It was strange walking with a dog in tandem. Edward wasn't used to it. He was used to walking alone, although the dog seemed obedient enough and content to follow him. He felt no resistance on the lead, as he walked past the Brangwyn Hall and Victoria Park, towards Oystermouth Road and the beach. At the traffic lights at the bottom, he crossed over to the seaward side. Very soon, he found himself walking past the guesthouse where he was staying on the other side of the road. He was amused to speculate what Alan or Gwen might think if they happened to look out at that moment. They'd no doubt wonder why he was walking a dog along the beach. Edward was rather wondering that question himself. The thought had certainly entered his mind. What was he doing? What had he got himself into? He had come away to be on his own. He was bonding with the locals rather better than he'd expected.

Edward continued down Oystermouth Road, past the civic buildings and Swansea Prison, with Beti dutifully trotting by his side. Both he and the dog walked quite slowly but made steady and good progress. Edward quite fancied returning to the Dylan Thomas Centre for his lunch, but he thought it unlikely they'd want a dog, even a well-behaved one, in that historic and pristine building. It was no matter. He could return there another day when he was alone. He had Beti with him now. She was in his priority. He had a responsibility for this ageing and amiable animal. She was his concern, at least for that part of the afternoon until he returned her to her owner. For once, Edward couldn't just think about himself. He couldn't just come and go as he pleased. He imagined they wouldn't want a dog in the two nearby museums he'd visited on his second day in the city either. Again, he could return to them another time if he so wished. That was the good thing about museums. No matter how often he visited, he always spotted something new he hadn't noticed before. That was part of the joy of returning over and over.

Edward stopped at one of the many café-bars that lined the side of the marina. He deliberately chose one which wasn't too busy, and he and Beti couldn't possibly disturb other customers, not that she was the kind of dog to start barking. Edward found an empty outside table away from other diners and sat down. Beti settled calmly by his feet. Edward gave her a couple of the treats from the packet he'd been given, to reward her for her good behaviour. He had a perfect view of the harbour's still waters and the many vessels that bobbed gently on its silvery, blue-green surface. There was a mixture of modern and historic craft, and both wind-powered yachts and motorised boats. Edward had never been much of a sailor. It was yet another thing he wouldn't have minded doing if he'd ever had the time. He could picture himself as the captain of a small sailing ship. He could see himself standing on the bridge with his captain's hat, handing out orders to his willing crew, perhaps his children and grandchildren, if he ever had them.

Perhaps he should consider getting himself a boat if he ever came to live by the sea. It wasn't as if he couldn't have easily afforded a modest one. A superyacht, of the type that Russian billionaires sailed around the globe in, might have been beyond his means. Other than that, he had more than enough in the bank to buy one worth the cost of several houses. Technically, Edward was a millionaire, though he never considered himself one. It no longer had the meaning it once had. If he added his home and all his assets together, including savings and investments, he was no doubt worth quite a few million. It didn't really feel like that to him. He just felt comfortably placed. He knew he could live out the rest of his life without ever having to worry about money, as long as he wasn't reckless and stupid with it. He was never likely to be that. If he had been, he wouldn't have had the money he'd gradually saved over the years. His clever business sense and acumen had just seen it gradually increase year on year, until he'd chosen to retire.

Edward cast his eyes down the menu. Plenty of things appealed to him. In the end, he chose fish and chips and mushy peas. He was by the coast after all. Fish from Welsh waters was considered a local delicacy. What he ordered was claimed to be locally caught. Edward had noticed much on sale in Swansea Market, but so far, he hadn't greatly availed himself of it. Perhaps it was high time he did. He noticed another customer's fish and chips being brought out. It looked very nice. It would more than do him. It was funny to think none of these upmarket café-bars had existed in Edward's day. The mouth of the River Tawe had been very different forty years before. It had been transformed in the time that had passed since Edward had left Swansea. He wouldn't even have recognised what was dubbed the Maritime Quarter in truth. It had still been the home of derelict and decaying industry. All that was gone, pulled down, wiped clean and redeveloped into something modern, shiny, and new. Some changes were for the better, Edward decided. This development, which included the National Maritime Museum, was one such example.

To his surprise, Edward found himself stroking Beti's coat, as he waited for his meal to be brought out. Beti wagged her tail back. The dog appeared to like him. Maybe he should get one himself when he got home to Oxford. They weren't such bad things. One like this would be all right. Beti had her own charm. Even Edward wasn't oblivious to it. She was no doubt good for Jill. She kept Jill company when she didn't appear to have much other company in her life. Of course, Edward only knew the few things Jill had chosen to tell him about herself. She might not have told him the whole story. She might have been harbouring dark secrets and hidden depths.

As Edward tucked eagerly into his food with relish, he broke off small bits of battered fish and the odd chip to throw down to Beti. He wasn't sure if he was meant to do that, but she seemed to enjoy them. There were no bones in the fish. It was properly filleted, so he assumed it couldn't do the dog any harm, even though fish and chips probably weren't part of her normal, daily diet. Beti seemed to be enjoying them almost as much as Edward was. She kept looking up for more. Edward found it hard to say no. He had a very big portion. There was plenty of his plate. It wasn't as if there wasn't enough for the both of them.

Edward was too full for dessert, although Beti would probably have liked one. Even Edward drew the line there. All that sugar, cholesterol and calories couldn't possibly be good for a dog. He'd read about overfed ones having to go to the vet to be treated for their rich blood. Edward didn't want to be the cause of that, even though Beti looked up hopefully. Edward told her no, it was time they were heading back. He was even more surprised to find he was speaking to her as he would another person. Perhaps that was what came of spending most of the last week on his own, in his own company.

Edward guided Beti back the way they'd come, past the civic buildings and prison, then along the coastal path that ran alongside the beach for the whole length of the bay, all the way round to The Mumbles. Edward understood that to be its correct, full name, though as students they'd always referred to it simply as Mumbles, with no prefix. Perhaps it didn't need one. Perhaps they'd been right all along. It was certainly easier in its simplified form. Edward now found himself caught between using the two, not sure which was grammatically and geographically correct. He couldn't even find a definitive answer when he endeavoured to check on his phone. He noted Jill, a local herself, called it The Mumbles.

Eventually, Edward passed the guesthouse where he was staying. That was his cue that he'd shortly have to cross over and head inland past Victoria Park and the Brangwyn Hall. He then continued along the back streets behind King Edward's Road and the parallel St Helen's Avenue, where Jill's second-hand bookshop was located on a side street, hidden away among the closely packed, terraced residences. Edward had no trouble locating it. He knew the way now, although it was hardly obvious to potential customers. It was no wonder business wasn't exactly booming. Still, it seemed to suit Jill well enough. Edward presumed she lived above the shop. That kept things simple for her. She could combine work and homelife together.

'Did you have a nice time?' Jill asked, when Edward finally returned Beti safe and well and in the same condition that he'd taken her, bar the consumption of a quantity of fish and chips Edward didn't see fit to mention.

'We did,' Edward replied, truthfully.

'Did she behave?' Jill continued.

'She behaved impeccably,' Edward answered.

'How far did you take her?' Jill enquired.

'Down to the marina, where we stopped for lunch, and back, just as I intended,' Edward confirmed.

'Well, thank you very much. I really appreciate it, and I'm sure Beti does too,' Jill said.

'I can take her out again tomorrow if you like,' Edward suddenly blurted out, before he'd really given much thought to what he was saying.

'Where are you going to?' Jill asked.

'You know I haven't actually decided yet, but I'm sure Beti can come along,' Edward offered.

'Have you been to Cwmdonkin Park on your travels so far? It's a lovely, quiet place to sit,' Jill suggested.

'Where's that?' Edward enquired. He'd heard of it, but he wasn't quite sure where it was.

'It's in the Uplands,' Jill replied.

'I used to live in the Uplands, so how come I don't know it?' Edward wondered.

'It's a bit like my shop. You wouldn't notice it, unless you were looking for it,' Jill explained. 'The entrance isn't on the main road. It's tucked away behind the shops.'

'I have heard of it though. Why's that?' Edward puzzled.

'Ah, that's because it was the childhood playground of Dylan Thomas and quite famous for its literary connections. It virtually backs onto the house where he lived. He played there all the time as a child, and it inspired a lot of the stories he wrote as an adult. He claimed it was his biggest inspiration,' Jill said.

'I didn't know that, but in that case, I shall definitely visit,' Edward agreed. 'I shall go there tomorrow if the weather stays fine. I'll pick up Beti in the morning on my way.'

'I'll see you then,' Jill told him.

Edward knew he'd have to go for his customary coffee and cake first. He could collect the dog on his return after that.

'Indeed, you will,' he confirmed.

'Beti says thanks and goodbye,' Jill said.

'Thank you and goodbye to you both too,' Edward said,

Outside, Edward looked at his watch. It was mid-afternoon. He decided to wander back to his room, where he'd rest for a while. Later, he'd pop out to get something to eat. He'd probably finish his evening with a quick drink with Alan and Gwen in the bar. He imagined they were probably expecting him. He didn't wish to disappoint them. His mind was already turning towards visiting Cwmdonkin Park the following day. He was already looking forward to it. To his surprise, he was also looking forward to seeing Jill and Beti. They'd almost pushed Alice out of his mind altogether. He had to reprimand himself for forgetting her and for forgetting for a moment he was a married man. He was still that whatever Alice had done.

Day Nine (Tuesday)

Edward started his day with his usual lukewarm shower and cooked breakfast. He still hadn't had the heart to tell Alan the water was a little tepid. He had no doubt Alan would have tried to fix it. He always did his best to please. Edward had been there over a week, and he wasn't quite sure how much longer his stay would continue. It was a bit too late to mention it now. If he was going to, he needed to have done so on his first or second day. It would seem pedantic at this point. Otherwise, his little room was perfect for his needs, regardless of its modest dimensions. Despite his wealth, Edward didn't need luxury. Basic and functional was all he required. In most things, he only sort adequacy not opulence. He wasn't by nature an extravagant man.

Edward looked out of his bedroom window. There was enough blue sky poking through the grey cloud. It was fortunate he'd chosen May not October or February. From memory and previous experience, there would have been little but rain then. That didn't mean Edward was about to forego his raincoat. He wasn't about to anytime soon. He rarely left home without it and would take it with him as a precaution now. He knew how quickly the weather could change in Swansea. Thick cloud and heavy rain could soon blow in from the sea across the bay. He checked the forecast on his phone. There was a small risk of showers. Otherwise, it was expected to stay reasonably fine.

Breakfast eaten and preparations for going out complete, Edward set off. As on most days, he took the costal route into the centre, with the beach on one side of the Oystermouth Road and his and other guesthouses on the other. It was a lovely walk on a day like today, one he'd no doubt miss when he was back in Oxford. He'd miss the salty sea air in his lungs and the light brush of fine, windblown sand on his face. It was reviving and invigorating. It made Edward think once again that staying in the city might have been better for Angela's health. It was odd they'd never given it more consideration. They'd been in too much of a rush to get back and launch their burgeoning careers. They'd been highly successful in their chosen professions, but there had been a price to be paid for that success.

Edward left the bay road at the junction with West Way and headed up towards the Quadrant and Swansea Market via the Grand Theatre. Edward hadn't forgotten Meredith would have an Eccles cake waiting for him and he was heading straight there. He was already licking his lips in anticipation, despite not long having eaten his breakfast. Edward reached the coffee shop and walked straight in. It was a little busier than some mornings. Edward assumed it was at its busiest at lunchtime. He'd only been once then.

'Good morning,' Edward greeted Meredith.

'You've come for your Eccles cake, I expect,' she commented.

'I have indeed, and a latte if I may,' Edward said, offering his debit card to pay.

'Just find a seat. I'll bring them straight over,' Meredith promised.

Edward placed his phone on the table. He hadn't checked for more calls and texts from Alice. It was still on silent mode, so he wouldn't hear it ringing anyway. He could have blocked her number, he realised, but that seemed a tad childish. He wasn't about to do that. He just wasn't ready to enter into communication with her either as yet. Time was the great healer. Eventually, he'd have to speak to her and ask about Paul. There was no particular hurry. All that could wait for another day. Instead, Edward got out *The Rum Diary*. He was continuing to make good progress with it. It was an entertaining read. When Meredith brought his coffee and cake to him, she studied the cover quizzically.

'So, what's this one about?' she asked.

'That's a very good question,' Edward said, pausing to think for a moment. 'You could say it's the story of the kind of man I might have been in another life.'

'What do you mean by that?' Meredith wondered.

'I mean it's about a man not afraid to live spontaneously in the moment, with little thought for the future,' Edward said. 'That's quite brave. I was never brave enough to be like that, though my son is. I always planned everything in advance. I had just about every small detail of my life worked out before I lived it.'

'That doesn't sound like a bad thing,' Meredith commented.

'Not a bad thing, but perhaps a little restrictive, like a straitjacket,' Edward noted. 'Of course, I couldn't plan for every eventuality, my first wife dying for one.'

'Oh, I'm sorry to hear that,' Meredith said. 'It sounds like you remarried?'

'Indeed,' Edward confirmed. 'Are you married, Meredith?'

'Not married, but I live with a partner - another woman actually,' Meredith explained. 'I've had both male and female partners in the past. I'm pansexual.'

'I understand it's the modern way. You'll have to forgive me but some of these terms are new to me,' Edward admitted.

He was aware attitudes towards gender and sexuality were much more fluid than in his day, but he was yet to grasp all the terminology. Forty years ago, there had only really been straight, gay, bisexual and trans. He could perhaps add to that list androgyny, celibacy or abstinence by choice, and perhaps asexuality or no interest in sex. Now, there were a host of new terms to describe gender and sexuality. By his own admission, it was a whole new world to Edward, which he was only just coming to grips with and learning. He had a vague idea what pansexuality was. It was a more inclusive form of bisexuality, he understood.

'That's OK. It's never too late to learn, Edward,' Meredith smiled.

'So, I'm often being told,' Edward chuckled. 'What is good is that people have greater freedom to express themselves these days. When I was a young man, people were afraid to admit to being different. At least society has broken down those sorts of prejudices and barriers.'

Edward recalled several gay friends from his youth who'd been scared to come out. Others who did had encountered bigotry for their honesty. Edward couldn't have imagined turning up at his local rugby club forty years earlier and announcing he was gay. He would have been shunned in all probability. Now, no one would bat an eyelid. They wouldn't care anymore. That at least was a good thing. Some changes were positive, it seemed. Society had quite rightly become more accepting about certain things. People were more able to be true to their nature, their sexuality, and their gender. It made Edward feel sad for those gay friends of his childhood who'd been forced to live much of their lives in the closet. It was cruel and unfair. Edward realised he was out of touch with many of society's changes. He did know he'd always disliked discrimination and injustice of any kind and always would do. He'd fight against such until his dying breath.

'Thank goodness for that. We don't want to return to the Dark Ages,' Meredith said, jokingly.

'Indeed, we don't,' Edward agreed, returning to his book.

He really needed to get more with-it and up to speed with the times. He really was an old fuddy-duddy at heart, he realised. In his beautiful house in Oxford, away from other people, he'd lived in splendid isolation. He'd mainly worked with white, middle-class, middle-aged folk, which hadn't helped. He was a bit clueless about the ideals and beliefs of the younger, more diverse, multicultural generations. What little he did know was what he gleaned from newspapers and television. He had a lot to learn about modern attitudes and thinking, he appreciated. Perhaps his trip would enable him to make a start on that process.

'I'll probably see you tomorrow,' Edward said, as he downed the last sip of his coffee and hoovered up the remaining crumbs from his plate.

It really had been a most delicious Eccles cake.

'I'll make sure I have something nice for you,' Meredith promised.

From the coffee shop, Edward headed back out of the shopping centre, along Oxford Street and then down St Helen's Road. At the end, he turned towards Jill's bookshop, where he presumed that she was patiently waiting for him to pick up her dog, Beti, to take her out for a walk. Edward walked neither slowly nor quickly. It was only mid-morning. He was in no particular hurry. He figured he had ample time to visit Cwmdonkin Park, before finding a little café in the Uplands, hopefully one that didn't mind taking dogs, where he could have a spot of lunch. When Edward arrived at the bookshop, he found Jill dashing about in a slightly disorganised manner. He wondered for a moment if she'd forgotten he was coming. Apparently, she hadn't.

'Just looking for a book I promised to put back for someone,' she explained. 'I know it's here somewhere. I just can't immediately put my hands on it.'

'You want to get all your stock catalogued on computer, then placed on the correct shelves,' Edward suggested.

'I know, I know, maybe one day,' Jill promised. She then stopped her search for a moment and rested her glasses on her forehead. 'So, are you taking Beti to the park today?' she asked.

'I thought I would,' Edward replied.

'Would you like me to make you a cup of tea before you set off?' Jill offered.

'I tell you what, I'll have one when I get back. That can be my reward if you like,' Edward said.

'Well, I hope you both have a lovely time,' Jill said, attaching Beti's lead to her collar and handing it to Edward.

'I'm sure we will,' he replied.

'Oh, here's my number just in case you have any problems,' Jill said, handing Edward a small business card. 'I forgot yesterday.'

'Hopefully I won't need it, but thanks anyway,' Edward said, before leading Beti out of the door. Again, just as on the previous day, she followed dutifully.

Edward walked down King Edward's Road before turning right into Rhyddings Park Road, and continuing up the steepish hill, towards the Uplands. He passed one of his old student residences in Gwydr Crescent, which he and Angela had shared in their second year with some fellow friends. He stood outside for a moment. It brought back all kinds of memories, just to see the house again after forty years. They'd enjoyed many happy times there. It almost brought a tear to his eye to recall them.

At Uplands Crescent, Edward continued past the shops along Glanmor Road and then into Park Drive. He spotted several cafés where he might have his lunch, as he walked. He had little difficulty finding the bottom entrance to the park. Jill had described it to him in detail. He'd also double-checked on a map, to make sure of his bearings. An impressive metal gate and signpost painted in a vibrant shade of light green welcomed Edward and Beti. He knew they'd come to the right place. A steep path led in. It soon opened out into more formal gardens, with water features to the left and more open parkland to the right. He could see an attractive, ornamental shelter in the distance, with clear, blue skies hovering above.

Continuing further into the park, Edward encountered an elegant tearoom, with a pleasing vintage look. It was constructed of white, painted bricks, and pale green, wooden beams, in the traditional style of Victorian and Edwardian parks. Adjacent, was a carefully mown bowling green and tennis courts. Some students were having a game. They weren't beginners. Neither were they quite as good as they thought they were. If Edward had been dressed more appropriately and hadn't had Beti with him, he might have been tempted to take them on and challenge them to a game. He had a half a mind to anyway. He was confident he could have surprised them and taught them a thing or two. Despite his age and his erratic heartbeat, he still had a pretty solid forehand and backhand. His volley wasn't bad either. He had little doubt he could have disposed of these young upstarts without too much trouble. He'd been a local champion in his day. Those days were well and truly gone, but he could still play well enough when he had to.

Edward sat on a bench and watched for a bit, with Beti by his feet. They both seemed content to sit and enjoy the sunshine. After a while, they moved on. Edward noticed a small, carved, wooden bust of Dylan hidden among the trees. It wasn't difficult to see what had inspired and enthralled the great Welsh poet so much as a child. It would have been easy for a child to get lost there, both literally and spiritually. Edward could see how easily it would be a place of dreams. Dylan Thomas had lived just across the way at 5 Cwmdonkin Drive. Doubtless, he'd gone there all the time as a child. Strangely, when Edward had lived in the Uplands he hadn't even known of its existence. It was his loss. He could have come here with Angela. They would have enjoyed the peace and quiet in the morning, particularly after a heavy night of drinking. Perhaps he could have found a little of the inspiration it had given Dylan. He'd still take a fraction of that inspiration now.

Edward and Beti gradually meandered their way back down towards the exit. Edward deliberately chose the route past the shelter on the opposite side to the path they'd gone up. Edward took a few photographs as he went. He was sorry to say goodbye to the park. It truly was a magical place. He wondered if Beti was sorry to be leaving too. He realised Jill must be a very trusting person, to leave him in charge of her dog. She obviously had more faith in Edward as a dog walker than he had himself. So far, he'd just about managed. Beti seemed content enough. It was now time for lunch.

There was of course the *Uplands Tavern*, which had stood proudly on the main Uplands shopping street even back in Edward's day, but Edward wasn't after a pub lunch today. He'd had plenty of them already. More accurately, he'd eaten most of his evening meals alone in pubs. He preferred a nice café in the daytime if he could find one. On the bottom right of the small stretch of shops and other business premises that formed the Uplands mini shopping centre were a succession of posher restaurants. There had been some there when Edward had lived nearby, some forty years earlier. They were no doubt different restaurants from those Edward had often walked past and had presumably changed hands many times in the years since. Edward had never been able to afford to go in any of them back then, as an undergraduate of limited financial means. Even now, they seemed more suited to a birthday meal out or a romantic evening date. They weren't really the places for a quick lunch with a dog in tow. Instead, Edward headed back towards a pleasant-looking café they'd passed on their walk there. It was neither posh and foreboding, with a crisply dressed if slightly surly host to greet them, nor the kind of greasy workmen's diner, specialising in chips and huge cooked breakfasts. It was down to earth, yet warm and welcoming.

'Is it OK if I bring a dog in?' Edward asked meekly, before daring to enter further.

'Of course, there's plenty of room upstairs,' a lady with brown hair of a medium tone, probably in her early forties, who Edward took to be the proprietor, told him kindly.

She handed him a menu. All the tables downstairs were taken, mainly by retired folk of Edward's age or older. They chatted happily among themselves, calling out to each other, even though they weren't sitting at the same table. They all seemed to know one another. The proprietor seemed to know them all by name too. Edward guessed many of them came there for their lunch most days. Immediately, he decided it was his kind of place. He felt comfortable, at ease and relaxed with the world and life in general, even with Beti by his side and Alice back at home with Paul.

Edward found a corner upstairs, where he and Beti could sit away from other customers. Although she was very well behaved, it seemed to be the decent thing to do in the circumstances. Dogs weren't to everyone's liking, including his own usually. Edward had no wish to impose a dog on someone who might not appreciate them. There had been enough incidents with Victoria, who was afraid of dogs as a child, not to want to do that, and for Edward to have a healthy awareness not everyone's heart instantly melted at a dog's charms. Victoria had jumped out of her seat to avoid them in cafés and public places or tried to run past when they'd approached her in the street. They had on occasion left her fearful and shaking. Of course, it only led to inquisitive dogs giving her more attention than they otherwise would have done. All that because an overeager dog had once jumped up and knocked her over in the park as a toddler. It had been a major reason Edward never considering getting a dog himself.

Edward sat and studied the menu. It was mainly traditional fayre, to cater for the tastes of the principally more mature clientele. A few trendier, modern dishes were thrown in for the sake of variety. Edward also noticed they seemed to do a good trade in takeaway baguettes and sandwiches for the local workers. It was the kind of place Edward imagined cottage pie and similar would be popular. Edward settled for cheese and potato pie with salad. It would suit him perfectly. He went downstairs to order. He told Beti to *stay*. He thought he knew her well enough now to presume she wouldn't follow him. It wouldn't matter all that much if she did. In fact, she stayed under the table where she was, until Edward returned. Perhaps like Edward she was happy to have a rest.

Edward veered from his usual tea or coffee for once. He noticed healthy, fresh juices made of real fruit were a house speciality, so he ordered one of those. He hoped it would refresh him for the walk back and give him some much-needed energy for whatever else he chose to do that day. As he sat and waited for his food to be brought, he got his book out. He'd only read a few pages when his meal arrived. It was placed before him. Steam rose enticingly from the pie. Edward cut into it. Of course, Beti looked up eagerly and with expectation.

'You'll have to wait for it to cool down,' he told her.

When it did, he threw her a few pieces of pastry. Naturally, she gobbled them up. It made Edward wonder if she was more used to a human diet than a dog one. He presumed she didn't share Jill's vegan meals, or maybe she did. She was certainly happy enough to share his pie, which on this occasion was vegetarian. Maybe he was changing little by little and hadn't even noticed the changes that were happening within him.

After lunch, they meandered their way back. Edward chose a different route, down Brynmor Road. He was keen to pass other houses where friends had once lived and he used to visit them there. He was interested to see if he could even remember where they were located and if they looked at all familiar to him. He was pleased to find they did. His memory wasn't as bad as he feared. More and more snippets of forgotten information were slowly coming back to him. The longer he stayed, the more he remembered. It was only natural, he supposed. It was the logical way of things.

'Did you have a nice time?' Jill asked him, when he finally returned Beti to her, just as she'd asked the previous day.

'We certainly did,' Edward confirmed. 'She behaved perfectly again. She was excellent company for me.'

'I'm very glad to hear it,' Jill said.

'I may not be able to take her tomorrow. I maybe out of town, but I can take her again later in the week,' Edward explained, with a hint of apology.

He already had a little trip out of Swansea in mind for the following day. He wasn't sure if he could take Beti.

'That would be lovely. I'm very grateful you can take her out at all,' Jill said.

'I'm more than happy to when I can,' Edward told her.

'Now, tell me, Edward. You've now been back in Swansea for over a week. After visiting Cwmdonkin Park, do you finally accept Dylan Thomas is a better writer than George Orwell?'

Edward laughed. 'My views may have changed a little, but I'm not quite ready to admit that,' he said.

'Well, we don't have as many great writers here in Wales to celebrate as you English do. We have to treasure those few we have,' Jill said. 'I think there's a bit of an anti-Welsh bias among the English literary critics,' Jill added.

'You could be right,' Edward admitted. 'Besides, even if you don't have as many acclaimed writers as us, you have history, heritage, beautiful landscapes, and Welsh hospitality in abundance.'

'Yes, we have all those,' Jill agreed. 'Now, I'd better get you that tea I promised you.'

Later, Edward sat in a pub on the same Brynmor Road he and Beti had walked down earlier, eating his evening meal alone. He thought in retrospect he should have invited Jill along. He very much doubted she was doing anything, though she had mentioned in passing she was a member of a local book club and did the occasional evening class. One of those could have been meeting that night. Edward imagined if they were, Jill would have said. She hadn't. No, she was probably sat in a room above the shop on her own with Beti, watching television or reading.

It would have been polite to ask her. Edward just hadn't thought to, until it was too late. Now he was sat eating by himself, he realised he would have been glad of her company. She was a very nice lady, and her companionship would have made the night complete. He'd been rude not to say something. Perhaps he would another time. Of course, he had to remember he was still married. Alice was at home waiting for him, or perhaps not. Any offer might have been misconstrued. Jill might have seen such a suggestion as an unwelcome and unwanted advance on Edward's part. He certainly didn't want that and didn't want it perceived as such. They were just two lonely people who'd both experienced bereavement in life, who could perhaps have benefited from someone to talk to. Edward knew he could, though he was happy enough in his own company.

Perhaps it was best in retrospect he hadn't asked. That didn't mean he might not another time. It was just something that required more thought. He needed to think it through a little more fully before asking. He didn't want Jill to think it was a date. That wasn't his intention. Edward had in mind something more innocent entirely. It would just be two friends, with something if not a lot in common, enjoying a drink and some food together. It would be nothing more, nothing less. It wasn't fair Jill was sat in every night by herself when Edward could do something about that if he so chose to. No, he would ask, only not just yet. Perhaps at the weekend would be better timing.

Back at the guesthouse Edward had a quick drink with Alan and Gwen, before heading to bed. A scotch and soda would be a fitting conclusion to the pleasant meal and tasty pint of real ale he'd just enjoyed at the pub, he decided. He didn't want to be late going to sleep, however. It was sure to be another early start in the morning. He'd have breakfast sometime after eight, before setting out on his travels. He certainly wouldn't be idling away the hours in his room. Such ideas would be far from his mind.

'Did you have a nice day?' Gwen asked, as he sat down to join them.

'I did. I seemed to have acquired a dog,' Edward replied jovially, as he awaited the questions and comments that he felt certain would surely follow his unexpected announcement.

In fact, Alan and Gwen let the remark pass and Edward didn't mention it again. Instead, they chatted amiably about other things, until Edward decided it was time to turn in.

Day Ten (Wednesday)

'Are you still finding plenty of things to keep you occupied in Swansea?' Alan asked, over breakfast.

'It's not been a problem so far,' Edward replied, happily. 'I've even found places to visit I didn't even know were here. I should have been aware of them, after three years, but a few escaped me, like Swansea Botanical Gardens and Cwmdonkin Park. I went there yesterday.'

'Nice places,' Alan nodded. 'I suppose you have to be a real local to know everywhere though.'

'Yes, as students, we had other priorities,' Edward agreed. 'When we weren't in lectures, it was mainly about going to the pub, I'm afraid.'

'All students are like that, or most are anyway,' Alan said.

'They were in my day. Perhaps a little less so now,' Edward commented. 'Being back here now as an older man, it makes me realise we didn't make enough of the area's natural beauty. I suppose our only excuse was perhaps we were generally home in the summer months, when we could have done more sightseeing and that kind of thing.'

'Well, I'm glad you're making up for it now,' Alan said.

'I certainly am. I thought I might head over to Neath today, to have a little look about. It's only a short train ride, one stop,' Edward explained

'Not a lot of people choose to go to Neath. It's not the usual destination for holidaymakers,' Alan laughed.

'I know,' Edward said. 'That's why I'm going there.'

In his student days Edward had mainly restricted himself to Swansea and Cardiff. They were the most regular shopping destinations of choice. On Saturdays in his first year, he'd often gone to football or rugby matches, depending on which team was at home. It could have meant a trip to the nearby St Helen's Rugby and Cricket Ground or further afield to the Vetch Field, then home to Swansea City. After he met Angela, he went to matches much less often. Frequently, they got the train into Cardiff, where they shopped in the pleasing historic arcades or visited Cardiff Castle or Cardiff's National Museum. Once or twice, they'd visited the Aberafan Shopping Centre in Port Talbot, or gone as far as the shops in Newport or Bristol further down the rail line, just for a change. He never recalled stopping at Bridgend, though it was possible he had done at some point or other in time.

Edward only recalled going to Neath once, when they'd visited The Gnoll, to watch Swansea play rugby, although he might have been more than that. He recalled it as being a not disinteresting, minor, provincial, Welsh, market town. He could see it wouldn't be everyone's cup of tea, but it had shops, cafés, a nice park, and the ruins of its Norman castle. Edward would enjoy looking about. It would be a real, Welsh, small town community and not the picture postcard beauty of the Gower, Snowdonia, and the Brecon Beacons. Edward was often slightly perverse and contrary in his choices. He liked to go to places others wouldn't bother with. He found interest and pleasure in the kind of grey, former industrial towns others found unattractive. Perhaps he was spoilt living in Oxford, with its history and elegant buildings. It made him seek out places that were the opposite, but still had their own humbler, basic charm. Edward had read Neath had experienced trouble with rowdy teenagers on the streets at night. He trusted he'd be safe in the daytime hours and wouldn't see that side of the town.

'Well, have a nice time anyway,' Alan said.

'I'm sure I shall. It will interest me, even if it wouldn't others,' Edward said. 'By the way, I'll definitely be here until the weekend. Beyond that, I don't know. I may have to think about heading home and sorting a few things out.'

'No problem,' Alan said. 'You can stay as long as you like. You're an impeccable guest.'

'As you and Gwen are hosts,' Edward said, returning the compliment.

After breakfast, Edward pottered about in his room for a while, catching up on one or two jobs before heading off. Shaving was one. He realised he'd gone a few days without. That wasn't really like him. He was normally most particular about such things. He'd had to be in his job. To his surprise, a bit of stubble on his face quite suited him. He might let it grow again. Perhaps he'd even grow a beard. That would be a shock for Alice, just as she'd shocked him with her announcement about Paul. At work, Edward had always been immaculately dressed. It had served its purpose, creating the impression he meant business. Since coming away, he found he was slowly dressing more casually, some might even say scruffily, as least by his usual standards. Gone were the stiff collars and suits. He was favouring T-shirts more than formal, collared shirts under his sports jacket or raincoat, and why not? He was on holiday, not going to work after all.

As always, Edward checked the weather forecast before setting out. It would be fine until early afternoon when rain was expected. By evening, it would be moderately heavy. Edward planned to be back by then. He took his usual early morning bay walk down the Oystermouth Road. He always preferred to cross over to the seaward side, where he had a good view of the beach and the waves, as they gently lapped the sand. He guessed the tide was on its way out, as it was still quite high now. In a few hours, it would be out a good mile or more, so flat was the bay at this point. As on most other days, Edward stopped at Meredith's coffee shop. He'd have a coffee and cake there and a little read of his book, before heading up the High Street to the railway station. He hadn't checked times of trains, but he knew they were very regular to Neath. Just about everything heading east stopped at Neath first. Even if he just missed one, he wouldn't have long to wait for another.

'I'm afraid I haven't got anything special for you today,' Meredith told him sadly, when he walked in.

'That's OK, as I know what I'm having anyway. I'll have two of your lovely Welsh cakes and a latte, please,' Edward said, opening his wallet.

Edward realised he hadn't had a single traditional Welsh cake since being back in Wales. Today, he'd change that. He used to buy them quite regularly in Swansea Market as a student. They brought back fond memories of visiting his long-deceased grandparents in Cardiff as a child. His grandmother had almost always bought Welsh cakes for him and his younger sister when they visited. He'd loved them. It had always been a source of regret that they couldn't get them back in England, though his father had often tried. It wasn't as if they were difficult to make. There just wasn't much call for them in the Home Counties' town where they lived as children. There wasn't much call for them in Oxford either. Edward had grown up largely in Buckinghamshire, where his father had commuted into London, just as he himself had during his working life. It was that proximity to Oxfordshire that had eventually led he and Angela to settle there. It was a good compromise, not too far from either of their families.

Edward's Welsh relatives had gradually died off. No doubt, there were some distant cousins and nephews and nieces still there somewhere, but none he was in touch with. He hadn't kept in contact with enough of his more distant relatives, he realised. He'd been too busy in his working days. Angela's illness and bringing up two teenagers by himself had rather occupied him. Perhaps that was something he could now rectify in retirement. Perhaps he could trace those still living when he got back home. He knew one branch of his family had come from Yorkshire to Merthyr during the 19th century, to take advantage of the growing industrialisation of Wales. Having made their money, they'd eventually settled in Cardiff, although branches of the family had spread out across South Wales. It was possible some were here in Swansea, although Edward wouldn't know them, even if they passed him in the street.

Edward got out his book and began to read. He was now three-quarters of the way through *The Rum Diary*. It wasn't a long book and it had been a good read. He'd found it most entertaining. Edward had read quickly and turned the pages eagerly. He was keen to get to the end, for all the right reasons not the wrong ones, not because it was hard going. It was the opposite. The action had gleefully skipped along at a pleasing pace, as Paul Kemp had got himself in some new scrape immediately after extricating himself from the previous one. Disaster was never far away, as he just about kept his head above water, living each day by his wits. Edward had been a much more considered person. He'd also lived by his wits in a manner of speaking, but in a much more orderly fashion.

After finishing his coffee and Welsh cakes, Edward closed his book. He'd be starting a new one very soon. He said cheerio to Meredith and continued on his way. He walked to the end of Oxford Street and past Castle Square, where he turned left onto the High Street, towards the railway station. It wasn't very far. It wasn't one of those annoying out of town ones he often encountered, where it was still a two-mile taxi ride into the town centre. The whole point of taking the train was that it should be convenient. It wasn't that if it stopped miles away from anywhere. Luckily, that wasn't the case in Swansea, and it was conveniently located at the top of the High Street. The railway station was also conveniently located in Neath, only a short distance from the shops. Edward remembered that much, even if he didn't remember much else about the town.

When Edward got to the railway station, he checked the timetable. A train was leaving in just over ten minutes. He knew he wouldn't have long to wait. It would just give him time to get a ticket and visit the toilet, to relieve himself. At his age, tea and coffee went straight through him. Perhaps he'd buy a newspaper from the shop. He'd rather lost touch with what was happening in the world. It was time he caught up. The weather was still fine when Edward boarded his train. It was only a very shirt distance before he got off again. There would be no time to get his book or paper out. Travelling by train, it was very hard to see where Swansea finished, and Neath started. They just seemed to run into each other. There was no clear divide.

When the train made its first stop, Edward got out. Just a couple of locals joined him. One was a young woman who Edward guessed from her look was returning from a night out. Perhaps she'd stayed overnight in Swansea, probably with a young man. With her short skirt, dyed, blonde hair and multiple tattoos on display, she looked unashamedly sexually driven and not afraid to flaunt her physical attraction. Such things were very much beyond Edward's limited knowledge and experience, he chuckled wryly to himself, but not really minding one bit. He'd had his time once. Young women looked very different in his day, he reflected. They perhaps dressed rather more modestly. They certainly didn't go in for piercings and body art. Times had certainly changed a lot.

At Neath Station, or Castell-Nedd as it was known in the Welsh language, Edward headed down Alfred Street and then along Orchard Street past Victoria Gardens, towards the shops and Neath Castle. He was keen to get his bearings, before visiting anywhere in particular. He thought he'd take a look at the castle and river first. Afterwards, he'd look around the shops and perhaps get a bite to eat. He might wander down to The Gnoll, home of the mighty all-conquering *Welsh All Blacks* rugby union team of the late 1980s, early 1990s, before finishing in the park, where he planned to read for a bit.

To his pleasant surprise, Edward found Neath Castle not only open but free to enter as well. He'd fully expected it to be closed, in which event he'd planned to take a couple of photographs of the outside walls, to add to the numerous snapshots of his holiday he'd already taken on his phone. That wasn't the case, and he was able to look around at his leisure, viewing the historic battlements from both inside and out. Only one other middle-aged couple shared Edward's interest and were also taking the trouble to explore the site and subject it to further investigation. Edward had the feeling that passing drivers were viewing him with mild suspicion. The castle was a piece of living history, around 900 years old. Why shouldn't he wish to take a closer look? To Edward, it was the most natural thing to do in the world.

He then took a few photographs looking down onto the slowly flowing waters of the River Neath. No doubt that would also have seemed odd to some folk. This wasn't the most attractive point of the river's winding course from its source in the Brecon Beacons National Park. Edward didn't really care. It was one of the joys of getting older. You could do odd things without attracting much attention. People just presumed you were either a little eccentric or perhaps had the early stages of dementia. Edward wasn't yet in either category. He wasn't overly concerned if people assumed he was.

The other joy of getting older was of course being able to complain and feeling you had the right to do so. Edward didn't complain about trivial details, but part of him enjoyed complaining that things weren't as they had been in his day. He liked to insist to anyone who'd listen, like Alice or his children, that everything had been better when he was a young man. In reality, he realised that wasn't entirely the case. Some things had changed for the better, some hadn't. He just preferred to view the past through rose-tinted spectacles. He'd quite enjoyed playing the role of *grumpy old man* to his younger wife. On holiday, perhaps that was changing a fraction. He was finally moving a little with the times. He was getting hip, he might say. Whatever happened with Alice, he'd still go back a slightly changed man now. He'd eaten a vegetarian meal. He'd befriended a person who was pansexual. He'd made friends with a dog. He wasn't quite ready to be a vegan but was even willing to give that a go if Jill ever wanted to eat out with him.

Edward then walked back into the town's shopping centre. He'd remembered it as being modest. Compared to Swansea and Cardiff, of course it was. But it wasn't so bad. There was plenty to occupy Edward's interest and more shops than he recalled. There was a pedestrian part running down from Wind Street, quite different in feel to Swansea's famous one, which was busy with weekday shoppers. Many were middle-aged or elderly, but Edward also spotted a few young mums, pushing toddlers in pushchairs. There was no sign of the juvenile delinquency he'd read about with alarm in *Wales Online*, though he observed some empty business premises and vacant buildings. Edward wasn't expecting Covent Garden, so all in all he was pleasantly surprised. He even popped his head in one or two shops, as he wandered from street to street with quiet, understated pleasure.

Edward was impressed to pass a number of small independent cafés and coffee houses with distinctive and stylish outside décor he hadn't really expected. He was sure they hadn't been there on his last visit, when there had been more cafés of the greasy, all-day breakfast variety. Edward's eye was drawn to one particular café, where he stopped and went inside. There, he ordered a gourmet toasted sandwich, followed by a crepe for dessert. He didn't generally bother with puddings, but he was working on the possibly false assumption the toasted sandwich might not be that big. Edward got out his book and newspaper to read, whilst he waited for his food to come. He wasn't disappointed. The food was very good. He needn't have worried about it not being enough. He left feeling very full indeed.

Leaving the café, Edward walked out of the shopping centre towards Neath's famous, old rugby union ground, The Gnoll. It was easy to find and only a short walk from the shops. In fact, Edward had already caught sight of it in the distance, as he wandered around the town. The Gnoll had been an iconic sporting venue in the late 1980s, early 1990s, when Neath had been not only one of the strongest club sides in Britain but in the whole of Europe. Domestically, they swept virtually all before them then. Crowds of 15,000 or more eager fans had packed into the famous old ground, to see them rout their local rivals and many visiting touring teams. It was truly a sporting fortress in those days. Now it was just home to the local amateur or semi-professional Neath side. The main team had merged with Swansea to form *The Ospreys* and played at the Liberty or Swansea.Com Stadium. The Gnoll still had its place in history, that could never be taken away.

Edward had taken a special interest in that team, as several of his former teammates from his Swansea days had gone on to play for them. Of course, they'd been much better than Edward and had played a part in his giving up rugby, to focus more on football instead, not that he was much better at that. He'd still followed their progress with pleasure and was pleased when several former Swansea students he remembered had eventually made the Welsh national team. Edward by comparison was barely good enough to play for the university thirds or fourths back then. It didn't matter. He'd enjoyed the playing that he'd done. Sometimes, taking part was what mattered most. Besides, sport wasn't the big priority to Edward that it was to some. He just played a bit of football, rugby, tennis, and badminton when he could, purely for fun. Angela had been his main concern. That and drinking and going out and at least finishing with an adequate degree that would land him a decent job at the end of all that. Edward took a few photographs of The Gnoll before heading on.

His next destination was the picturesque Victoria Gardens. He'd already passed it once. Now, he was going back for a proper look. He'd read the gardens were very pretty. They came highly recommended in one of the guidebooks Edward had glanced at in the guesthouse, when he'd been looking for places to visit. They were described as a must if visiting or passing through Neath. That was recommendation enough for Edward. Like his lunch, the gardens didn't disappoint. They weren't huge but were ornamental in nature and pleasingly laid out to the eye, with attractive floral beds to admire and enjoy. A traditional bandstand stood as the centre point. Edward sat on a nearby bench and got out his book to read in the sunshine. Others were sat on benches too, some eating late lunches, or making the most of the sunshine whilst it lasted.

Edward stayed in the park for nearly an hour, until it started to cloud over. The skies above him began to darken. Rain had been forecast for later in the day. It was evidently coming. That was his cue to get moving again. He closed his book and made his way out of the park, back through the shopping centre, towards the railway station. Edward knew he wouldn't have long to wait before a train was heading in the direction of Swansea. When he got there, he found he'd only just missed one. It didn't matter. When he checked the times, he didn't have long to wait for another one.

Edward read his newspaper, *The Guardian*, on the platform whilst he waited. There had been another high school shooting in America and a number of students had been slaughtered. Edward had been totally oblivious in the solitude and seclusion of his holiday for one. It was a tragedy that such things took place and would continue to do so, as long as people were allowed to own guns. Edward could never understand the logic of private citizens bearing arms, but that was America for you. It was a country that had always mystified him, with its strangely contrary take on liberty. He viewed the USA as a mixture of both good and bad, the best and worst of what democracy had to offer.

In other news, the lead singer of a band Edward had liked as a teenager had died from complications of pneumonia. It struck a chord in Edward. It made him realise he wasn't getting any younger, although the singer had been a little older than he was and not in the best of health. Edward had seen the band in concert once many years earlier. They'd been excellent. Thinking about it now brought back the memories of excitement and flowing adrenalin that attending gigs and watching live music had generated at the time. He'd loved it then. In his teens and twenties, he'd watched every band going. He seldom went these days.

On occasion, he'd been to see some of the gentler rock acts he liked in his youth, like Van Morrison, Elvis Costello and Squeeze. Anything more than that he now considered too noisy. At home, he often listened to jazz and classical music. He had been to see the veteran sixties' Scottish singer-songwriter, Al Stewart, when he'd played locally, and very much enjoyed that. Al Stewart had once been a controversial act, one of the first to include swear words in his recordings. Edward was now pleased to see he dressed very much as he did himself, like a bank clerk. Gone were the psychedelic clothes. He wore a collared shirt, and sensible, grey trousers. Like Edward, he was the epitome of British decency and respectability. Edward had always had a fascination for history. Most of Al Stewart's songs which weren't about love concerned historical events and famous factual figures.

By the time Edward's train arrived, it had begun to rain. By the time the train pulled into Swansea ten minutes later, it was raining quite heavily. Leaving Swansea Station, Edward decided to take shelter in the nearby Glynn Vivian Art Gallery, whilst the worst of the rain passed over. He'd been there once already, but he knew there would always be more to take in and appreciate. One visit to a gallery or museum was never enough in Edward's mind. He could always manage another, without undue feelings of boredom and repetition.

Before looking around, Edward treated himself to a pot of tea in the café. He remembered from his previous visit that the gallery didn't shut until 5pm, so he had plenty of time to look around. Whilst he sipped his tea, he got out his book. He'd nearly reached the end of *The Rum Diary*. He'd be ready to start a new book the following day. He tried to remember what others he'd brought with him. He couldn't immediately recall. He'd just flung a small pile into his travel bag, as he'd hastily made his escape. He was sure to have included something interesting. He only bought quality fiction and reference books as a general rule. When he wasn't reading an acclaimed novel, he wasn't averse to a well-written biography or autobiography, if it was about someone he admired.

Edward reflected quietly on his visit to Neath. He'd very much enjoyed it. Some would have seen it as a slightly depressing, shabby market town, best avoided. It wasn't in Edward's eyes. It was quite the opposite. With the increase in independent cafés and small, boutique businesses, he could see the seeds of rebirth and the potential and possibilities of growth. It was a town of contrasts. It reminded him a little of Paignton in Devon. He'd stayed there a few years before, whilst attending a business conference in adjacent Torquay. Some viewed Paignton as squalid and rundown, with its best days very much in the past. In fact, it was full of little gems and buildings and sights of interest and character for those like Edward, who took the trouble to look beneath the surface decay and poke about a bit. He'd found much to enjoy in Paignton, including the harbourside, the gardens of Oldway Mansion, the medieval Kirkham House, the Victorian Palace Theatre, and a bounty of small, independent cafés. In the same way, he'd enjoyed Neath and the modest attractions it had to offer.

Edward left the gallery shortly before closing time. He didn't want to outstay his welcome. He always considered it impolite to remain anywhere until he was asked to leave. It was good manners in his mind to leave before that. He was fully aware staff would be ready to lock up and depart by then. He disliked selfish people who didn't appreciate that and only began to make their way to the exit when requested. Edward would never be one of those. He was back outside a good five minutes ahead of time. Unfortunately, it was still raining quite heavily. It would take him about twenty minutes to get back to the guesthouse. He was likely to get rather wet, he realised, even more so if he took the coast road, where he'd be additionally exposed to any breeze blowing across the bay. At least the buildings of the inland route along St Helen's Road and past the Brangwyn Hall would provide some cover.

When he got back to his room, Edward had to immediately change out of his wet clothes and put fresh, dry ones on. He hung the wet ones up to dry. Gwen had kindly offered to wash a few of his dirty clothes for him and he was anticipating their return imminently. He felt like he was almost a resident of the guesthouse. He was aware some elderly folk did that. They sold their houses and moved into a small hotel for their final years. Perhaps Edward would end up doing just that. It wasn't a total impossibility. He could give the house to Alice and live out his days travelling from town to town.

Later that evening, Edward sat in a nearby pub eating his evening meal, with a large glass of *Rioja* in front of him. Football was on the big screen behind him. It was the Europa League Final, one of the last games of the season. Edward was only half watching. He wondered how long he'd remain in Swansea. He'd told Alan and Gwen he planned to stay at the guesthouse until the weekend at least. After that, he was uncertain. He'd reassess his situation then. Perhaps he'd return to Oxford on Sunday and face Alice. He'd have to have it out with her eventually and decide if they had a future together or if it was divorce.

Edward wondered what he'd do with his last few days in Swansea. He still hadn't visited Clyne Gardens. That was one thing on his list. He also recalled Brynmill Park as being very pleasant. He used to walk through it almost every morning on his way into campus from one of the student houses where he'd lived. It would be lovely to go back again. If he remembered correctly, there was even a small coffee house on the corner at the bottom end where he could get a light lunch. He'd stop at the bookshop on his way, to see Jill and offer to take Beti with him. He could also take the dog when he visited Clyne Gardens, he realised. When he got back to the guesthouse, Edward had a quick nightcap with Alan and Gwen, as he had done on most nights since arriving, before heading up to his room. He got inside the soft duvet on his bed, finished reading *The Rum Diary*, before turning off his light and falling asleep.

Day Eleven (Thursday)

'So, where are you off to today?' Alan asked Edward, as they chatted amiably at breakfast.

As usual, Edward was down in good time and had his favourite seat in the window, where he could look out at the passing cars and people. There were many more cars than people. The bay road was long and only the hardy and fit walked it generally. The guesthouse had been quite quiet all week. In truth, that was how Edward like it best, with just a handful of other guests. He preferred that to the busier weekends, when the noisier families arrived. He really did feel like a resident now, although he realised his stay might be gradually drawing to its end.

'I'm staying quite local, I think,' Edward replied. 'I want to have a look at Brynmill Park and take a few pictures of the lake perhaps. I used to walk through there on my way into college from the house I was living in during the last term of my second year. It will be quite nostalgic for me. I don't think I've been back since then. I've pretty much forgotten what it's like, except that there is a big lake on one side.'

'We occasionally enjoy walks there, as it's not too far away. It's lovely and quiet, one of Swansea's best kept secrets,' Alan commented.

'Like the Botanical Gardens,' Edward suggested.

'We go to a little coffee house on the corner afterwards,' Alan explained.

'Funnily enough, that's exactly what I had in mind,' Edward said. 'I'll probably have the dog with me too. Do you know if they allow dogs inside?' Edward enquired.

'As far as I know, as a lot of people go there before or after they've been to the park. Dogs wouldn't be unusual' Alan said. 'So, who is this mysterious dog you're looking after?' he wondered.

'She belongs to a bookshop owner I've befriended,' Edward answered. 'I've been taking the dog for walks as a favour, as she has no one else to do it for her. It doesn't greatly inconvenience me. Beti, the dog, is very well behaved.'

'That's very kind of you,' Alan commended Edward.

'It's the least I can do really,' Edward responded. 'The bookshop owner, Jill, is on her own there, and the dog stays in the shop with her, unless I can take her out.'

'I expect she's good company on your walks too,' Alan observed.

'She certainly is,' Edward agreed, realising he'd missed the loyal company of Beti the previous day. Edward had been less loyal. He hadn't taken her out the day before, whilst he'd been off on his strange, solitary wanderings to the town of Neath. He'd try and make up for it today if he could.

'So, how was Neath?' Alan asked, changing the subject.

'Actually, it was very nice and much more interesting than it's given credit for. There are some new, independent businesses there these days,' Edward replied.

'Well, I think you're the first of our guests to go there by choice,' Alan laughed.

'It's got some hidden gems, like the castle and Victoria Gardens, and there are a few nice shops and cafés. If you find interest in small, market towns, it has plenty to look at. I'd happily go back,' Edward said.

'I think Gwen and I will stick to Swansea and the Gower,' Alan confirmed. 'We quite often drive through Neath. I don't think we ever stop there.'

'Perhaps you should. You may be pleasantly surprised,' Edward suggested.

'Maybe next time, just for you,' Alan agreed, smiling.

After breakfast, Edward readied himself in his room for going out. He hadn't spent a single lazy day there, just reading and watching television, as he could have done. Every day he'd done something. That would continue until he went home, he was determined. Life was too short for wasted time. That had been his general principle during his working life. It was the same in retirement.

Edward picked out another book to read, from the small pile he'd brought with him. It was another comparatively short one, *The Country of the Blind and Other Science-Fiction Stories* by HG Wells. He'd read all the English author's well-known classics over the years and enjoyed them – *The Time Machine*, *The Invisible Man* and *War of the Worlds*. He'd never read *The Country of the Blind*, even though its title had always intrigued him. It was meant to have had a biblical origin, and there were various other historical versions, amounting to the same thing, but the quote it came from was generally credited to the Dutch, Renaissance philosopher, Erasmus. *In the land of the blind, the one-eyed man is king.* Edward had always liked that concept, although it was Edward's understanding that HG Wells turned the idea on its head in his famous short story. He'd have to wait to find out, he supposed. It wouldn't take him very long to read, and then he'd be starting yet another book, he imagined.

As always before leaving, Edward checked the weather forecast. Again, it was mixed. There would be some sunshine, but also clouds and the risk of rain showers. Edward had got very wet on his way back from Neath. A few rain showers he could cope with. It wasn't too bad, as long as he didn't end up wet to the skin. That seemed unlikely. Any rain that did fall was expected to be fairly superficial and not long lasting.

Of course, Edward wouldn't head straight to the bookshop. He aimed to get there around mid-morning. First, he'd have to head into the shopping centre for a coffee and cake as usual and a few pages of his latest book. Edward walked down the Oystermouth Road on the beach side with a slight spring in his step. Was he walking a little quicker than he usually did? His legs and feet had hurt a bit during the first few days of his break, as he walked much further than he normally did. Perhaps he was getting used to it. Perhaps he was getting fitter. It no longer hurt so much. His legs felt stronger. He perhaps felt slightly healthier. The sea air of Swansea Bay was doing him some good. Perhaps it suited him better in some way than the airs of his Oxfordshire village. Edward headed straight for Meredith's coffee shop. He wondered what treat she'd have in store for him today.

'I've made a nice lemon drizzle cake,' she told him, as he stood at the counter.

The thought of a slice of lemon drizzle cake certainly whetted Edward's appetite and filled him with a mild sense of joy. 'That sounds delicious,' Edward said, approvingly.

'I'll bring it over, and a latte?' Meredith asked.

'Oh, yes please,' Edward confirmed, passing her his money.

'Another new book?' she commented, as she placed his coffee and cake down before him.

'I'm afraid so. I do read a lot,' Edward said, almost as if it was something to be ashamed of. 'I have time on my hands these days.'

'What's this one about?' Meredith enquired, with a hint of suspicion in her voice.

'I couldn't really tell you yet. I'm just about to start it,' Edward admitted. 'I was attracted to the title. It's based on a famous old saying. You've probably heard of the author, HG Wells.'

'I have heard of him,' Meredith said, her face suddenly lighting up. She felt momentarily pleased with herself. Perhaps she knew more about classic fiction than she thought she did. 'We studied *The Time Machine* at school,' she remembered.

'Very good. I expect this one to be not dissimilar, in style at least,' Edward said.

Meredith then left Edward in peace. He wondered how many visits he'd already made to the coffee shop. He couldn't quite recall. It must be six or seven easily by now. He'd only missed a few days. It could in fact be more than that. There might not be many more visits, however. It was Thursday and he'd been away eleven days. He'd have to return home at some point, perhaps this coming weekend. In the back of his mind, he had the vague notion that might be the right time to leave. It still wasn't definite. He remained uncertain. He might stay longer if the mood so took him. He might hang around for another week. He could if he wanted. If he did, he might have to look at doing other things with his time. He might have to make trips further afield, to Cardiff and Newport, perhaps into West Wales towards Pembrokeshire, or inland to the Brecon Beacons. He could always hire a car. It would be no great expense for a man in his financial position. So far, he'd relied mainly on his own two feet to get about, with the occasional bus or train ride. It had always been his intention to keep things simple, to go back to basics. That was why he'd taken the train and not driven in the first place. He'd generally taken the train as a student, and as far as he could it had been his plan to do things the same way. He'd largely achieved that so far, and would continue to walk for the time being, whilst his destinations remained local.

'Will I see you tomorrow?' Meredith asked, when Edward brought his empty cup and plate back.

'I expect so, though it could be my last time, at least on this visit. I may be going home at the weekend,' Edward said, with a tinge of regret in his voice.

'I'm sorry to hear that,' Meredith said. 'You've become one of our regular and best customers.'

'It's not definite and I will be back to stay again in the future, I'm sure,' Edward promised. 'I won't leave it so long this time. I'll see you tomorrow anyway.'

'I'll see you then. I'll have to make something special for you,' Meredith said.

'I can't wait,' Edward replied.

As on other days, having taken the coast road into the shopping centre, Edward took the inland route back to Jill's bookshop, passing the myriad of takeaways, many Middle Eastern, along St Helen's Road, before meandering through the side streets behind King Edward's Road to the shop. Edward wasn't quite certain in his own mind if he really planned to return to Oxford that weekend. Was it too soon? Had he already stayed too long? Perhaps he'd ask Alan and Gwen for their opinion that evening. They seemed like sensible, down-to-earth people, who'd give him good advice. Perhaps he'd consult Jill. She might have a take on the matter. She didn't seem in the least surprised to see him when he walked into the shop.

'Beti missed you yesterday,' she said, by way of greeting. 'I missed you too,' she added.

'And I missed you both,' Edward said. 'I got a train yesterday and I wasn't sure about taking Beti on with me.'

'She'd be fine,' Jill said, nonchalantly. 'I've taken her on trains a few times in the past.'

'Another time then,' Edward promised.

'Where did you go to?' Jill asked.

'Only a short distance, one stop to Neath,' Edward said.

'Why did you go there?' Jill enquired, looking slightly confused by Edward's unusual choice.

'Why not? Just to look about really. Actually, I found it an interesting, old town, with its own unique character. It wouldn't be for everyone, but I find places like Neath quite fascinating,' Edward explained.

'Where are you going today?' Jill continued.

'I thought I'd have a look at Brynmill Park. I used to walk through it going to college as a student. It will be nice to go back, to see if it's changed at all. I thought I'd get a bite to eat and then bring Beti back after,' Edward said.

'Not going too far then,' Jill commented.

'Does that sound all right?' Edward asked.

'It sounds perfect. It's a nice park. Beti likes it there. She probably knows her way around by now,' Jill said, jovially.

'She can show me then,' Edward laughed, as he took hold of Beti's lead.

'I'll make you a cup of tea when you return,' Jill promised.

'I look forward to it,' Edward said, as he led Beti out of the shop and up the road.

From the bookshop, Edward walked to the end of King Edward's Road. He was saddened to observe another pub he used to drink at had now been converted into accommodation. It was a sign of the times, he reflected. Pubs were closing everywhere. Students didn't go out quite as much perhaps as they once had done. In Edward's day, students drinking both at lunchtime and in the evening had helped to keep the local pubs going. It was where they normally met up as soon as lectures and tutorials had finished. There had been no all-day drinking back then, however. Licensing laws had forced pubs to close in the afternoon, before opening again for the evening session. It had been a case of getting a few pints down before three, and then resuming at around six. It had been possible of course to go to an off-licence in between, and sometimes Edward and his friends did that. He rarely turned down the opportunity for a drink if it was offered to him.

The pubs around King Edward's Road had once overflowed with spectators flocking in their droves to watch matches at St Helen's Rugby and Cricket Ground. It no longer attracted the crowds it once had. That in turn had a knock-on effect on the quantity of pints consumed in the local pubs on match days. As a result, many pubs that had been there forty years earlier hadn't survived to the present day. Edward crossed over by the rugby ground and continued with Beti on her lead along Bryn Road. He'd never lived there, but other friends had during Edward's time in Swansea. It had been a popular place to rent a room or get a place in a shared house. At the end of Bryn Road, Edward turned right into Brynmill Terrace, which ran adjacent to the eastern edge of Singlelton Park. Edward remembered Byrnmill Terrace as being quite a steep road, which took longer to walk than logically it should have done.

Eventually, Edward emerged by the corner coffee shop, where he planned to have his lunch later, and the bottom access to Brynmill Park. It was quite narrow at its entrance. This was deceptive, however. It was much bigger than it appeared at first sight. Edward led Beti along the path, passing neatly tended, ornamental flower beds on either side. Edward suddenly had a flashback to a winter many years before, when he'd taken photographs of fallen snow, blanketing the park's trees and vegetation. Snow had been a rare occurrence in Swansea. In one year only whilst he'd been there, it had snowed quite heavily. Edward remembered it being late January, shortly after he'd returned from his Christmas holiday. Lectures had been cancelled for the day. Instead, Edward and

Angela had headed to their nearest park, to take pictures for posterity and to record the moment. Being back in the park, Edward was struck by a wave of nostalgia that almost knocked him over.

He recalled he'd once come across the photographs many years later, when doing a bit of sorting out in the house. He and Angela had looked so young in them, little more than children. The pictures had seemed so tiny and dated, compared to more modern ones. They looked like they were from another era or lifetime. They were from another century, Edward reflected. All that really was so long ago. Angela was dead now. She was just nineteen or twenty then, with her whole life and her whole future ahead of her. They'd spent that future together. Now it was over. Edward resolved to find the photographs again when he got home. He'd take them out to examine again. He'd take a few now to see how the park had changed. It didn't seem all that different to him. The path he and Beti were walking seemed just as it had when Edward had walked it to and from the university campus. He mainly recalled hurrying along in the early morning, keen to get to lectures on time, having cut things a little fine. No doubt, he'd been up late drinking. That was usually the case. It had been most days of the three years he'd spent in the city. That was how things were for students in those distant times.

Eventually, the park began to widen out. A huge expanse of water lay to Edward's left. It suddenly came into view. Edward understood it had once been a reservoir, providing water for the city's population. During the reign of Queen Victoria, it had formally been opened as a public park and open space, the first of its kind in the city. It was strange to think that such a huge volume of water existed there, as it was virtually hidden from the road that ran alongside the park. The trees that lined the water's edge kept its presence a local secret. Gradually, the path meandered round to the left, following the contour and outline of the lake. There were benches at the top end. Edward sat with Beti to rest. He looked out across the gleaming, watery surface. It was an impressive sight, reflecting the sun's orange rays back into Edward's eyes. Swans and ducks skimmed about, looking for insects and other small creatures to eat.

Edward and Beti continued their way round. Edward occasionally paused, to take a picture or two on his phone. He imagined the texts and messages from Alice were continuing to build up, but he had no wish to check them. One day, he would, one day. At regular points, where the path opened out to reveal the full expanse of water, there were more benches to sit and enjoy the view. At one point, they passed a small kiosk selling drinks, snacks, and ice creams. Edward didn't stop for one. It would soon be lunchtime. He'd eat then. He'd give Beti something too.

The park reminded Edward of the many times he'd taken Victoria and Henry to parks back in Oxford when they were children, in those carefree, joyous days when Angela was still alive. At this moment, Victoria would be busy at her public relations job in London, Edward imagined. Henry would be on his travels somewhere. Edward didn't see enough of them anymore, not as much as he'd have liked. Victoria was too like him. She was anxious to get on and make a name for herself in her chosen profession. Henry was a wanderer, a bit of a lost soul, in truth. He'd been thirteen when he'd lost his mother, Victoria fifteen. They'd both put on brave faces for their father. It was the British way, stiff upper lip, and all that, to suffer in silence. They'd all done that, but it had been hard. They'd soldiered on as best they could and rarely spoke about it, each trying to come to terms with their own personal sorrow and devastation in their own individual way, but always failing.

It had probably hit Edward hardest. He had to keep going for the sake of the children. He had to look after them. Even now, he was still coming to terms with what had happened and how fate had cruelly cut short their family happiness. Perhaps Henry was also, he now realised. His son had turned inwards and internalised his feelings afterwards. He'd gone quiet for months, even years. Perhaps he was still working through it. His wandering would eventually cease when he finally achieved acceptance. Perhaps Victoria's answer was to throw herself into work. Perhaps she worried the same fate of early death lay in store for her. She needed to do things now before it was too late. The pair were very different, but Edward loved both his children. He wished he saw more of them. He resolved to do that too on his return.

Edward was in a mood of quiet, melancholic reflection, when he finally led Beti out of the park. Some welcome nourishment at the coffee shop wouldn't go amiss and would no doubt cheer him. He ordered a sandwich and a flapjack and a coffee to go with it. He hadn't forgotten a tea was waiting for him back at Jill's bookshop. Beti sat quietly at his feet. He stroked her a few times, telling her what a *good girl* she was. She was a good girl indeed. When his food arrived, Edward broke a few pieces off for Beti, which she quickly devoured. He also gave her a few of the treats he always carried in his pocket when he took her out. Edward continued to sip his coffee, after finishing his food. He looked about. It was a nice place, one he'd be more than happy to come back to, if he ever visited the park again. He had a feeling he would do. Edward read a few pages of HG Wells, before emptying the last drops from his cup and continuing on his way.

Beti left with him obediently, as Edward continued up Alexandra Terrace into Rhyddings Terrace. In Gwydr Crescent, he again paused for a moment outside his old house. It brought the memories flooding back and he felt another tinge of heavy nostalgia. Sometimes, the memories seemed to weigh him down. Other times, he gladly embraced them. Overall, they gave him a warm feeling. They were also tainted with a slight sense of loss, as he recalled days he'd never get back. Putting his memories aside, Edward led Beti down Rhyddings Park Road and eventually back to the bookshop. Jill already had the kettle on. When it had boiled, she handed Edward a cup. She didn't inform him it was vegan milk. It then struck Edward that during all his visits he'd never once seen another customer.

'They see you coming and run away,' Jill joked. 'No, I do have them. I just need a few more. It's a lot of the same ones, a bit like you. I have regulars who come back time and again, always looking for that special, old book they can't find anywhere. I try to keep lists of what they're after in case any ever turn up. Occasionally they do.'

'And I thought I got special treatment,' Edward said, feigning a sense of hurt feelings.

'You do. You're the only one who gets a cup of tea,' Jill told him.

'Glad to hear it,' Edward said, sitting down.

'So how was she?' Jill asked.

'Perfect, as always. We had a lovely time,' Edward replied.

'Have you been to Clyne Gardens yet?' Jill enquired. 'It's another place Beti likes to walk.'

'It's on my list. In fact, I'm thinking of going there tomorrow, if it's another fine day. There would be no point going in the rain,' Edward said.

'I think it's meant to stay like this until Sunday, so you should be OK,' Jill said.

'Would you like me to take Beti with me?' Edward asked, knowing the answer before he'd even posed the question.

'If you're offering,' Jill answered.

'I'll pick her up at a similar time then,' Edward confirmed.

'That will be lovely,' Jill said.

'You know I may have to go home at the end of the weekend,' Edward said, raising the prospect cautiously, as if it were a slightly delicate matter.

In the short time they'd known each other, he and Jill had grown quite close in their own funny way, despite being very different people. Edward now considered her a friend. Jill paused for a moment, before responding to Edward's announcement.

'That's a pity. Beti will miss her walks. But of course, you have to go back sometime. We knew you would eventually. It's just we've both got used to seeing you most days. It won't be quite the same without you,' Jill said, with a touch of sadness.

'I know. It won't be the same for me either,' Edward admitted. 'It's not definite anyway. It's just a possibility. I may stay longer. It's something I have to weigh up over the next day or two. There's a lot to consider. I promise I'll come back soon whatever happens. Hopefully, Beti won't have forgotten me.'

'I'm sure she won't. I won't forget you either,' Jill said. 'I didn't realise how much I've missed having someone to talk to, until you turned up.'

Edward left the bookshop with much to think about. It was something he could chat about further with Alan and Gwen when he shared a drink with them later than evening. Perhaps they'd have some great wisdom to impart on his situation. Perhaps they'd know when it was a good time for him to leave and confront Alice. It was now Thursday. He had at least two more full days in Swansea and perhaps Sunday morning and afternoon. He had to make the most of the time. It was only right to mention it to Jill. He was anxious not to feel like he was suddenly leaving her in the lurch. He needed to give her some warning about his eventual departure.

Day Twelve (Friday)

'In case it is my last visit, I wanted to thank you personally for all your delicious coffees and cakes, for welcoming me so warmly and for your unfailing courtesy and good humour,' Edward told Meredith, when he visited the coffee shop that morning.

He wasn't certain it would be his last visit, but it was a distinct possibility. He wanted to say his goodbyes, just in case. Anything less would have been unforgivably rude in Edward's eyes. He was a man of good manners if nothing else. He was always unfailingly polite in his dealings with people, even when he didn't particularly want to be. He expected politeness back in return. In the twelve days he'd known her, Meredith had never been anything but courteous to him. She was a warm-hearted and good-natured woman. She was another person Edward would miss tremendously.

He'd got up early that day, showered and had his usual cooked breakfast, before taking the coastal road into the city centre. Even though he was eventually planning to head in the other direction, to the picturesque Clyne Gardens, he couldn't possibly do so without seeing Meredith first, just in case it proved to be his last visit to the coffee shop, at least during his current stay in Swansea. He was sure he'd be back soon enough, at least if he had any say in it. He'd left it too long before returning. Work and other things had got in the way. He'd never leave it as long again. It would become a regular holiday destination for him.

'I've actually made two special cakes, just in case it is your last day, so you have a choice,' Meredith said, her eyes lighting up, eager to see Edward's reaction to her baking.

His eyes started to light up too, even though all these cakes weren't good for his waistline. Luckily, all the walking he was doing was helping to counterbalance any extra calories he was consuming. Judging by the mirror alone, he'd neither lost nor gained weight. Of course, he didn't have any scales in his room. He was judging by visual impression alone. He was sure Alan and Gwen would oblige him and lend him some if he asked them. So far, it hadn't been necessary.

'You do spoil me,' Edward replied.

'Well, you can either have an indulgent chocolate cake or a pineapple upside-down cake I've baked,' Meredith explained. 'Which do you fancy?'

'It's just too hard to decide,' Edward said, weighing up his options. 'You know what, I think I'll have a slice of both. Why not, eh? You only live once. Just in case I don't get a chance to sample your delicious cake making again for a while. I'll have a light lunch to compensate.'

Meredith laughed.

'It's up to you,' she said.

'Yes, cut a slice of both, before I change my mind,' Edward said. 'And a latte to go with them.'

'Of course,' Meredith confirmed, taking Edward's payment.

Edward found himself a seat and got out his book. He'd nearly finished *The Country of the Blind.* In this version, eyesight proved a hindrance and a source of suspicion rather than a blessing. The story's protagonist, the lost mountaineer Nunez, was soon to discover it was better to be blind than have sight in his new surroundings, not the outcome he was confidently anticipating. Edward wondered if he'd been blind all along to Alice's faults. Had she been nothing more than a gold-digger all along? Had she ever really loved him? He was beginning to suspect she hadn't.

Edward was almost ready to move on to the other short stories in the collection, by the writer affectionately known as the *father of science fiction.* Edward enjoyed the works of HG Wells, at least the ones he was familiar with. He found them well-written, entertaining, and thought-provoking. That was all he could hope for in any book. Wells had also written on history, politics, science, social commentary, and biography, but Edward knew nothing of that output. He only knew the fiction of Wells. It was fiction Edward was mainly drawn to. Perhaps he could write a novel himself. He could set it in London's financial world. He'd seen enough in his working days to fill a number of books. Perhaps it was another thing to add to his to-do list when he got back to Oxford.

'Thank you again,' Edward said to Meredith, as he got up to leave. 'I hope to see you again before too long.'

'I hope so too, and I'm sure I shall,' Meredith said.

She came round from her counter to embrace him briefly, before allowing him to go. Edward returned her hug. It was a sign of mutual affection and appreciation. There was nothing wrong with embracing warmly, Edward reflected. Too many people were afraid to express their emotions and grasp those they loved. Edward had been like that in the past, a bit too aloof for his own good. He wouldn't be anymore. He would show his true feelings. The only thing about saying such a public goodbye to Meredith was that it would make it difficult to go back if he decided not to return to Oxford at the weekend and to stay another week in Swansea. He'd just have to find another temporary coffee shop, he decided. That would be the prudent thing to do in the circumstances. There was no doubt he would go back to see her the next time he was in the city. He'd make a point of doing so.

Edward made his way out of the central shopping area and down Oxford Street. Overhead, the skies were grey. It was meant to brighten up later, hopefully by the time he got to Clyne Gardens. Edward took a shortcut through Picton Arcade and onto the Kingsway. He noticed a couple more small, independent cafés he might try one day if time permitted. At the roundabout where the Kingsway ended, he crossed into St Helen's Road and continued towards Jill's bookshop. It was a bit out of town. It was hardly in a prime location. It was no wonder it attracted so few customers.

'She's all ready for you,' Jill told him, when he walked in through the front door.

By *she*, Edward knew Jill meant her dog, Beti. As always, the shop was empty. It was just Jill and Beti. Who else would there ever be? It was a wonder Jill stayed open at all. She had mentioned she sold a bit online but didn't have a proper website set up. That was another thing she needed to do. Her email address was just listed on a few book sites, where potential customers could get in touch. A few did, some from abroad. That was the beauty of the internet. It helped to keep her afloat, though there was no doubt she'd benefit greatly from a proper website, with all her books catalogued according to author and subject. That would never happen, whilst it remained Jill on her own.

'I expect she's got used to her daily walk,' Edward commented.

'She certainly has. She looks forward to them,' Jill agreed. 'Is it still Clyne Gardens today?'

'That's the plan, as long as we both have the energy to get there and back,' Edward said.

'You can always get the bus if you're tired,' Jill suggested.

'We might do that if we're flagging or if it starts to rain,' Edward confirmed. 'I think she's helping me to get fit, although I've been eating too much cake, I'm ashamed to admit. I go to the same coffee house every morning, to read for a bit, before coming to get her. At least I go as often as I can. I'll miss my coffee and cakes if I do go home.'

'I stick to the vegan coffee houses,' Jill said. 'Surprisingly, there are a few of them about, more than you'd expect in a city the size of Swansea.'

'I'll have to try one out with you one day,' Edward promised.

'That would be nice,' Jill said. 'I normally have to go on my own.'

'I'm trying to open myself to new things and new experiences, including trying veganism,' Edward said. 'More to the point, I'd be very happy to keep you company.'

'We'll definitely do that then. It will be my treat,' Jill said.

'I couldn't hear of you paying,' Edward said. 'Let me treat you. I have very little to spend my money on.'

'Only holidays with no apparent endings,' Jill teased.

'The guesthouse is very reasonable,' Edward said. 'I'd spend almost as much back home. Besides, my holiday may be about to end. I'll have to decide very soon.'

'Well, as long as you've had a pleasant time here,' Jill said.

'I certainly have. It's been more than that. In fact, it's been wonderful,' Edward beamed.

'I'll have the kettle on and tea ready for when you get back,' Jill assured him, as she followed Beti and her new, temporary, daytime master to the door.

'See you in a bit,' Edward said, as he stepped back into the fresh air.

He'd remained careful not to tell Jill about his true financial position. He didn't want to use the term millionaire or multi-millionaire even. The house on its own must be worth more than a million at current market value, perhaps two. Then he had some millions tied up in investments and another couple in the bank in various accounts. That was hardly extraordinary these days. It was quite normal for someone in Edward's former line of work, who'd been successful over many years, and who'd carefully managed the money that had come his way. Edward had never been anything less than generous to friends and family. Neither had he thrown his money away on silly, indulgent expense. That way, he'd preserved the bulk of his income and now had a mixed portfolio which was able to flourish in good times as well as ride out the bad.

In truth, he didn't know his true worth. It no longer really mattered to him. He just contented himself with the thought he was a millionaire. He was actually worth a lot more than that. He just couldn't be bothered to figure it out, largely because he just wanted to be seen as an ordinary man in the street. That was how he wanted Jill to view him. He wanted her to like him for who he was and not for any money he might have. Unfortunately, Alice had been told at their first meeting he was rich. Perhaps in retrospect that might have encouraged her interest in him. He'd let her keep the house for the duration of her lifetime if they did split up. He'd also give her some kind of generous divorce settlement. He'd go and live somewhere else, somewhere altogether humbler, and more basic. He wasn't bothered. It was all he really needed. He'd never really needed the big house he had. He'd only ever really needed Angela and the children.

Edward led Beti past the St Helen's Rugby and Cricket Ground and its's long car park, past the entrance to Singleton Park and the Swansea University Campus. Beti didn't complain or try to pull back on her lead. They only ever maintained a modest pace, appropriate to their ages in human and dog years. They were probably of a comparable relative vintage. Edward wasn't a young man. Beti wasn't a young dog. She had grey in her fur, just as most of his remaining hair was grey. Neither of them was quite decrepit either. They both still had a few years left in them.

They continued along the Mumbles Road, past the boating lake and athletic track, where they crossed over to walk on the beach side and enjoy views of the bay all the way round to Mumbles Pier. Eventually, they reached the car park for Clyne Valley Park on the right and Blackpill Lido on the left. There, they crossed back over and headed for the entrance to Clyne Gardens. It could easily be missed by those who didn't know its location. There was a pub on the corner, which provided a convenient signpost to the park. It was one Edward remembered from his student days. They'd gone there on occasion when Angela had still been staying in Clyne Halls. It would make a perfect choice for a spot of lunch, Edward thought. He could get a bit to eat there, before deciding whether to walk or get the bus back.

Clyne Gardens was busier than the other parks he'd been to on his stay. It was clearly very popular with local, retired walkers. A number stood by the entrance with their hiking sticks. Edward had no need for one of those just yet. The terrain wasn't quite that steep. He had no doubt he could manage it unassisted and in his normal clothes and shoes. He didn't even have walking boots, as all these other eager walkers had. Some looked at if they'd just completed their trek around the grounds. Others looked just ready to start. All looked content to be in the open air and keeping healthy and active. They were a good example to those of Edward's age and older.

Edward began his walk through the bog gardens, that followed the watercourse that dissected the bottom edge of the estate. Classically shaped leaves, extending from huge bog plants that he recognised by sight but the names of which eluded him, surrounded him on all sides. They were intermingled with splashes of fragrant colour. Occasionally, the path opened up, allowing glorious views of what resembled a tropical rainforest. Edward took pictures as he went, Beti waiting patiently by his side as he did so. Edward had closely examined the map on entry and observed if they followed the watercourse to the top of the gardens, they would eventually reach its most famous feature, the Japanese Bridge, at the north-western edge. It proved to be quite a long walk. Edward had done it in his youth. It seemed much further as a retired man of sixty.

When they finally reached the stunning, red Japanese bridge, Edward took more pictures, before finding a bench for them to sit and rest on. It had been quite a trek. Perhaps hiking boots and sticks might have been helpful after all.

Once they recovered their breath, they made their way through the Bluebell Wood and Heather Beds, past the striking gazebo on the left, stopping to sit again at the Italian Bridge. Luckily, it was downhill all the way now and the path was much easier to traverse. The estate castle stood proudly behind them, and stunning views lay in front of them. Eventually, they made their way back down past the wildflower meadow on one side and the tower on the other. They'd managed to walk the entire grounds. Even he and Angela had rarely done that, forty years earlier. They'd normally just walked a little way, before finding somewhere to sit, hold hands and look longingly into each other's eyes. Those days were over. He just had Beti now, and perhaps Jill.

Despite eating a cooked breakfast and two cakes, Edward suddenly started to feel the pangs of hunger coming over him. It was almost one-thirty in the afternoon, past his usual lunchtime. It was time to head to the pub and get something to eat. No doubt, he'd find himself feeding titbits of whatever he had to Beti. She was highly unlikely to refuse them. She seemed happy to eat anything he ordered. She clearly had sophisticated tastes and didn't restrict herself to the vegan diet Jill enjoyed.

At the pub, Edward ordered chicken in breadcrumbs, chips and peas and a pint of ale to go with it. He knew Beti would be pleased with his choice. He recalled dogs had to be careful with chicken bones, but this was all carefully filleted, as had been the fish at the marina restaurant. There would be no awkward bones for he and Beti to contend with. When his steaming plate of appetising food arrived, it looked mouth-watering. The chicken and chips were done to golden perfection. He couldn't wait to tuck in. Beti evidently felt the same, as she eagerly looked up at him. The smell of his meal had clearly made her feel hungry as well. Edward had admitted to Jill that he fed titbits to Beti, and she was fine with it.

'I can hardly expect Beti to be vegan, can I?' she'd responded.

That had given Edward the green light and he shared everything he had with Beti after that, until she seemed full too or they'd mutually cleared his plate. She was always happy to have more. Having eaten, they meandered their way back onto the bay path and walked for a bit, to let their lunch go down. Eventually, Edward tired of walking. He looked down and sensed that Beti felt the same. They decided to wait for a bus that would take them most of the way back to the bookshop. If Edward remembered correctly, one stop was by the Brangwyn Hall. That would suit them perfectly. As promised, Jill had boiled the kettle and was getting a cup of tea ready to hand him as he walked through the door to drop Beti off.

'Did you have a nice walk?' Jill asked.

'We certainly did, though we got the bus back, as you suggested. We were both tired after lunch,' Edward said.

'You must have walked a pretty long way still,' Jill commented.

'Far enough,' Edward agreed. 'My feet can definitely feel it. We walked as far as the Japanese Bridge. I'm certainly ready for a cup of tea.'

Beti was lapping at a bowl of water on the floor by her basket.

'I think Beti was ready for a drink too, by the look of things,' Jill observed.

'She did have water in the pub. I had a pint,' Edward admitted.

'You do surprise me,' Jill said.

'Busy day?' Edward asked, as all three settled down to enjoy their drinks.

'Not too bad, just a few in, but I sold a couple of things,' Jill said.

'That's good,' Edward said, approvingly.

Jill then paused, before replying.

'I've been thinking,' she said. 'You don't have to return home.'

'What do you mean?' Edward asked, suddenly looking up, with a slightly perplexed expression on his face.

'Well, it's obvious really,' Jill said. 'You like books and there's too much to do here for me to keep on top of. I'm barely coping at the moment. I can't even keep the books sorted and catalogued, as you keep pointing out. I need help.'

'I can see that. What were you thinking of?' Edward wondered.

'I thought you might like to look after the shop for a day or two a week, or a couple of mornings or afternoons, whatever you like really. I'm open to suggestion. It would mean I could take Beti out more myself and do some of the other things in my life, that are currently getting neglected. You seem like a very organised person. I'm sure you'd quickly get the shop running as it should be.'

Edward thought about it for a moment. He'd noticed Jill was much in need of help. He'd never seriously thought he might be the one to give it her. The notion was absurd and impossible. He had a wife and a home back in Oxford, or did he? Was it such a silly idea? Was it a total impossibility? He might like pottering round in a bookshop a couple of days a week. He could certainly get all the books sorted and up on the shelves in their rightful place, and perhaps improve Jill's presence on the internet.

'It's a lot to think about,' Edward said, at last.

'I know. You don't have to give me an answer straight away,' Jill said quickly, almost embarrassed she'd made the suggestion in the first place. It had just been on her mind. With Edward thinking of leaving, she'd been left with no choice but to come out with it.

'It is an intriguing thought,' Edward acknowledged. 'I can see there is a lot I could do with this place. It has potential. It could be the best second-hand bookshop in South Wales.'

'Well, Swansea perhaps,' Jill laughed. 'There are only a couple of them.'

'How long would I stay and where would I live?' Edward suddenly blurted out.

'I've thought of that,' Jill said. 'You can stay as long as you like. Regarding where you live, you could stay on in the guesthouse. Alternatively, with Megan gone, I've got space upstairs. I've got two spare rooms in fact I hardly use. You could have one of them. I'll give you reduced rent and everything. You can take a look now if you like.'

'It does all sound very tempting,' Edward recognised. 'I think we are both forgetting one thing. I do have a wife, Alice, back home in Oxford. I also have a rather big house there.'

'Do you want to go back?' Jill asked. 'I sense I'm not sure that you do.'

'The truth is I don't know myself,' Edward admitted. 'I came away to decide that, and to reflect on my former life here with Angela. It's been two weeks and I'm no nearer deciding what I want. I was always so decisive during my working life. Now I don't know my own heart. I don't know what I want. What I will say is I'll consider your suggestion. I'll give it some thought overnight, and I'll let you know tomorrow if that's all right. How does that sound?'

'It sounds fine to me,' Jill said. 'Of course, it doesn't have to be permanent. You could just do it for a few weeks, until we get the shop sorted and you decide what you want to do next with your life.'

'That too is a possibility,' Edward nodded. 'I guess I've got some hard thinking to do tonight.'

He was suddenly struck by the thought he'd already said his goodbyes to Meredith in the coffee shop. It would indeed be a bit embarrassing to go back there now. If he did, he'd probably leave it a few days, before making an unexpected appearance, to announce that he was planning to stay in Swansea after all. Not that he was certain that was what he wanted to do. It was a massive decision. There was much to consider, many pros and cons to weigh up. Oxford and the little village outside where they resided was his home. He had friends there. He was a popular member of the tennis club and other local bodies and organisations. Victoria wasn't far away in London, even if he didn't see all that much of her. Perhaps the crux of the matter was, did he still love Alice? Did she love him, or did she now love Paul?

'Just let me know when you're ready,' Jill said. 'Just promise me you won't leave without saying goodbye.'

'I can promise you that,' Edward assured her. 'I'll pop by tomorrow afternoon with my answer, one way or another. Will you be here?'

'What do you think? Of course, I will. I wouldn't miss that,' Jill said. 'But don't let me influence you. Do what's right for you.'

'OK and I'll see you tomorrow,' he said, putting his teacup down and getting ready to leave.

Edward left a little more quietly than he'd arrived. It was a bit of a bombshell Jill had dropped. It had rather taken him by surprise. To an extent, it made perfect sense. In other ways, it made no sense whatsoever. What was he to do? He had no idea. He thought about ringing Alice and asking her advice of all things. Perhaps it rather hinged on whether she was with Paul now, or did that really matter? Didn't what Edward want also matter too? Did he want to go back to Oxford and fight for Alice, or did he want to stay here in Swansea with Jill and Beti? Were he and Jill just friends, or were they slowly becoming more than that? Edward didn't know. They did seem to have formed some kind of mutual understanding that transcended mere friendship. Perhaps he was just imagining it. Perhaps Jill simply wanted some help in her bookshop and nothing more than that.

Edward sat quietly in the pub that night, pondering all these thoughts and trying to sift his way through them as best he could. He'd had a light evening meal, washed down with a glass of red wine. He hadn't really been in the mood to drink, but that had changed. He'd now moved onto the beer and would probably have a whisky with Alan and Gwen before the end of the night. It really was a pretty pickle he'd managed to get himself in, and a dilemma he was struggling to resolve. Should he stay or should he go? He still didn't know the answer. Should he follow his heart, or should he allow his head to rule? Which one was right? What were each telling him to do? Did he even know that much? He suspected his heart was telling him to stay, whereas his logical side said he should go back. Another course of action was of course to return to Oxford, get things sorted with Alice and then return to Swansea. He hadn't thought of that. It was a kind of third, compromise option. When he got back to the guesthouse, he invited Alan and Gwen's opinion.

'I've had an offer to stay in Swansea,' Edward announced.

'Oh, how's that?' Alan asked, intrigued by Edward's news.

'Jill, the bookshop owner, whose dog I take for walks, has asked me to help out in the shop,' Edward explained.

'Are you going to do it?' Gwen asked.

Her interest in the conversation had also suddenly been aroused and gone up a notch. It had moved on from the usual evening pleasantries, of Edward describing in detail what he'd done that day.

'I don't know yet. I honestly haven't decided,' Edward admitted. 'Either way, this weekend is likely to be my last in the guesthouse I'm sad to say. If I do stay in Swansea, it's been suggested I take a room over the shop,'

'Well, it's been lovely having you,' Gwen said.

'You've been a model guest,' Alan added.

'I want to thank you for looking after me so well,' Edward said. 'I really will be sorry to leave. I've had a simply marvellous stay here. It's been absolutely wonderful.'

'Well, you know where we are if you ever want to stay again,' Gwen reminded him.

'I shall certainly do that. Either way I'll still be here tomorrow night if that's OK. Sunday is the day of reckoning. I'll either be heading back to Oxford then or moving into Jill's place, I guess,' Edward said.

'Do what's best for you,' Gwen suggested.

'That's good advice,' Alan agreed.

It was indeed.

'Funnily enough, that's exactly what Jill said,' Edward laughed, as he finished his whisky and soda, put down his glass, said goodnight and headed off to bed.

Day Thirteen (Saturday)

Edward allowed himself an extra half an hour in bed as it was a Saturday, before heading down for breakfast. He guessed it would be a little busier than usual, with most of the tables taken, as it had been the previous weekend. It was a good base for trips out onto the Gower Peninsula. It was quite popular with families at weekends, it seemed. Edward presumed this one would be no exception. The weather had generally been fine for most of the week, apart from when Edward had got soaked on his way back from Neath. It was expected to remain nice until Sunday afternoon, when rain would blow in again off the bay. No doubt the good weather they'd been enjoying would bring the visitors flocking to the Gower in their droves, to take advantage of any sunshine before it inevitably turned. By Sunday afternoon, the clouds would struggle to rise above the higher ground overlooking Swansea and would happily empty their heavy contents on the city. It was a familiar pattern. It always had been during Edward's years living there. The basic topography of West Glamorgan hadn't changed, he imagined. It had probably altered little in eons.

Edward presumed most of the weekend getaway enthusiasts would be on their way home by the time the rain came. He might be on his way home too or moving his scant belongings into a room above Jill's shop, one he realised he hadn't even looked at yet. He'd neglected to accept Jill's suggestion to take a proper look around her home. In truth, he'd been too befuddled by her proposal that he move in and help her look after the shop. It had come out of the blue. It had taken him completely by surprise. His usual calm assuredness had momentarily deserted him. Everything else had temporarily slipped his mind.

Taking a look at the rooms would have been the sensible thing to do. At least then, he'd have a better idea of what he was getting himself into. Judging by the shop, he imagined Jill's home above could be something of a mess. Edward disliked disorder. Left to his own devices, he was an organised and well-ordered man. He couldn't imagine living anywhere that failed to meet his exacting high standards and was full of clutter. Then he shrugged to himself. Perhaps sorting that and making it tidy would just be an extension of sorting out the shop. Both were entirely possible if he set his natural efficiency to the task in hand. It wasn't in itself reason to decline Jill's offer. Besides, he liked a challenge. If things weren't a bit chaotic and been allowed to deteriorate somewhat, Jill would have no need of him.

Edward had been right. He didn't get his window seat. He hadn't expected to. He had to sit at a little table off to one side, which wasn't normally used. The guesthouse wasn't usually sufficiently busy. It didn't matter. There was just enough room for him where he was. He had room for his orange juice, his pot of tea, his cooked breakfast, and his toast. He dreaded to think how many sausages and rashes of bacon he'd consumed in the last fortnight. It was as many as he'd eaten in the previous six months, possibly more.

After breakfast, Edward had a quick shower in the lukewarm water, before heading out. He had a lot to think about. Big decisions needed to be made. He was running out of time in which to make them. He had much to weigh up in his mind. Things couldn't be postponed any longer. It was strange. He'd always been so decisive in the past. It had been an easy decision to settle in Oxford. He'd wasted no time embarking on a career. He'd proposed to Angela not long after they'd both graduated. They'd mutually agreed to delay having children until they were financially secure. All this had been straightforward. Edward had rarely been filled with doubt. He'd owed a lot of his success in the business world to quick, clear, concise thinking. He'd made big decisions on the spot, and they'd normally been the right ones. He'd been able to weigh up deals in an instant and make the correct evaluation and formulate an appropriate plan. He hadn't delayed asking Alice to marry him. He even knew when the time was right to give it all up. Now, he was struggling to find that same level of decisiveness. Perhaps because it had become more a matter of the heart than just the head.

Edward didn't go to Meredith's coffee shop. He couldn't bring himself to, even though he knew she wouldn't be working. By saying goodbye, he'd inadvertently brought the curtain down on that particular chapter of his time in Swansea. Of course, he would go back eventually if he extended his stay. He just couldn't do it straight away. He'd have to let a little time pass, a few days at least. In the meantime, he'd have to find somewhere else to enjoy his morning coffee. It wouldn't be as good. He was confident of that. Edward found a modern, hipster-style coffee house near the High Street to try. It had pleasant wooden décor and a nice ambience, that enticed him to enter. The cakes looked appetising, though they were more of the trendy, new variety than the traditional ones Meredith had made and sold. They were fine, but Edward knew which he preferred. He was perhaps showing his age.

Being an organised chap, Edward thought about getting a pen and paper and listing the arguments for and against both staying and leaving. He thought that might help him reach a decision. Then he thought that was no way to do it. He wasn't giving enough consideration to the part Alice had to play in all of this. Even if she planned to leave him, the house was still his, he supposed. He'd invited her in. He could just as easily invite her to leave, although that seemed harsh. That wasn't really his style, whatever she'd done. He was a gentleman after all. He couldn't just throw her out onto the street, although some might have been tempted to do exactly that. The house was in fact big enough, that they could live in separate wings and their paths barely cross. That was yet another possibility Edward hadn't considered. The more he thought about it, the more choices he seemed to have. The most pressing remained was he to return to Oxford the following day or was he stay put where he was? If he could decide that much, it would be a start.

Edward got fed up thinking about it. It frustrated him a little that for a supposedly decisive man, he remained so undecided. Was Jill the kind of woman he really wanted to share a home with? She was a vegan for a start, something Edward wasn't and was uncertain if he truly approved of. She was scatty and muddled and unlike Edward quite haphazard. She had a dog. She clearly wasn't a businesswoman, even though she owned a shop. She was pleasant, however, not unattractive, and quite charming in her own way. Alice on the other hand was a model of efficiency and feminine beauty combined. She had a good job, one she excelled in. She was someone he'd always been proud to be seen out with, lightly holding onto his arm, as they walked. She was refined, elegant, and always well-dressed. She could also be a little remote and cold. She maintained a façade which rarely dropped. Even when she'd been discovered in her affair with Paul, her composure had largely remained intact. She hadn't thrown herself at Edward's feet, to beg forgiveness. She hadn't seemed too bothered in truth. It was almost as if Edward had just caught her out in some small white lie, that perhaps she'd spent more on a coat than she'd first admitted, but it was nothing to get too het up about. It would all be glossed over and forgotten by morning. That was what she seemed to think.

Edward got fed up mulling it all over. Instead, he got out his book to read. He'd finished *The Country of the Blind* and had moved onto the other stories, *The Star*, *The New Accelerator*, *The Remarkable Case of Davidson's Eyes.* HG Wells had been a very clever man, as Edward was in many ways himself. Someone like HG Wells would have been sure to know what to do in Edward's situation. He'd been blessed with eloquence and brilliance in his lifetime. The answer would have been staring him in the face. He'd have known instinctively what the correct course of action was. Perhaps Edward should just trust his instinct also, as he usually had in his work. Perhaps he should give it no more thought for now. He'd enjoy a pleasant day by himself and when it came time to see Jill, he'd just somehow know what to say. The answer would doubtlessly present itself in due course, when it needed to. That was his earnest hope anyway.

Edward finished his coffee and cake and closed his book. He left the coffee shop and proceeded along High Street, past the ruins of Swansea Castle and down Wind Street. He hadn't reached an active decision in his mind where he was going, not that he was aware of. Yet, he somehow knew where he was going all the same. He was going back to the Dylan Thomas Centre. He'd try and get some inspiration from the great man, before perhaps enjoying a bite of lunch there. Sometime in the afternoon, he'd wander over to see Jill in the bookshop and give her his answer. She was probably waiting and wondering, or maybe the whole thing had slipped her mind. That would be embarrassing, if Edward turned up with some announcement of great significance and she had no idea what he was talking about. Hopefully, that wouldn't happen. Hopefully, her suggestion that he help out in the shop and take a room above had been a serious one.

Walking round the Dylan Thomas Centre, Edward was struck by the realisation that the great writer had never forgotten his roots, his happy, Welsh childhood and growing up in the Uplands area of Swansea. He'd lived in London. He'd travelled extensively in America. Yet, everything always came back to Wales and Swansea in particular. Even when writing in the remote boathouse in Laugherne, to the west of the Gower, Dylan Thomas still drew most of his inspiration from the observations he'd made of the people of Swansea, the characters, habits, and practices of those folk he'd encountered in their ordinary lives, that made the city and surrounding area what it was. Edward had never forgotten his roots either, or perhaps he had for a bit. That was the painful truth. He too had some Welsh blood in him. His father had grown up in Cardiff. Edward had spent his formative university years in Swansea. He'd put those years to the back of his mind for the last forty years. Now he'd returned and the memories had returned to the forefront of his mind too. Perhaps they were providing a hint that was telling him what he had to do.

Edward ate his lunch at the Dylan Thomas Centre. He had quiche, sautéed potatoes, and a mixed salad, washed down with a very agreeable glass of *Pinot Noir*. Fortified by red wine, he was ready to face Jill and give her his answer. He followed the River Tawe as it meandered it way past both the city's two museums and the stylish apartments of the Maritime Quarter. Leaving that area behind him, he passed Swansea Prison and the Civic Centre. Shortly after passing the guesthouse where he was staying, perhaps for just one more night, he turned inland. He followed Guildhall Road South, before branching off at Francis Street for Jill's shop. Once outside, he took a deep breath before stepping inside. He was rather surprised to realise he felt quite nervous.

'Hello, how are you today?' Jill greeted him.

She made no mention at all of the matter that was no doubt occupying both their minds. At least Edward assumed it was occupying her mind too. Perhaps it was just occupying his. That would be quite awful if that was the case, Edward thought to himself. He trusted it wasn't so, and his first instinct had been correct. She was just being polite. No doubt, they'd get round to discussing the truly important matters of the day in the fullness of time once niceties had been observed.

'I'm very well, thank you,' Edward replied. 'I've just been for coffee and then back to the Dylan Thomas Centre for lunch and to have another look round.'

'So, you are finally being converted,' Jill commented, making a little joke at Edward's expense.

'Just a little, perhaps,' Edward admitted.

'Would you like a cup of tea?' Jill asked.

'That would be nice,' Edward said.

Jill put the kettle on to boil. There was a momentary silence. Should he or should she break the ice?

'So,' she said at last. 'Have you given any more thought to my little proposal?'

That was a relief to Edward. She hadn't forgotten and indeed she'd brought it up first.

'I have, as a matter of fact,' Edward answered, without giving too much away.

'Is that all? Have you perhaps come to a decision?' Jill continued to quiz him.

'Well, there's a lot to think about and consider, but I think I probably have,' Edward said.

'Don't leave me in suspense then,' Jill said. 'Spit it out, man.'

'What I've decided is I'll stay at least for a while longer. I can help in the shop, until we get it properly sorted out. We can just take it from there and see how it goes week by week, I guess. Perhaps in that time my thoughts about everything and the future may become clearer,' Edward said.

'And will you take one of the rooms above the shop?' Jill asked.

'At least on a temporary basis,' Edward confirmed.

He didn't want to overcommit. He imagined it would take a few weeks to get the shop properly shipshape, perhaps a month or even a little longer. Everything might be clearer then. Perhaps Alice would have tracked him down and come to get him and drag him back to Oxford. She'd probably already guessed where he'd gone. There weren't all that many places he could realistically have gone to. London might have been another, to stay with old work friends, or perhaps to a cottage in the middle of nowhere. That also would have been a very Edward thing to do in the circumstances, somewhere Alice would never find him. Of course, in truth it was unlikely she was even looking. She probably didn't care very much that he'd taken off. It meant she could spend time with Paul.

'So, that's settled then,' Jill said. 'You can move in as soon as you like.'

'I thought tomorrow, a Sunday, might be as good a day as any, to bring my things over,' Edward suggested.

'Tomorrow will be perfect. I'll help you move them,' Jill said.

'You can if you like, but I've actually travelled very light,' Edward admitted.

'That's OK. I'd like to see where you've been living anyway, even if I only end up carrying one thing,' Jill told him.

'I fear it will be two bags at most,' Edward confessed. 'I guess I'll be needing to buy more if I'm staying longer. I've already had to buy more clothes since arriving here.'

'I'm sure we can sort that. Anyway, I for one am delighted you're staying. It will be a pleasure to have you aboard,' Jill said.

'Thank you, I'm delighted too,' Edward responded, still not quite certain exactly what he was agreeing to.

He'd find out in good time, he reasoned. That was all that really mattered. All his questions would be answered in the fullness of the passing days and weeks. He'd have to tell Alice he was staying longer. Perhaps he'd finally check some of her messages, those he hadn't deleted without reading. It might give him some idea of the lie of the land. Another month in Swansea in the early summer wouldn't be too bad at all. Perhaps he might even hire that car he'd thought about and get out and about a bit more. He could take Jill and Beti with him. He could get the shop sorted out. It really was the best compromise when he thought about. He could extend his stay without committing to anything permanent. That way, if things didn't work out in the shop or if he suddenly started to pine for Alice, he could head back at little more than a moment's notice. Of course, he wouldn't do that. He'd have to give Jill due warning of any changes in his intentions. That was the only decent thing to do. Of course, he might end up staying the whole summer or even longer.

'You know I think this calls for a celebration,' Jill suddenly announced.

'That sounds like a plan,' Edward agreed. 'What did you have in mind?'

'I was thinking I could shut the shop early and we could go for a celebratory drink, just somewhere local,' Jill suggested. 'What do you say to that? It will give us a chance to work out some of the details and practicalities of you moving in.'

'Why not? I rarely turn down the offer of a drink,' Edward laughed. 'I tell you what, I'll take Beti for a walk and when I come back, we can head off to the pub. How does that sound?'

'It sounds marvellous,' Jill said, enthusiastically. 'It will be my first drink in ages. It will probably go straight to my head.'

'Don't worry, I'll look after you,' Edward promised.

Why had he said that? he wondered. Perhaps he now felt some responsibility towards this slightly chaotic woman he'd agreed to share a home with, for some reason still not quite known to him. He'd done it now. There was no going back. He'd given his word. He couldn't break it. At the very least, he'd have to get the shop sorted and in good efficient, working order. Not only would he get it clean and tidy, with books off the floor and catalogued, he might even get some new shelves and bookcases for her and give the place a lick of paint whilst he was at it. He'd work out a plan of action once he got started. He had little doubt it would all fall neatly into place once he put his mind to it. Edward took Beti's lead and led her towards the front door.

'See you later,' Jill shouted, as he pulled it shut behind him.

Still no sign of any customers, Edward reflected. Did the woman live off thin air? She couldn't earn enough to keep a sparrow going, from what he'd observed. Perhaps she'd inherited from her late husband. Perhaps that was the only reasonable explanation. Perhaps she was just doing it as a hobby. It hardly seemed plausible she was making enough for it to be considered a viable business. Perhaps she was doing better on the mail order side of things than she let on. Perhaps like himself she was a person of hidden means.

Edward and Beti wandered onto King Edward's Road and continued to the end, where they passed the familiar St Helen's Rugby and Cricket Ground, continuing past its long car park, before reaching the bottom entrance to Singleton Park. Edward thought he'd do one traverse of the park before heading back. He started at the lowest point and slowly made his way upwards, passing the Singleton Abbey entrance to the university campus. He continued past the ornamental gardens and woodlands path, before eventually reaching the famous Swiss Cottage landmark. He could see Swansea Botanical Gardens above. He wouldn't go there today. Instead, he continued to the very top of the park, past Gorsedd Stone Circle, until he reached the northern Gower Road entrance that led to the residential area of Sketty. There, he made his way back down on the opposite side to the one he'd walked up, keeping Uplands and the top end of Brynmill to his left. He knew he was nearly back once he saw the shallow lake and wooded area that occupied the middle of the park. Edward thought about leaving via the Byrnmill exit, but instead continued all the way back to the bottom, where Singleton Park exited onto the beach road. Jill was true to her word. As soon as Edward walked through the door, she switched off the lights and got out her keys to lock the front door.

'Let's go then,' she said, with undisguised enthusiasm. Either the prospect of a drink or Edward moving in and helping with the shop had given her a new spring in her step and an optimism and energy for what lay ahead. 'There's a pub just round the corner, where they know Beti. They won't mind her coming in,' Jill continued, taking Edward's arm, and leading him along.

Edward still had hold of Beti's lead.

'Sounds ideal,' he said, happy to be directed to their destination.

'This is going to be such fun,' Jill said. 'It could be the perfect solution to all my problems.'

'I'll do my best, but don't expect too much,' Edward said.

'Don't underestimate yourself,' Jill said. 'I can see you're just the man to get the shop and house sorted. It's been missing a man about the place. There's been no one since John passed away.'

'No one?' Edward asked.

'Not really. I haven't even dated much. I've had one or two drinks with men, members of my Book Club and other groups, but just as friends and nothing more than that,' Jill said.

'How long's it been?' Edward asked.

'About five years since John died. Anyway, let's not think about that. It's time to celebrate and be happy,' Jill announced.

She brought him to a pub on Brynmor Road. It was opposite one of those where he'd often had his evening meal during the past fortnight, but not one he'd been in yet himself. This would be his first time. At the bar, he ordered himself a pint of ale and asked Jill what she was having. He thought she might ask for a glass of wine or a gin and tonic. Instead, she asked for a pint of cider. They found a table in a corner, sat down, and made themselves comfortable.

'Will you be eating?' Edward enquired.

'Will you?' Jill replied.

'I may have something,' Edward said.

'I may if you do,' Jill said.

'I'll get a menu then,' Edward said. 'It will save me coming out again later.'

Jill kissed Edward warmly on the cheek when he finally escorted her back to the shop. They'd both consumed a few drinks by then.

'I said it would go to my head. I feel quite tipsy,' Jill admitted. 'I'm not used to drinking anymore.'

'It's a Saturday night, so why not?' Edward said, encouragingly.

He himself still felt reasonably sober, although he was aware he'd had a drink or two. He'd paid. He'd insisted on it. He wouldn't allow Jill to open her purse once. She needed the money she had.

'I'll see you in the morning then,' Jill said, taking Beti's lead from Edward's hand.

'I'll be round after breakfast and we can go and collect my things, the few that there are,' Edward said. 'At least you'll be able to see my room and where I've been staying.'

'I'm looking forward to it,' Jill said.

Edward smiled back. He then watched her as she slipped inside the shop, before heading off himself. She was a nice lady. She was a bit odd, but she was good company. All that time she'd spent on her own. It didn't bear thinking about. It wasn't as if she old. She was only in her fifties. Her late husband had been older, just as Edward was older than Alice. Why did women often choose older men and men choose younger women? It didn't really make sense. Women as a rule lived longer. By rights, it should have been the other way round. Perhaps it was just the natural order of things, or unnatural order in fact. Back at the guesthouse, Edward joined Alan and Gwen for a final nightcap.

'I'm sorry to say this will be my last night,' he announced. 'I'll settle up for my second week in the morning if that's all right.'

'Well, it's been lovely having you to stay,' Alan said.

'It has indeed,' Gwen agreed.

'You've looked after me wonderfully. I couldn't have asked for more,' Edward told the couple. 'You've been perfect hosts in every way.'

'Perhaps you can leave us a review on *Trip Advisor*,' Alan suggested.

'I'll certainly do that,' Edward confirmed.

'So, what did you decide in the end?' Gwen asked. 'Are you staying on in Swansea or going home?'

Edward paused for a moment. Was he really doing so for dramatic effect? He wouldn't be that petty, would he? Truthfully, he couldn't quite believe the answer he was about to give himself.

'I'm going to stay with Jill for a bit, at least until I get the shop sorted,' Edward said. 'After that. I'm undecided. I guess it will depend on how things progress and work out. But I should be around for the first part of the summer.'

'You'll have to pop in on us when you're passing,' Alan said.

'Yes, you can come for a drink any night,' Gwen echoed.

'I'll certainly do that,' Edward replied.

With that, he downed his whisky and soda, before starting to make his way to his room and bed.

'Thanks again,' he said. 'You really have made my stay a special one.'

'Well, we're always here if you need a room,' Alan said.

'If I need a guesthouse in Swansea, I wouldn't stay anywhere else,' Edward assured them. 'I can absolutely promise that.'

What was more, he meant it. Whatever happened during his time in the bookshop, he was resolved on returning to Swansea more regularly in the future. If he did, Alan and Gwen's guesthouse was certainly the place he'd stay at. In the comfort of his bedroom, he got out his phone. He could see Alice had both rung and texted again. He started to read one text. *Where are you? What on earth do you think you're playing at? We have things to discuss and sort out*, it read. A proper reply could wait. Instead, he typed the following and pressed send. *I'll be staying a while longer. I'll be in touch when I'm ready and my long-term plans are a bit clearer. Take care and say hi to Paul for me, Edward.*

That last bit seemed a bit churlish, but Edward couldn't resist his small joke, though he realised it might come across as just sarcastic and bitter on his part. He was, he realised, also making a point. She'd created this situation after all. None of this would have happened if she'd remained faithful. He'd still be in Oxford, playing a spot of tennis, going for leisurely walks and lunches, reading his book, watching sport both on television and at local sports grounds, sitting in the garden when the weather was fine, doing the occasional crossword. Alice had chosen to turn his world upside down. He'd just decided to run with it for once in his life. It had brought him to a strange point in time, where he was about to move in with another woman.

Day Fourteen (Sunday)

Edward got out of bed and drew back the curtains. He knew it would be the last time he performed this particular ritual in this particular location. He felt a tinge of sadness to be leaving. He'd had a fabulous stay in this modest, little guesthouse, one he'd never forget. He'd remember Alan and Gwen and how kind they were to him for the rest of his days. He hoped to see them again. Indeed, he'd make a point of doing so. He'd accept their invitation to pop in on them from time to time, for a nightcap. If for any reason he did need a guesthouse in Swansea again, theirs would certainly be the one he'd choose. He had no doubt he would be coming back, even when his current stay ended. Whether that would be at Jill's or somewhere else, he was less certain.

Edward looked out of his window across the bay. It was a grey day in Swansea, how he remembered it best really. Even though it was grey, he could still see Port Talbot to the east and Mumbles Pier to the right. There was no sign yet of the rain that was to come. That was expected to blow in shortly after lunchtime. He needed to get the small amount of moving that needed to be done completed by then. That was unless he wanted to get rained on. Maybe a small part of him did, just for old time's sake. It was strange that he remembered the wet days, battling the elements along the bay road to the university campus, much better than the fine ones. There must have been just as many of those, when the sky was blue, and the air was still. Edward just didn't remember them as well.

Breakfast was a little later on a Sunday, so Edward had his shower before going down. It would be the last time he felt the lukewarm water on his skin. He really should have mentioned it to Alan. It just seemed such a minor thing. It would have felt petty bringing it up, as everything else was so nice. He could hardly expect perfection on the daily rates he was paying. He mustn't forget to settle his bill, and include all the whisky and sodas he'd had, before leaving. He certainly didn't want Alan and Gwen to be out of pocket. Edward would have rather paid too much than felt he'd paid too little. When he went down to the breakfast room, he encountered Gwen waiting for him, before seeing Alan.

'I just wanted to check it was scrambled eggs today?' Gwen asked.

'Yes, I did say that,' Edward confirmed. 'I had something different last Sunday, and thought I'd do the same today. Six cooked breakfasts in a row are probably enough for anyone. If I stay any longer, I'll end up getting very fat,' he chuckled.

'I think your walking has helped keep you in shape,' Gwen said. 'If anything, I think you've lost a bit of weight,' she complimented him.

'You really think so?' Edward said, surprised but secretly quite pleased by her remark. 'You're just being kind. I've also had a lot of cakes since I've been away,' he admitted.

'It doesn't show,' Gwen said.

'I have been walking the dog a lot, or perhaps she's been walking me,' Edward said.

'It must be keeping you fit,' Gwen commented, as she disappeared back into the kitchen.

'So last day, then,' Alan said, as he guided Edward to a vacant table. 'It won't be the same when you've gone.'

'It will seem odd to me too,' Edward agreed. 'The last fortnight has flown by. Although it also seems a while since I've been home in Oxford. That's starting to feel like another lifetime.'

'Well, I hope it all works out in the bookshop,' Alan said.

'I hope so too,' Edward answered.

'If it doesn't, you can always come back,' Alan told him.

'Thank you, that's good to know,' Edward said, taking a sip of his orange juice.

He didn't have a huge breakfast, just in case he ended up having another Sunday lunch in the pub. He would invite Jill of course. It would be the polite thing to do. Being a vegan, she might well not accept. A Sunday roast would hardly have the same appeal for her. Indeed, the thought alone was probably quite abhorrent. He imagined she could have the vegetables and some of the trimmings. Perhaps they did a nut roast or something similar, though Edward hadn't seen one on the menu. He'd ask her anyway. She could only say no. Not that he was certain he'd end up in the pub anyway. The day might pan out quite differently. Jill might have different plans for him altogether.

Back in his room, Edward started to put all his things neatly together. He took his clothes out of the wardrobe and chest of drawers and placed them on the bed. He gathered up his toiletries from the sink and shower. He'd arrived with one bag, now he had two. He'd also acquired a couple of extra items, like some books and small mementoes of some of the places he'd visited. It probably wasn't too much for him to carry by himself, but he'd humour Jill that it was. He'd formed the impression she was just looking for an excuse to see where he'd been staying. She was probably intrigued. He'd still given her no hint he could have afforded to stay somewhere much more expensive and markedly posher, even live there if that was his desire. It wasn't. Edward had decided he liked the humble lifestyle. Before heading over to Jill's, he went downstairs to pay Alan and Gwen the money he owed them.

'Do you have my bill?' Edward asked. 'Make sure to include all the drinks I've had from the bar.'

'I have it here somewhere, as I knew you were checking out today,' Alan said, looking behind his desk for the piece of paper he'd printed out. 'I think you've already paid for the first week anyway.'

'As long as you haven't missed any days that I've stayed. That's all I'm concerned about,' Edward said, anxious to pay what he owed in full.

Alan passed him the bill. It still seemed very reasonable, Edward thought, as he handed Alan his bank card, to take payment. Edward then reached into his wallet and pulled out one hundred pounds in crisp, new twenty-pound notes, which he handed to Alan.

'That's a small, personal thank you from me,' Edward said, in a hushed tone. 'Perhaps you and Gwen can treat yourself to lunch or dinner, if you ever get the time and opportunity,' he suggested.

'That's most generous of you,' Alan said. 'I'm sure we can do something.' He wasn't used to getting tips from guests and his face positively lit up.

'I'm just heading over to pick up Jill. Then I'll be back in a bit to collect my things,' Edward explained. 'I'll say goodbye then if that's OK.'

'That's absolutely fine, and you can keep your things in your room as long as you like. There's no hurry to leave,' Alan said.

Before vacating his room, Edward made sure everything was neatly packed and ready to take. He carefully checked he hadn't left anything behind. That would have been anathema to his naturally well-ordered mind. He even checked under the bed and in places he hadn't used, just to be sure. He then proceeded on his now familiar way to the end of Oystermouth Road, before turning right into Guildhall Road South and continuing along Francis Street, between Victoria Park and the Brangwyn Hall, to the bookshop. Of course, when he arrived, as it was a Sunday, the shop was closed, and he had to ring the doorbell. Jill soon appeared.

'Ready?' Edward asked.

'I'll just get a coat, in case it starts to rain,' she said, grabbing one off a hook and then pulling the door shut behind her. 'I'll show you round when we get back,' she said. 'I don't want you to be put off until it's too late and you've left the guesthouse. I've tried to tidy it up a bit,' she laughed.

'Will Beti be all right on her own?' Edward asked, with a slight tone of concern in his voice.

'She'll be fine,' Jill assured him. 'Besides, we shouldn't be too long.'

Edward led Jill back down the road, exactly the same way he'd just come, until they were standing outside Alan and Gwen's distinctive-looking guesthouse.

'Oh, this one,' Jill said, sounding pleasantly surprised. 'I've walked past it many times with Beti. I've always thought it looked the nicest.'

'That's exactly what I thought when I did a quick search on the internet,' Edward said. 'It was the one that I remembered best from forty years ago. It's only small, but it's cosy and comfortable. I was lucky they had space for me.'

He pushed his key into the front door lock and let Jill in.

'I'm near the top,' he said, leading Jill up the stairs, before letting her into his room.

The door was slightly stiff and hard to open. That was another small foible he'd brushed off during his stay there as simply quirky and adding to the general character of the place.

'It is cosy, but nice,' Jill said, bouncing down on the bed.

Edward was glad he'd packed his things into bags, or they'd have gone everywhere.

'I like it,' Edward agreed.

'Lovely view,' Jill said, pulling the curtains back and looking out across the bay. 'I could stay here myself.'

'There's nothing stopping you,' Edward pointed out.

'Now that would be silly. I only live around the corner,' Jill replied, with a reproachful look.

Edward handed her a bag, the lighter one.

'I guess we should be going then,' he said. 'Are you OK carrying that?'

'I can just about manage it,' Jill replied, slightly mockingly.

Edward picked up his other bag and belongings. He paused for a moment, before shutting the door for the last time. He wanted to say a final goodbye to the room that had been his happy home for the last fortnight. He genuinely would miss it. He wondered if he ever would be back. He would visit Alan and Gwen of course. He was less sure if he'd ever see this particular room again. With a somewhat heavy heart, he pulled the door shut and proceeded down the stairs.

At the bottom, he called out to Alan and Gwen. 'I'm off now,' he said. 'Just dropping off the keys.'

At the sound of Edward's voice, Alan and Gwen came running out together from the back room.

'This is Jill,' Edward said, undertaking the formal introductions. 'And this is Alan and Gwen, who've kindly been looking after me.'

'Hello,' they all said, in unison.

'Make sure you take good care of him,' Gwen remarked.

'I shall,' Jill promised.

'And make sure you pop in for a drink from time to time,' Alan reminded Edward.

'I certainly will. You haven't seen the last of me,' Edward promised. And thanks again for your hospitality. It's greatly appreciated.'

'It's been a pleasure having you to stay,' Alan said.

'Goodbye,' Gwen said.

She sounded a little sad to see him leaving. But it was time. It was time for him to go and embark on the next chapter of his stay in Swansea, at the bookshop, with Jill. When they got back, Jill paused for a moment before letting him in.

'Don't expect too much,' she said, welcoming him inside.

There was a side door to the property. There were also stairs at the back of the shop, that continued to the accommodation above and doubled as a fire escape, he was later to discover. Jill used these when she was working, but not when the shop was shut. She led him up to the first floor. There were two rooms, a bathroom, and a small kitchen. One room was clearly Jill's bedroom. The other was also a bedroom but was currently being used as a lounge. It was all a lot tidier than Edward had anticipated. Perhaps he'd misjudged her. Perhaps she'd had a massive spring-clean before letting Edward in. There were a few piles of clutter, but far less than he'd imagined. It appeared Jill wasn't a person of numerous, unnecessary possessions. Perhaps she sensed Edward looking around, taking it all in, judging by her subsequent remark.

'I had a big clear out when John died, and again when Megan left,' she explained. 'I gave a lot away to charity. I wanted to get rid of some of the memories, not that they were bad, quite the opposite really.'

The rooms had a slightly musty smell, as most older homes did. Jill had cleverly disguised it with a pleasant-smelling diffuser or by burning a mild incense. Overall, the impression was quite homely and quite welcoming. Edward nodded his approval. It was better organised than the bookshop. Perhaps Jill had just made a special effort, in readiness for his imminent arrival.

'I thought you could have the converted loft upstairs,' Jill suggested. 'It's not as bad as it sounds. It's actually my favourite room.'

'I'm sure it will be fine,' Edward said, allowing Jill to lead him up to the top of the building.

She was right. It was indeed the most spacious of the three rooms by some distance. The ceiling was a little low at the sides, but nothing Edward couldn't cope with. It would be more than adequate for his needs.

'Why don't you take this one for yourself?' he asked.

'I don't know. I just never have,' Jill said. 'I've just kept it as the spare room since Megan moved out.'

Edward put down his bags. He could unpack and make himself at home later. There was no immediate hurry to do any of that.

'It will suit me down to the ground if you're sure I can have it,' Edward said.

He could imagine himself already, sitting at what had been Megan's desk, reading a book or doing a spot of writing or research.

'I'm sure. I have my room, which I like,' Jill confirmed. 'Anyway, come down now. We can sit in the lounge, and I'll make you a nice cup of tea.'

Edward accepted her invitation and made himself comfortable on the sofa in the lounge, while Jill went off to the kitchen to boil the kettle. The lounge was located directly over the front end of the shop, with Jill's bedroom immediately behind. The lounge had a large window looking out onto the road. Jill's bedroom had a window view onto the backyard. There was no real garden, though Jill had scattered a few potted plants around on the mossy, weather-beaten, paved surface. The bathroom and kitchen were on the other side of the landing. At the end of the landing was a small staircase down to the rear of the shop. Edward's bedroom was the only room on the floor above. It had originally been a loft but had been cleverly converted into a large extra bedroom. For what appeared to be quite a modest property from the outside, the available space inside had been used quite wisely and for optimum efficiency. Jill returned a few minutes later with two steaming mugs of tea.

'So, what do you think?' she asked, at last. 'I wasn't sure you'd like it.'

'It's very nice. There's more space than I expected. I could feel quite at home here,' Edward admitted.

'I'm glad about that. I was a bit worried it wouldn't suit you, after dragging you away from the guesthouse you liked,' Jill confessed.

'I'm sure I'll be very happy here,' Edward assured her.

'There is one thing. I realise we haven't discussed what I'm to pay you for helping out in the shop. It totally slipped my mind until today,' Jill said.

'Well, I have been giving it some thought,' Edward announced. 'I don't want payment. I was thinking more along the lines that we could become business partners. We could share the cost of running the shop and the bills of the house, and then split any profit equally. I can work any day you need me. Indeed, I'll probably get on with sorting and cataloguing everything, even when you're there too. It will be more like a hobby. It will give me something to do with my time. How does that sound to you?'

Edward didn't let on he was a man of independent means and wasn't doing it for the money. Indeed, he had one or two ideas to put a bit of his own capital into the business, to raise its profile and hopefully make it more profitable.

'That sounds amazing if you're certain it's OK with you,' Jill said.

'I'm certain,' Edward confirmed.

'To be honest, after John died, I tried my best to carry on, but it was too much for one person,' Jill said. 'Gradually, more and more things ended up not getting done.'

'Well, not anymore,' Edward said. 'We'll gradually get everything back up to speed. Even if we don't, it won't be the end of the world. I was an investment banker in London in my working days, quite a good one. If selling books isn't working out for us, perhaps we'll branch into something else.'

'Sounds like you've got it all planned out,' Jill said. 'I'm very glad to hear it,' she added

'How about I take you out for Sunday lunch, to cement our new partnership?' Edward suggested.

Jill pulled back the curtain and peered out the window. It had started to rain quite heavily, just as was forecast.

'I have an even better idea,' she said. 'Why don't I cook for you?'

'You really don't have to, but if you want, you can,' Edward said.

'It will be vegan though,' Jill explained. 'Can you cope with that?'

'Why not?' Edward replied. 'It will be my first vegan meal, at least that I know of.'

'Well, let's hope it's not your last,' Jill joked.

'I'm sure it won't be. As I say, I'm a new man. I'm trying new things. Perhaps you'll see me in a whole new wardrobe one day. Perhaps I'll grow my hair, what's left of it. I am considering growing a beard. It will be my new, bookish look,' Edward laughed. 'I feel I need a new identity, to go incognito for a bit. I like the idea of wearing disguises, so Alice won't find me. Besides, being a vegan might be good for me. It may help me lose a bit of weight. I quite fancy getting in shape. I had too many cooked breakfasts at the guesthouse, and a few too many cakes at the coffee shop,' Edward confessed.

'It will be a whole new world living under the same roof as a vegan,' Jill said. 'Hopefully, you'll get used to it.'

'Technically, as Beti is a meat eater too, you're still outnumbered,' Edward reminded her.

'Yes, but I don't see you as someone who ventures into a kitchen too much,' Jill said. 'How are your cooking skills?'

'Not great,' Edward admitted. 'I ate out a lot when I was at work. I didn't have much choice really. Even after retirement, it wasn't that much different. Alice wasn't a keen cook either. We probably dined out most nights if I'm honest. Sometimes we ordered a takeaway or even a hamper for the weekend. When we did dine in, it was often easy things like cold platters. We rarely ate anything which required a lot of preparation.'

'I make most of my own food. I have to,' Jill said. 'It's not so bad these days. You can get most of the ingredients from the local supermarkets. Those you can't, I get from the health food shop.'

'How long have you been a vegan?' Edward asked.

'I've been a vegetarian since my late teens, early twenties. I used to like the band *The Smiths*, who were active supporters of animal rights. That probably influenced me to give up meat. I gradually gave up dairy and eggs too. I suppose I've been totally vegan for about the last fifteen years,' Jill explained.

'That's pretty impressive,' Edward acknowledged. 'Do you ever get bored of a limited diet?'

'Not really, I'm always looking out for new vegan products and recipes to try. As more people are becoming vegan, choice is less of an issue than it was,' Jill said.

'Did you go to university, Jill, or did you go straight into work after school?' Edward enquired, suddenly realising he didn't know all that much about Jill's pre-married life.

'I did A-Levels, and I did an art foundation course afterwards. I was going to do an art degree, but I suddenly lost interest. I was seeing a guy at the time who had a job. I think I became jealous of the money he was earning, so I decided to get a job too,' Jill said.

'Have you always lived in South Wales?' Edward asked.

'Pretty much, I'm Swansea born and bred really,' Jill replied. 'I've lived in a few places round and about, but none too far away. I did try England once. I got a job in Swindon. I didn't last very long. I was back after a few months.'

'You must have been here when I was at university,' Edward pointed out.

'I must have been, but I would still have been at school then,' Jill said.

'If you'd been a few years older, we might have bumped into each other in one of the local pubs,' Edward suggested.

'That's a funny thought,' Jill said. 'I started going out when I was fifteen or sixteen, so we probably only missed each other by a year or two.'

'Yes, I'd probably just graduated and gone back to Oxford by then' Edward nodded. 'Of course, I met Angela in Swansea, so I didn't notice other girls as much as I might have.'

'You might have noticed me. I looked pretty crazy in those days,' Jill laughed.

'I'd like to have seen it,' Edward said.

'I'll see if I can find a picture when I get a moment,' Jill said. 'I was quite arty and punky back then. I wore outlandish, colourful clothes and had wild, spiky hair. It was the fashion among the art students. I've calmed down a bit in the time since.'

'I'm pleased to see it,' Edward noted.

'You were lucky to find Angela so young. I didn't meet John until my mid-thirties. It was probably why we only had the one child together. I was a bit old to have more. I'd had one or two stupid, bad relationships before I met John. He gave me the pleasant, settled life that I needed. Things were a bit haphazard for me before that. I was always changing jobs. I didn't really know what I wanted. My parents despaired,' Jill said.

'Are they still alive?' Edward asked.

'My mum is, not my dad. But she's getting on, well in her eighties now. She's still local and has her own place,' Jill said. 'What about yours?'

'Both gone now. They have been a while. They weren't that young when they had me. My dad passed nearly twelve years ago, my mum about five.

I still miss them. They both outlived Angela. I still miss her too,' Edward said.

'I miss John, but I've learnt to live without him,' Jill said. 'Anyway, this is a day of happiness not sadness. You make yourself comfortable here, watch a bit of television, whilst I rustle something up in the kitchen.'

'As long as you're happy to,' Edward said.

'I am,' Jill confirmed, heading off to get the cooking started.

Edward looked at his watch. It was about half-twelve. They'd been chatting awhile. He hadn't noticed time pass, but it had. He looked outside. The rain was falling in heavy drops against the windowpane. It had come early. It wasn't originally forecast until afternoon. He could hardly complain. Arriving in May, he'd been generally lucky with the weather so far and had only experienced a few drizzly days. It was a good job they'd moved all his things first thing in the morning, however. If they'd hung on and waited, they'd have got very wet indeed.

Edward became absorbed in the television. A food programme was on. It was making him feel hungry himself. He was ready to eat, even something vegan. Edward was surprised how relaxed he felt. It was almost like being in his own front room back at home, although not quite as big and expensively decorated. Alice insisted on only the best furniture, fittings, and ornamentation in their house in Oxford. It had never been that important to Edward. He guessed it wasn't to Jill either. After about twenty minutes had passed, Jill appeared with two steaming plates of food. She handed one to Edward and some cutlery. She then went back to the kitchen for a bottle of white wine and two glasses.

'I know it's not your usual red, but it's all I have,' Jill said. 'I don't usually keep much drink in the house. I've been saving this for a special occasion.'

'I'm sure it will be lovely,' Edward said, almost surprised to get wine too.

He took a sip from his glass and then started to tuck into his food.

'It's very nice. What dish is it?' he asked.

'It's tofu and vegetables in a satay sauce on brown rice, with naan bread,' Jill said. 'It's the kind of thing I eat a lot.'

'I wouldn't have known the little lumps weren't meat,' Edward admitted. 'I could soon get used to it.'

So, Edward's time in a vegan household began. After helping Jill with the washing-up, he spent the rest of the afternoon settling himself in. He unpacked his two bags and lined his small pile of books up on the bookshelf. He put his scant toiletries out on top of the chest of drawers. Judging by the roughness of his chin, he was overdue a shave again. He'd so lost the habit of shaving daily that he no longer noticed when he was sporting stubble. Perhaps he would just leave it and allow it to grow into a full beard. It might even suit him, he reflected. It might give him a noble look.

By late afternoon, the rain had eased. Edward offered to take Beti out for a short walk. When she wasn't with Jill in the shop, she wandered between the kitchen, the lounge and Jill's bedroom, wherever she felt most comfortable. Beti had a basket in each room apart from his, as well as the one downstairs. She hadn't had a walk all day, so Edward walked her through Victoria Park and down to the seafront. He took the coastal path as far as the university campus, where he crossed and walked back on the other side of the road, past the entrance to Singleton Park and St Helen's Rugby and Cricket Ground, up onto King Edward's Road, before eventually returning to the bookshop. By timing his run, he'd managed to dodge the worst of the rain.

When he got in, he slumped down on the sofa. He looked at his phone. There had been more missed calls from Alice. He ignored them. He'd get in touch in his own good time. Whilst he'd been out, Jill had thoughtfully popped to the shop to pick up a bottle of red wine and some snacks to share. They spent the evening watching television together. Already Edward was feeling like they were some old, married couple. The strange thing was it wasn't a bad feeling at all. It was really quite nice in fact.

Day Fifteen (Monday)

Edward slept remarkably well in his new bed. He woke up around eight o'clock, with the knowledge that he'd be going to work for the first time since he retired several months earlier. Except that it wouldn't really be work. It would be more of a hobby, to keep his mind occupied, which he could pick up as and when he wanted, and presumably put down again when it no longer suited him. Of course, he wouldn't leave Jill in the lurch whatever happened. There were certain basics he was committed to undertaking, to get the business on a firmer footing. He wanted to get better procedures and organisation in place. He wished to consider some rudimentary marketing. He intended to get a better understanding of all the stock Jill had, a lot of it still unsorted in various makeshift boxes, as well as numerous piles, scattered around the shop. He'd try to source new stock when he could, which they could then sell on at a tidy profit. He'd also look into simple methods to repair and clean damaged and tarnished books where possible, to make them more sellable.

He'd approach the task of selling books with the same methodology and attention to detail he had his regular job. His methods and careful planning for every eventuality had brought him ongoing success in the financial world. Edward hadn't been a flash in the pan. He'd had the ability to ride out market fluctuations, peaks, and troughs. Not only had he had a good business head, he'd had a fair degree of flair and ingenuity to bring to the table too. He'd now bring all those skills to bear on Jill's bookshop, until either she or he had enough and one or other of them cracked. Edward laughed to himself. Of course, it wouldn't be like that. He intended to keep it all pretty casual and relaxed, as much as his nature allowed. He hoped they would in fact have some fun together, getting the whole thing sorted and shipshape.

Jill had told him the previous night there was no need for him to get up early. She didn't usually open the shop before 10am, even later if she had chores to do and errands to run. She admitted the hours had been somewhat laissez-faire since her husband John had died. Despite being fond of a tipple, he'd insisted that the shop be open according to its advertised opening hours, as far as possible. Jill saw them more as an informal guide. There was a sign in the window, giving a telephone number for customers to call if they found her closed. In fairness, she'd always been in when Edward had called by. Of course, that had been a little different. Apart from the first time, she'd generally been expecting him. When taking Beti out for walks, he'd always endeavoured to give a rough time of arrival. Where he could, he'd stuck to it. It had normally just been a case of factoring a walk to the shopping centre for a coffee and cake at Meredith's coffee shop, before returning to pick up the dog.

When Edward got up, he realised for once in his life he was woefully unprepared. At the guesthouse, he'd been used to going down when he was ready for a hearty, full, cooked breakfast, prepared by Alan's wife, Gwen. There would be no cooked breakfast waiting for him today, no eggs, bacon, or sausages. He could be pretty sure of that. Jill had admitted she didn't even really like having meat in the house. She could just about tolerate milk, butter, and cheese. She actually suggested Edward get his own fridge long term, which he could keep in his room for the storage of such items, if he really wanted them. Edward had yet to decide what his approach to Jill's committed veganism should be. On the one hand, he didn't want to offend her. On the other, he wasn't sure that he could go without meat and dairy products altogether. Sixty years was a long time to give them up completely, especially at the drop of the hat without warning. It would be like going cold turkey.

The problem was Edward had neglected to do any basic grocery shopping, before moving in. It was most unlike him to forget such a thing. Of course, he hadn't needed to during his first fortnight in Swansea. Breakfasts had been prepared for him. The rest of the time he'd mainly eaten out. Jill had been kind enough to provide for him on his first day. He could hardly expect her to do that every day. He resolved to go to a supermarket later and pick up some essential provisions, enough to keep him going and ensure he didn't go without entirely. There was still the issue of what he'd do in the meantime. When he went downstairs, he found Jill in the kitchen. He needn't have worried. She hadn't completely forgotten about him and seemed aware that he was yet to undertake any food shopping.

'I've made some toast. There's also cereal and some fruit in the bowl. It's not a lot, but it's hopefully better than nothing,' she said, almost apologetically.

'I'm sure it will be lovely. It's good of you to think of me,' Edward said. 'I realise in my haste to move in, I'd rather forgotten about all the practicalities, like buying food. I'll pick up a few things when I finish at the bookshop today,' he said.

'There's tea in the pot,' Jill said, enthusiastically. 'Of course, I only have oat milk.'

'Oat milk will be fine,' Edward said. 'Although I don't really know what oat milk is.'

'You get used to it,' Jill promised him, pouring Edward out a cup of steaming tea and topping it up with some plant-based liquid from a carton, that to Edward looked slightly off-white in colour. 'In fact, you already have. It's what I've been giving you in the shop, that or soya. I should have told you before.'

'Oh,' Edward said, slightly taken aback.

It certainly didn't look like the pure, white cow's milk he was familiar with. Edward took a sip. Analysing it in greater detail, it didn't quite taste like tea either. It was hot and wet but not like the stewed brew he was used to. He would have described it more as a tea-like drink than tea itself. He supposed Jill was right. He'd get used to it in time. He'd have to or give it up. He was surprised he hadn't noticed when drinking it in the bookshop after dropping Beti back. He must have been distracted and his mind on other things. He'd probably been grateful to have any drink at all.

'I think I saw a coffee shop just around the corner. I can always pick up a proper coffee there before we start work,' Edward suggested.

'There is, but as a matter of fact, it's vegan too,' Jill laughed.

What was the world coming to? Edward thought. Bloody vegans! He was surrounded by them.

'They do a nice soya latte there, and a nice vegan sausage in a bap. You can barely tell the difference,' Jill assured him.

'I suppose a soya latte and vegan sausage bap will have to do then,' Edward said, grudgingly. 'Tell me, do you own the vegan coffee shop too?' Edward ventured, adding a bit of welcome humour to the conversation.

'Not yet,' Jill giggled. 'Perhaps if the bookshop starts doing a bit better, it could be how we branch out.'

'Perhaps,' Edward said, not wholly convinced.

He then thought he should get serious for a moment. It was a business venture they were embarking on, even if he hoped it would retain an element of fun at the same time and not be too earnest in its nature. He was trying to view it as an adventure. He kept that thought in mind when considering what needed doing most.

'I thought today, if you can show me the ropes and how to open up, you can have a little time off to yourself,' Edward suggested. 'You've certainly earned it and it's well overdue. You can just come back later and show me how to lock up. Just make sure we've got each other's telephone numbers to hand, before you leave. Just in case there's any problem and I need to ring you, or you have to ring me. What do you think?'

Jill's eyes lit up. Apart from Sundays and the occasional other day, she hadn't really had a proper day off in weeks if not months. She certainly felt in need of one.

'That sounds lovely if you're sure it's OK,' Jill said.

'I'm sure,' Edward confirmed. 'Just tell me what I have to do.'

'There's not all that much in truth. I just have a basic cash till, which I leave a small float of loose change and notes in. There's also a portable credit card machine, which just needs to be kept charged. I normally just make a note in the ledger on my desk of any sales. All the prices are written in pencil on the inside of the books. If they haven't been priced yet, I just make a price up. Other than that, there's not a lot to it. You might get the occasional phone call, but probably not that many customers in person. There are keys in the till if you need to leave the shop unattended for any reason,' Jill explained. 'Oh, and there's a laptop on the desk in case you get bored. I also use it to check any emails and enquiries to my work email account. I can show you how to do that.'

'I think you said you haven't got a website,' Edward said, just seeking confirmation of that fact.

'Not as such, but my work email is listed on a few bookseller sites, and I get some sales from that,' Jill said.

'No matter,' Edward responded. 'That's something we can perhaps look at long term. It's not urgent.'

'Most importantly, there's a kettle in the back office for tea and coffee breaks,' Jill said. 'I normally leave a few nibbles there too in case I get hungry.'

Edward chuckled.

'All vegan, of course,' Jill pointed out.

'Naturally,' Edward said. 'Well, I suppose I'd better go and get ready,' he said, finishing his tea and toast. 'Time waits for no man.'

Jill already looked dressed for the day and ready to start work. Edward wasn't, though he didn't take very long to go up to his room and come back down again raring to go. They took the back stairs down into the shop. Jill turned on the lights. She showed Edward where everything was. Beti followed them down and took up her usual position in her basket by the side of Jill's desk, or was it Edward's desk now? Jill was right. There wasn't too much to learn. There didn't seem to be all that much to it in truth. He realised he'd got a good idea where everything was from his many previous visits to the bookshop, both as a customer and a dog walker. Before Jill left, Edward briefly popped to the nearby coffee shop, to purchase a soya latte and vegan sausage bap. He'd have them when Jill had gone.

'Is everything really vegan?' Edward asked what he considered to be a relatively young man who served him.

He was a lot younger than Edward at least, probably in his mid to late thirties or early forties.

'It is,' Edward was told.

'Even the cakes?' Edward continued. 'They look very nice.'

'Even the cakes,' the man said, as if he was a little bored by Edward's somewhat facile questions.

Edward placed his order. 'I think I'll have a cake too,' he added. He was sure to get hungry later and want it.

When he got back to the bookshop, he laid his bounty down on the desktop.

'Are you sure you'll be all right?' Jill asked, before leaving him.

'I'll be fine.' Edward assured her. 'You just go off and enjoy yourself. I'll ring you if I need to, but hopefully that won't be necessary.'

They'd previously exchanged telephone numbers, for when Edward took Beti out for walks. Edward had checked he'd tapped in Jill's correctly by giving it a quick ring. He had, though to date he'd never needed to use it in anger as it were. Jill had also switched on her laptop and opened her mailbox, so it was all ready for him to use.

'When you need the toilet, just turn the latch on the front door, so it's locked and pop upstairs,' Jill told him. 'Is there anything else you need?'

'I don't think so,' Edward answered. 'If anything occurs to me, I'll be in touch. I'll text if it isn't urgent. If it's more important, I'll ring.'

'OK,' Jill said. She hesitated by the front door, as if she was reluctant to leave him. It had been years since anyone but her had been left in charge of the shop. Edward could sense her nervousness.

'You really don't need to worry,' he told her. 'I'm sure I'll be OK.'

'I hope so,' Jill said.

'Anyway, how are you spending your morning?' Edward asked, sensing the need to change the subject.

'I'm going to the shops and then I'm off to see my mum. I may even take her out for lunch,' Jill said.

'Sounds lovely,' Edward commented.

'By the way, if you want lunch, just make sure to lock up and take as long as you like,' Jill said.

She'd already given him the spare key to their lodgings above. The one for the shop was in the till. She also kept another on her key ring, which was with her at all times in case of emergency.

'I will,' Edward said.

'I'll be back early afternoon,' Jill told him.

'Take as long as you need to. That's why I'm here,' Edward said.

When Jill finally left him, Edward sat down at the desk to survey his surroundings. He was temporarily at least in charge of all he surveyed. Before he did anything, he took a sip of his soya latte and a bite of his vegan sausage bap. They weren't too bad. They were quite tasty in fact. Beti looked up eagerly, aware he was eating.

'OK,' he said, reluctantly, breaking her off a piece and throwing it down on the floor, for her to hoover up. 'Not quite the real thing,' he added, as he watched her chewing.

When he'd finished eating, he carefully wiped his hands. He didn't want to get any grease on the books. That wouldn't be a very good start. He looked at his watch. It was 10.15am. He then checked the sign on the door. It did indeed say open. No customers so far. That wasn't exactly a surprise. Edward took another sip of his coffee. He should check any emails first. He knew in time he would establish a routine. He always did, wherever he was and whatever he was doing. It would just take him a few days to establish a new one.

There were a handful of emails, mostly enquiring about rare books. The problem was Edward didn't know for certain if they had any of them. He could check on the shelves, but he was fully aware only a fraction of the stock had been put in its correct place. Most hadn't. A couple of emails enquired where the shop was located and its opening times. He could at least answer them. The others might have to wait. Whilst he was looking at the laptop, he opened a new spreadsheet. At least any books he did sort and price up, he could record on that too. It would be a small start.

It would be a way of introducing a degree of order to Jill's rather haphazard approach to selling.

Before starting to go through some of the unsorted books, Edward made some attempt to familiarise himself with the various shelves and bookcases on display, to get an idea where the different subjects were kept. He took a few random books out to inspect them. He looked at the prices on the inside covers. Jill was selling them far too cheaply for a start, he thought. That was something he could address on any books he priced up. She might then at least start making some kind of profit. Edward then settled himself on the floor to start going through the various piles, to see if he could begin to introduce some order to them. He started by sorting roughly according to whether they were fiction or non-fiction for starters. He found himself becoming quite absorbed in the task. He liked old books. Some he sifted through were little better than pulp. Others had a commercial value and an interest. Edward was only distracted from his work when the door opened and in walked his first customer of the day, his first customer ever in fact.

'Is there anything special you're looking for?' Edward asked, courteously.

'I was just passing and thought I might have a little browse,' the customer replied.

He was an older man, not unlike Edward. It reminded Edward of his own first visit to the shop when he hadn't been looking for anything in particular but had been happy just to look all the same.

'You go ahead,' Edward said. 'I've got plenty to be getting on with.'

Eventually, the man left without purchasing anything. That was the general fate of the bookseller, Edward supposed. He had to wait an age for another customer to come in. In that time, he'd made some progress with a basic sorting of some of the piles into subject matter. His second customer was after a rare book of the poetry, long since out of print, by the late Liverpool poet, Adrian Henri. Of course, Edward didn't have it, not that he could see. He explained a lot of the books weren't out yet and the customer was welcome to pop back, just as Jill had said to him. Edward promised to look out for the book too, just as Jill had done. He was getting the hang of this selling malarkey, he told himself. There was nothing to it really.

Edward then heard his phone beep. It was a text from Jill. *How are you getting on?* It read. *Fine, no problems*, Edward replied and signed it with a kiss before sending. *Have you sold anything?* Jill continued their conversation. *Not yet*, Edward replied, truthfully. He did sell one book, however, before Jill came back. It was a book on flora and fauna. He carefully recorded the sale with a tinge of pride in the ledger. It was his first one. At least he'd have something to show Jill, he thought. He also realised he'd been so absorbed in what he was doing he hadn't stopped for lunch. He hadn't fed Beti either. He'd rectify both oversights as soon as Jill returned from her trip out. It was now gone two o'clock in the afternoon. Edward looked out of the window. It had started steadily raining. Wouldn't get many customers now, he reflected. If they were wise, they'd stay at home. The next time the front door opened, it was Jill.

'Everything OK?' Jill enquired.

'I did sell one book, after you texted,' Edward said, proudly.

'Very good,' Jill congratulated him. 'We'll have to do a bit better than that though if we're both to make a living from this,' she added.

'I know, but it is a start,' Edward said, refusing to have his optimism and sense of accomplishment dampened.

'By the way, I picked you up a cheese and onion pasty from the bakery, in case you haven't eaten yet,' Jill said. 'It's still warm if you eat it now. I couldn't quite bring myself to buy a meat one,' she admitted.

'You must have read my mind,' Edward said. 'I'm starving, but I didn't fancy another vegan sausage bap just yet. Beti needs to eat too.'

'I'll go and get her something,' Jill said, heading off towards the kitchen via the back staircase.

Edward settled down to eat his pasty. It was just what he needed. He realised he was also rather thirsty. He was ready for a cup of tea, even one with vegan milk, and he put the kettle on to boil. When he'd made it, he sipped suspiciously at the light brown liquid that occupied the mug he held.

'I don't know why you're looking at it like that,' Jill laughed, when she returned with Beti's food. 'I told you I've given you soya or oat every time I've made you a cup of tea, and you didn't appear to notice. I don't have anything else. You didn't complain at least.'

Edward laughed. It was true. He hadn't really noticed, though he realised it had tasted slightly odd now he came to think about it. He'd wondered if it was just a different brand of tea to his usual one. He'd just been too polite to say anything. Generally, after a long walk, he'd been glad of any liquid refreshment afterwards, with cow's milk added or in this case an alternative.

'You've got me there. I have to admit it,' Edward said. 'I only really became aware when you mentioned it and I could see it being poured from a different package at breakfast. It just goes to show how fickle I really am.'

'Could you tell the difference with the food from the vegan coffee shop?' Jill asked. 'Did it taste that different?'

'I could taste the sausage wasn't real sausage. The coffee was still nice and creamy like a latte should be, so not really. The cake just tasted like a normal one,' Edward said.

'So, there's hope for you yet,' Jill said. 'Give it a couple of months and you'll be as vegan as me.'

'That will never happen,' Edward insisted, but without total conviction in what he was saying.

'You've got me drinking again, so making you a vegan will be my revenge,' Jill warned him.

Edward smiled. He was open to change, but he'd never change that much. It was impossible. It was out of the question. Jill just smirked back knowingly at him. Maybe she knew something he didn't. Maybe she knew him better than he knew himself. Although he generally didn't keep pets, it was true he's always been quite fascinated by animals and the animal kingdom. He enjoyed natural history programmes. Maybe it was actually high time he stopped eating the blessed, furry things. Even if by some remote chance that happened, he'd still eat cheese and eggs, he was resolved. Even so, he was amazed how quickly a woman with the right mindset and principles could change someone as set in his ways as he was himself.

'Do you want me to take over this afternoon, or do you want to carry on?' Jill asked, after putting food in Beti's bowl.

'I'll carry on if you like,' Edward said. 'I just need you to show me how to shut up at about five o'clock.'

'I can do that,' Jill said. 'Meanwhile, I've got one or two jobs to get on with upstairs if you're sure that's all right.'

'I'm sure. How was your mum by the way?' Edward asked.

'She was fine. She'd like to meet you in fact,' Jill explained.

'I look forward to it,' Edward said.

'She knows I've been on my own for a long time. She's probably wondering what kind of man I've left into my home,' Jill said, only being partially serious.

'Well, I hope she approves of me,' Edward said, cautiously.

'I'm sure she will,' Jill assured him.

'Is she vegan?' Edward asked.

'No, she isn't,' Jill answered.

Edward nodded approvingly. 'You're still a minority then,' he observed.

'For the time being,' Jill agreed.

'That reminds me, once we've locked up, I'll pop to the supermarket to pick a few things up. I can take Beti too if it's stopped raining,' Edward suggested.

'I'm sure she'd love a walk,' Jill said. 'Right, I'll leave you to it. Just shout if you need anything. You know it really is nice to have a bit of time to myself for once.'

'I'm glad of that,' Edward said.

After Jill had gone, Edward quietly continued his sorting. He even started pricing a few books up and putting them in their correct place on the shelves. He added a pound or two to the price he imagined Jill would probably have given them. He considered her prices to be unrealistic and no way to run a business. They weren't getting anywhere near enough sales. They had to maximise the profit from those few they did get. As the afternoon wore on, to his surprise Edward did sell a couple more books. He also had a couple of enquiries, which he duly made a note of. All in all, it hadn't been such a bad first day's work. He'd got quite a lot of sorting done and familiarised himself with the basic procedures Jill had in place to run the shop. Around 5pm, she came down to help him lock up.

'So, how was your first day?' she asked.

'Very good,' Edward replied.

She was pleased to learn he'd even made a few more sales.

'You've done very well,' she told him.

'Onwards and upwards,' Edward said.

After they'd locked up, Edward headed for the supermarket. There was a *Tesco Metro* on St Helen's Road, so he went there. As it had stopped raining, he took Beti with him for her daily walk. As he browsed the shelves in *Tesco*, Edward found himself subconsciously resisting the meat products. He didn't want to offend Jill, although he did buy himself a carton of normal milk and some cheese. He'd have to gradually ween himself off those. Everything he bought was at least vegetarian. He got no meat at all. He purchased sufficient basic items to keep him going for a few days at least. He made sure to stock up on decaffeinated tea and coffee just in case Jill didn't have any. He also bought a nice bottle of red wine he could share with Jill if they ended up watching television together again. When he got back, he found Jill had kindly already done the cooking.

'It's just something I rustled up quickly, nothing special,' she told him, as she handed him a plate of steaming pasta in tomato and onion sauce and what he presumed to be vegan cheese sprinkled on top and ciabatta bread on the side.

'It looks excellent,' Edward complimented her. 'You know, you really don't have to cook for me every day,' he added.

'I know, but if I'm cooking anyway, it's just as easy to cook for two as it is for one,' she said.

'That's very kind, but let me treat you some days,' Edward insisted. 'I'm happy to take you to the pub or a nice restaurant any evening you like. You only have to say.'

As they ate, Edward poured Jill a glass of fine red wine. It was a good quality one for *Tesco* at least, around twenty-five pounds a bottle, if not for Edward. He'd shared five-hundred-pound bottles of wine at exclusive London wine bars during his working days. He wouldn't be doing that again, he reflected. After they'd eaten, they continued drinking and watching television. They were enjoying each other's company while it lasted. Later, Edward retired to his room, where he resumed reading HG Wells. He'd nearly finished *The Country of the Blind and Other Science-Fiction Stories*. At least he'd never again be short of a book to read during his remaining time in Swansea, he noted with mild amusement. As he switched off his bedroom light, he was already looking forward to his next day back at work. He was no longer truly retired, he realised.

Day Sixteen (Tuesday)

Edward got up around eight. He made himself decent and wandered down to the kitchen, stopping at the bathroom for a quick wee on the way. He'd got up once in the night, or was it twice? He couldn't quite recall. It was the fate of men of a certain age like himself. It was an affliction he just learned to deal with. He didn't empty his bowels. He wasn't sure he was comfortable with such things with Jill just a room away. He could do that if he needed to when she was out. Not that his bowel movements weren't normal. They were as normal as could be expected for a man of sixty, who'd indulged in rich food and copious amounts of expensive alcohol, as he had during his working life. It had been the norm then. He'd cut back since retiring and since discovering the irritation of atrial fibrillation, that he suffered from in a manageable form, but rarely mentioned to anyone. A couple of pills a day was usually enough to keep him ticking over and on the straight and narrow. He would of course run out eventually and either look to get his prescription sent from Oxford or pick one up locally. He assumed such things were a possibility. He couldn't be the first person in the world to find himself on an extended stay away from his regular supply. When Edward walked into the kitchen, Jill was already sitting at the breakfast table, enjoying her breakfast of cereal and toast. She appeared showered and dressed too.

'You're up bright and early,' Edward observed.

'Beti's my alarm clock,' Jill said. 'She normally comes in about seven and nudges me if I'm not already awake.'

'It prevents you oversleeping at least,' Edward commented.

'It used to be handy before you became the primary dog walker,' Jill said. 'Most days, I used to take her for a quick walk before opening the shop. I still do sometimes. I think she still half expects her walk straight after breakfast. More often than not, she's disappointed ha. It doesn't really matter, as long as she gets out at some point. She's not a young dog, so once a day is now enough for her.'

'I can take her again after work,' Edward offered.

'I'm sure she'd be very happy to go with you,' Jill said. 'Now, what did you want to do in the shop today? Morning, afternoon, both, or neither?' Jill asked.

'Is morning OK?' Edward responded. 'I want to pop to the shops this afternoon. There are a couple of things I'd like to pick up. Does that work for you?'

'Anything you can do works for me,' Jill said. 'If you weren't here, I'd have to do the whole day by myself. Now, what do you want for breakfast? There's tea, coffee, toast, cereal, and fruit. I think you know where everything is anyway. You can just help yourself.'

'That's very kind,' Edward said. 'I'll certainly do that if you don't mind.

He'd also bought one of two goodies himself, including some rather appetising chocolate brioche buns. He knew Jill wouldn't eat them, as they contained butter. He was slowly beginning to get the hang of what vegans could and couldn't have. He hadn't realised at first that chocolate, most cakes and many biscuits, even some crisps and snacks were out. Jill had to carefully check the ingredients of anything that wasn't normally on her shopping list before buying it, she explained. Milk powder was contained in numerous products that wouldn't obviously contain milk. A lot of dark chocolate for example, even salt and vinegar crisps often contained milk, he'd learned, which had caught Edward by surprise. Why on earth was that? It made no sense. Apparently, Jill was OK to eat plain ones. Edward's education in such things was continuing apace.

That morning, he put normal cow's milk in his tea, although he felt a pang of guilt in doing so. He thought he saw Jill give him a slight look of disapproval, although he might have imagined it. Perhaps he was just being disapproving of himself. It was Jill's house after all, so it really should be her rules. Long term, he was intent on weening himself off anyway and learning to resist. In deference to Jill, he would stick to the soya and oat as long he could stomach the taste. As she'd pointed out, he'd never noticed when she'd handed him a cup or mug of tea in the bookshop, after returning Beti from her walk. His mind had been on other things. He'd drunk it down, grateful for anything, and it had tasted quite nice. It had tasted like tea then and not just a tea-like drink.

'Do you need any help setting up today?' Jill asked.

'It's probably better if I do it myself,' Edward answered. 'It's the best way to learn, and I think I know what I'm doing. I can always shout up if I've got a problem.'

'I'll be around for most of the morning, although I might pop out before I take over,' Jill said.

'Be as long as you like. I'll be fine,' Edward assured her. 'You know what, I might pick up a couple of those vegan sausage baps before I start. I can have them for my lunch or as a snack if I get peckish. I can see when you're on your own, it isn't always easy to get out to buy something.'

'It isn't,' Jill agreed. 'Most of the food shops are at the other end of King Edward's Road or on Brynmor Road. There's not much at this end. I normally just pop upstairs and make a sandwich or something simple like beans on toast when I'm on my own. You can do that too if you like.'

'I probably will once I get more into a routine,' Edward agreed. 'What we need is a really good sandwich shop nearby. Perhaps that's something we could open if the books don't work out,' Edward suggested.

Jill didn't reply immediately. She just laughed at his suggestion instead. Hadn't she suggested something similar herself? She wasn't really being serious at the time, though the possibility of combining books with coffee and light food wasn't entirely ridiculous. It could work and might give her something to ponder in the future.

'It's not such a bad idea,' she said, at last. 'Another to add to those we already have, I suppose.'

'Indeed, one way or another we'll make this a success,' Edward agreed. 'Well, I suppose I'd better get on with it. No peace for the wicked,' he added.

'It's still early. You don't have to open up yet,' Jill told him.

'I know, but I want to get down a bit in advance, just to familiarise myself with everything,' Edward said, rising to his feet, with the thought in his head there was work to be done.

In truth, he wanted to make an early start, so he could get on with going through some of the unsorted books, before any customers came in. He also wanted to make a start on the database he'd created. It was just a simple spreadsheet more accurately. Even if he just began listing some of the authors they had in stock, if not all the titles, it would be something. Edward was already getting frustrated with being asked for books he had no idea if they had or not. If he knew that much, it would make him feel a whole lot better and more efficient than he did at present. For the most part, he felt he was just scratching around in the dark, when asked a question. That didn't sit comfortably with Edward at all. He wanted to be able to reply with a degree of confidence and certainty.

Edward didn't spend long getting ready in his room. He just made himself presentable. He spent a few minutes in the bathroom, washing his face and cleaning his teeth. He checked to see he wouldn't scare any prospective customers off. He didn't look as pristine as he had in his banking days, but he looked tidy enough. With some days' growth of stubble on his chin, he looked every inch the fusty, old bookseller. He was exactly that, he supposed. That was his new identity. He genuinely was going incognito or in disguise. Alice wouldn't recognise him if she saw him now. She'd wonder just who this stranger was. He felt almost like he was undercover, a spy or a mole, waiting to be activated. His time would come. He was just waiting for the call, to spring into action. Except there would be no call. This was his life from now on or least for the foreseeable future.

Edward stood in the shop, master of all he surveyed. He switched the lights and laptop on. He also filled the kettle and put it on to boil. He imagined he'd want a hot drink at some point. Would he use the plant-based milk Jill had left in the small fridge in the back office, or would he go upstairs to the kitchen to get the real stuff? He was undecided. Edward looked at his watch. It was only nine o'clock. He was an hour early. He didn't have to open until ten. It would give him a chance to check the emails and perhaps even answer some this time. He'd also carry on with the book sorting. Those he did price up and put on the shelves he made a note of on his spreadsheet. Around 9.45am, Edward popped round to the vegan coffee shop just around the corner, to pick up his food supplies before opening up. He also bought his customary, daily latte. It would give him the caffeine hit he needed, to help get him through the morning. He then went back to the bookshop, to open its doors and wait for the first customer of the day.

He wasn't so much waiting as getting on with things. He wasn't really expecting a flurry of customers. He began checking the emails. There were only a handful. Once they were done, he continued with the sorting, cataloguing, and pricing. He was gradually getting through it, though there was still much to be undertaken. He could at least tell where he'd been. There was now more room on the floor. He could actually see more of the well-worn carpet, poking up underneath. Perhaps in time, he'd buy Jill a new one. He still hadn't let on he was a significantly wealthy man. He imagined Jill would just find out for herself in due course. It meant the business would never go bust at least, not whilst he was there. Edward's first customer of the day was actually a telephone one. It was the first occasion the phone had rung. It was a general enquiry, asking about opening times and whether they stocked much on philosophy and world religion. Not a great deal but some, Edward answered, truthfully. The customer was welcome to come and look at what they had, Edward said. He hoped to have more out on the shelves by then, he explained. He was still in the process of sorting stock. Edward's first physical customer walked through the doors just after eleven. After browsing for a bit, he turned to Edward to ask a question. He was an older man than Edward, probably seventy or more.

'What I'm actually looking for is a copy of *The Great European Treaties of the Nineteenth Century* by Oakes and Mowat,' he said. 'It's not the most fascinating book, but I studied it as a student,' the man explained.

'Not that I know of, but you're welcome to have a look in our history section,' Edward said, directing the customer towards the appropriate part of the shop.

'I'll certainly do that,' the man replied.

'I expect you can get a copy on the internet,' Edward suggested, helpfully.

'I expect so, but I don't really bother with that web business. It's more rewarding to find a copy in a second-hand bookshop yourself, don't you think?' the man said, in his elegant, middle-class accent with English overtones, not unlike Edward's own.

He certainly wasn't a local by birth at least. He sounded like an academic. Perhaps he'd studied at the university like Edward, who was suddenly struck by a thought. He could source a copy on the internet himself and then sell it on at a profit. Indeed, he could do that with every enquiry. It could be the way forward, to making the bookshop the success he'd promised Jill it would be.

'I tell you what. If you can you pop back in a week or so, I can probably get you a copy by then,' Edward suggested.

'I can do that,' the man said. 'Say, same time next week?'

'That should be fine. The book will be around twenty pounds. Is that OK?' Edward asked.

'That will be fine,' the man said.

Edward got the firm impression money was no great object to this customer. just as it wasn't to himself. As soon as the man had gone, Edward searched the internet for the book in question. Immediately, various editions came up. Whilst some were priced at more than he'd quoted, around the £25 mark, others were as little as between three and seven pounds. Edward immediately placed an order for the one he'd have chosen if buying for himself. Even with postage, it would leave a very healthy profit. He couldn't wait to tell Jill what he'd done. As long as the customer was able to return to the shop, it couldn't really go wrong. Even then, Edward could post it on. Of course, there might be occasion when the requested book simply wasn't available or was more expensive than Edward expected. He could always do a surreptitious search on the computer first, on the pretext of searching his own database, to get an idea of likely cost and availability. All in all, it seemed a pretty fool-proof plan. It was no wonder he'd been such a successful businessman in his time. When Jill popped down to see how he was getting on, she was duly impressed by his suggestion. She wondered why she hadn't thought of it herself.

'You're not just a pretty face,' she told him.

'You may be, but I'm definitely not pretty at all,' he replied, feeling a little embarrassed suddenly.

'You are in your own way,' Jill insisted, doubling down on her intentionally somewhat cryptic statement.

It was out there now, for a moment. Edward blushed. It was the first time they'd got at all personal with each other. Jill was pretty, he realised, just not in the way he was accustomed to. He didn't consider himself handsome at all, but he held himself well. It came from years of practice. Jill was attractive, however, and had her own style and way of presenting herself, which was appealing, even to an old duffer like him. To save him further embarrassment, Jill swiftly moved the conversation on.

'You're doing really well,' she said. 'Now, I've just got to pop out for a bit. As soon as I get back, I'll take over if you're happy for me to.'

'I'm happy indeed,' Edward said.

When she'd gone, Edward thought again about what she'd said. Was he really a pretty face? He very much doubted it. She on the other hand was undoubtedly so. Not in the obvious way like Alice. Alice was tall, slender, and always immaculately presented. There was never a hair out of place on her head of shiny, strawberry-blonde hair. It was always kept perfectly washed and brushed. She rarely went anywhere without the application of red lipstick and red, polished nails, flawlessly painted and manicured. Jill, on the other hand, had a natural, understated beauty. She wore little or no make-up and let her medium-length, slightly greying hair fall any way it wished. She favoured functional, comfortable clothes, and what level of attraction she achieved, she did so apparently without making any great effort. Perhaps that was the mark of real beauty, Edward reflected.

Why was he even thinking of Jill in this way, he wondered? He hadn't before. Now they were living under the same roof, he felt the first indications he was starting to see her in a different way. Was she also seeing him slightly differently too? Nothing definite had been said. They'd spent the last two nights watching television and drinking wine together. That much was the case. Now, for the first time, they'd made small compliments to each other. Was it the first sign of mutual interest? Edward knew he had to remain cautious. He was still a married man, at least for the time being.

Several more customers entered the shop in relatively quick succession before Jill returned. The first two were just browsing and left without buying anything. Despite Edward's best efforts to strike up conversation, they didn't seem keen to give Edward any notion of what books they were seeking. He made it plain he was more than happy to endeavour to track anything down for them. They refused to take the bait. Perhaps he wasn't quite as good at this game as he thought. He still had a lot to learn. The third customer was a woman Edward guessed to be in her mid-forties. She had a somewhat brusque, no-nonsense manner about her. He couldn't exactly call it unpleasant. It was more business-like, as if the time she had to spend was limited. Edward realised she was also his first female customer. That was something else to work on. They needed to attract more women into the shop, not just old has-beens like himself, with too much time on their hands. She flitted about the shop at high speed, putting books on the counter, or Edward's desk, whilst barely looking at them and with apparent little consideration as to what she was choosing. As far as Edward could tell, she'd made a wholly random selection. As she chose, she muttered to herself. *This one for Sara. This one for Owen…*

'How much for this little lot?' she asked, when she'd finally finished grabbing a hotchpotch of books from the shelves.

'Oh, I'll just have to add them up,' Edward said, putting on his reading glasses and getting out a calculator.

He checked the inside page of each book and made a quick note of the book title and price to enter later in his ledger. The total price came to £54.95.

'We'll call it fifty pounds, for a bulk purchase,' he told the customer. 'That's a discount of £4.95.'

She looked pleased.

'Can I put it on a card?' she asked.

'Of course,' Edward told her.

'I don't have a lot of time for shopping. I have a few birthdays coming up and I have to grab a few things when I can,' she explained.

'I'm glad we had something for you,' Edward said. 'Let me get you a bag to carry them in. Knowing Swansea, it will be sure to rain if I don't.

In fact, the weather forecast was for it to remain fine. Edward knew Jill kept some carrier bags in a drawer. He'd seen them earlier when he was looking for something else. He got one out and started carefully placing the books carefully inside. He then handed the bag to the customer.

'Thank you very much,' she said.

'Hope to see you again,' Edward replied.

He'd be very happy to see any customer who spent fifty pounds return. If only they had more of them. She was welcome back any time she wanted. Jill would be pleased he'd sold so many books in one sale. Edward started to enter the details in the ledger. When he'd finished that, he returned to the seemingly endless task of cataloguing and pricing up the piles of unsorted books. He hadn't done that many more when Jill walked through the door.

'Fifty pounds from one customer,' he announced, proudly.

'Excellent,' Jill said, heading straight towards the kettle in the back office. 'Do you want one?' she asked.

'Why not? I can have it with my vegan sausage bap and cake,' Edward answered. 'I guess it's time for Beti's lunch too.'

She'd spent the time since Jill had gone sitting quietly in her basket. No doubt, like Edward, she was ready to eat. Once the kettle had boiled, Jill handed Edward a mug. In return, he passed her one of his vegan sausage baps. It was a good job he'd got two, he reflected, as he started to munch into his. Beti whined, sensing she'd been forgotten.

'OK, Beti,' Jill conceded, putting her tea and bap down and going to get Beti some food, to put in her bowl.

'I think you're better at this than me,' Jill told Edward when she got back. 'I mean, using your initiative to order customers books and making bulk sales.'

'I wouldn't go that far. I really am just a novice,' Edward said.

'To be honest, it was John's business. It was never really mine,' Jill admitted. 'I just carried it on when he died. I might have been better off selling it or turning it into something else. It's just I've always quite liked reading and books myself. I thought I could make a go of it, and I've just about kept it afloat, I suppose.'

'You've done very well, and we're going to do even better,' Edward told her.

When he'd finished his bap and had another sip of tea, Edward generously broke off half his cake and passed it to Jill.

'I don't want to eat all your lunch,' she said, nonetheless still happy to accept the offering.

'It's fine. I can always get something else in town. I'll just have to remember to get more next time,' he laughed.

After eating, Edward headed off to the shopping centre, with Beti in tow, leaving Jill to mind the shop. He was already starting to think of it as his own. He wondered what would happen to it when he finally went back to Oxford. Would Jill continue with the new procedures he slowly planned to put into place, or would she gradually fall back into old, bad habits? He didn't know. He guessed it wouldn't be his problem if he was no longer around to care one way or another. Of course, he would care. He'd always care about Jill and the bookshop now. He'd just be too far away to do anything about it.

'You can see where I've got to with the sorting if you want to carry on,' Edward said, as he was leaving. 'No worries if not. I can do some more tomorrow.'

For once, Edward didn't take the scenic route. He knew where he was going. He had business to attend to. In fact, it wasn't so much business as pleasure or leisure perhaps was the best way to describe it. He was going to do something that had been on his mind to do for some time, but he hadn't yet got round to doing. No more delays, no more putting it off, no more procrastination on his part, he decided. He'd go there now without further delay. He'd seen what he wanted on one of his walks to the shopping centre via the Uplands. He recalled passing an art supplies shop, which was exactly what he needed for the purchases he had in mind. He'd head there now post-haste. There were a few things he was anxious to buy. Among them was a sketchbook, paper, some pencils and crayons, even some watercolours and brushes. He also wanted to pick up a notebook.

It would fulfil a long-time ambition of his. Once he was retired, he'd always intended to do a bit of writing and painting. Now was his chance. Even coming out of retirement to help manage the bookshop, he'd have more than enough time on his hands. There were no excuses. In fact, being surrounded by books and culture had finally prompted him to do it. It was time for Edward to join the ranks of writers and artists too. He'd dabbled a bit at university. Now, he was ready to take it to the next stage. He'd started to look the part, dressing down and sprouting the beginnings of a beard. He would finally see if he could actually produce anything creative of worth or merit.

Edward spent more than a hundred pounds in the art shop. He was unconcerned. If he was going to do it, he might just as well do it properly. Besides a hundred pounds to him wasn't really anything. He'd left that much as a tip in the guesthouse. His next purchase would be a decent camera, although that could wait for another day. On the way back, Edward picked up a few more provisions at the supermarket. He tried to make sure they were things that Jill could eat too, although he was certain he'd got some of them wrong. At least he was trying. He was endeavouring to fit in with her ways. He also bought a couple more bottles of good quality wine. It was the least he could do after all she'd done for him. If she didn't want any, he'd drink them alone. Jill was still working when Edward returned. It was only just gone four and technically the shop was open until five unless Jill decided to shut early. She often did, especially if it was quiet. Edward left her to it, whilst he furtively took his purchases upstairs.

'What have you been buying?' she asked, looking up.

'You'll have to wait and see,' Edward replied, deliberately vaguely.

He wanted to surprise her with a poem he'd written or a drawing or painting he'd done. She'd probably be surprised in a bad way, he feared. He'd have to be careful he didn't just end up making a complete fool of himself. He wouldn't show her anything he wasn't at least adequately satisfied with. In the sanctity of his room, he started to jot down a few ideas and make a few notes that could eventually make poetry in his notebook. He was happy and relaxed, he realised, probably more than he had been in years. He truly had landed on his feet. Somehow, without trying, by chance he'd fallen into a new life. He'd lost one and fortuitously another had come along. Later that evening, he found himself sat down in front of the television, drinking wine with Jill.

'It's lovely having you here,' she told him.

'It's lovely being here,' he replied, the wine making him feel warm inside.

Day Seventeen (Wednesday)

'I didn't expect to see you again, at least not for a while,' Meredith said, greeting Edward with a look of mild amazement.

'I know, I feel a bit sheepish coming in, after we'd said our goodbyes,' Edward admitted. 'The truth is I've decided to stay in Swansea, at least for a bit. I've actually taken a part-time job, in a second-hand bookshop. That's why you haven't seen me. I've been busy there.'

'Wow, you do surprise me,' Meredith said. 'I thought you'd only recently retired. Bored already?'

'Not exactly, I'm just helping out a friend for a little while,' Edward explained.

'Where's the shop?' Meredith asked.

'It's in a little side street off King Edward's Road,' Edward replied.

Meredith looked quizzically for a moment, as if she was trying to place it in her head.

'I don't think I know it,' she said, at last.

'That's the problem. Not many people do,' Edward said.

'But then, I don't often buy books,' Meredith acknowledged.

'The owner, Jill, is on her own. She just needs someone to help out and take some of the workload from her,' Edward said. 'That's where I come in. It quite suits me, as I like being around books.'

'I've noticed that,' Meredith interrupted, in a jocular manner, with a smile on her face.

'And I don't really have anything more pressing to occupy my time,' Edward continued. 'I've been to all the museums, art galleries and parks now, as far as I know. I was just starting to run out of things to do.'

'It sounds very generous of you. I hope she appreciates what you're doing for her,' Meredith remarked.

'She's doing me a favour too,' Edward said. 'I've now got my own room above the shop.'

'As long as you're not being taken advantage of,' Meredith said.

'It's definitely not like that. We're just two slightly lonely people of a certain age, who enjoy each other's company and can be of help to each other,' Edward responded, trying to formulate his friendship with Jill into some kind of words.

'It sounds idyllic,' Meredith commented.

'I guess it is,' Edward nodded.

'So, how long do you think you'll stay there?' Meredith asked.

'I'm not really sure,' Edward answered, truthfully. 'Maybe for the duration of the summer, whilst I get a few things sorted for her. After making a start this week, I can see there's quite a lot that needs to be done. It's unlikely to take less than a couple of months.'

'So, will I still be seeing you regularly?' Meredith wondered.

'When I get a morning off like today, you probably will. I couldn't keep away if I tried,' Edward said. 'I may have a dog with me in future, by the way. Jill has one called Beti I've been taking for walks.'

'That's all right. We allow dogs if they're well behaved,' Meredith said.

'This one's very well behaved,' Edward assured her.

'So, what are you having today?' Meredith enquired, aware another customer had walked in behind Edward and was also waiting to be served.

'Oh, the usual please. A latte and whatever cake you recommend,' Edward replied.

'I've got a nice fruit cake or a raspberry and lemon sponge,' Meredith said.

'They both sound nice, but I think I'll have the raspberry,' Edward said.

'I'll bring it over,' Meredith confirmed, after taking Edward's payment.

Edward found a table and made himself comfortable.

'Something's missing,' Meredith commented, when she brought him his coffee and cake.

'What's that?' Edward asked.

'No book,' Meredith pointed out.

'Ha, you're right,' Edward confessed. 'I've just finished one and I forgot to pick another up.'

'There's no excuse for that now you're working in a bookshop,' Meredith laughed.

'I know,' Edward conceded. 'It's most remiss of me.'

Meredith then left Edward in peace, to enjoy his coffee and cake. As he had no book on him, he decided to check a couple of things on his phone. It had occurred to him that if he was to stay a while longer, he might join a local art or photography class or something similar, if he could find one. To his mild disappointment, he did find a few things, but it looked as if most were about to break for summer. There were, however, a couple of venues running summer courses he might consider. At least he now had a better idea what was on offer and where in Swansea such classes as there were took place. It was another thing to think about if he was to make a temporary, new life in the city.

'Lovely to see you again,' Meredith told him, as he readied to leave. 'When will I see you next?'

'When I get another morning off, I expect,' Edward said. 'Until then,' he called out, as he headed towards the door.

'Bye for now,' she waved after him.

Edward waved back cheerily. It was always nice to see Meredith, but other errands were awaiting him. He started to wander the shopping streets, looking for charity shops. In each he passed, he proceeded immediately to the book section. He was looking for bargains and rarities he and Jill might be able to sell on for a significant profit. In all, Edward went in around a dozen charity shops. He found three or four books he thought were worth a punt on. They cost him almost nothing and he thought there was a chance at least they might be of interest to a collector. Potentially, he could sell them on at many times what he'd paid for them, or Jill could, if they hadn't sold before he left.

On his way back to the bookshop, Edward popped into a camera shop, to pick up a decent camera. He wanted something a bit better than his phone, to take pictures on. In his mind, he had a vague notion of taking high-definition photographs he could ultimately blow up and frame. Perhaps he could have his own exhibition in time. Maybe that was going a bit far. He hadn't taken one photo yet, let alone enough for an exhibition. If any were any good, perhaps he could hang them in the bookshop. They might give it a new, more modern air, like a gallery, if he could only take the right kind of photographs, not that he knew exactly what they might be. He just had some unclear concept in his head of taking something *arty*.

Edward was happy to be guided by the camera salesman. He didn't know exactly what he wanted. He just wanted something of reasonable quality, capable of taking what he termed *professional* photographs. He wanted a camera a professional photographer would be happy with, he explained. He ended up spending over a thousand pounds in the shop. Of course, it was nothing to him. It was the same as someone of less wealth spending fifty to a hundred. He'd be careful not to show Jill the receipt. He'd say he'd got it reduced or in the sale or wouldn't show it to her at all. He could claim he'd had it with him all along. One day, when the time was right, he'd tell her he was a wealthy man, and that money wasn't really a concern to him. It was no great matter whether the bookshop made money or not, as far as he was concerned. It only mattered in so far as it mattered to Jill. As it mattered to Jill, it mattered to him. For that reason alone, he would help make it more profitable, or try his best to. Otherwise, he could have just given Jill the money, enough that she'd never have to work again. He could have written the cheque now. When he got back to the bookshop, he asked Jill how the morning had been.

'Pretty quiet,' she replied.

'Did you manage to sell anything?' Edward enquired.

'Only one thing, although there are a couple of emails asking for books that I think we might have somewhere,' Jill said.

'We're not going to get very fat on that,' Edward joked. 'No matter, I picked up a couple of books in the charity shops, we might be able to sell. I thought I might try car boot sales next,' he said.

'That's a good idea,' Jill said.

'Did you do any more sorting?' Edward asked.

'I did a bit,' Jill said. 'I spent too much time talking to Beti and daydreaming if I'm honest. I actually fear you're better suited to this job than I am.'

'Don't worry. I can do some more this afternoon,' Edward said. 'Do you want me to take Beti for a walk today or will you when you go out?' he asked.

'I can if you like. I've got a few things to do, and she can tag along. I'll take the car today. You know you can always borrow it too if you want,' Jill said.

'That's really kind. I might just do that,' Edward said. 'I didn't actually know you drove. I was thinking of hiring a car in fact.'

'I hardly ever use it anyway, only to visit my mother and take her out, or to go the supermarket,' Jill explained. 'I'm not a confident driver. It's just handy to have here if there was ever an emergency. I forget I have it myself sometimes, as with the bookshop I'm never able to go out in it very much.'

For some reason, Edward hadn't really taken in the fact that Jill owned a car. He'd simply assumed she relied on public transport and her own two feet, just as he did. He'd never seen her drive and she hadn't ever really mentioned it. It made perfect sense though. She'd said she'd been to see her mother. She must have taken the car then. It should have occurred to him before. He had to admit it would be nice for him to take the car out occasionally, or indeed go with Jill sometimes if she was up for it. That much was abundantly clear to him. It would be of huge potential benefit for the pair. It would open up a whole new avenue of possibilities for them, to explore the surrounding area together.

'Have you had lunch yet?' Jill asked.

'I was going to make a sandwich or something quickly upstairs, before I start work,' Edward said.

'I tell you what, you hold the fort and I'll go up and make something,' Jill offered. 'I'll bring it down when it's ready.'

'If you insist,' Edward agreed, taking his now familiar seat behind the front desk.

He hadn't put his camera away yet, he realised. Luckily, it was hidden in a bag with the books he'd bought. He'd slip it upstairs to his room later, hopefully without Jill noticing, not that it really mattered if she did see it. She just might wonder why he'd spent so much on a camera, when there were probably better things to spend money on. If she did notice his purchase, he'd just have to come clean and confess he wasn't short of a million or two. He'd drop it casually into the conversation. He was quite intrigued to see what her reaction would be. Knowing Jill as he did, she probably wouldn't care that much, or be too bothered either way. She'd probably just think it was his business that he was choosing to live in a single room and not the mansion he could have rented, even if his choice was a little odd.

Jill sat with Edward, whilst they enjoyed their lunch together. It was some kind of mixed bean stew, with crusty bread. It was nice. The herbs and spices Jill had added made it very tasty. She was a good cook, much better than he was. There was no culinary comparison between the two of them, in truth. She was very competent in the kitchen. He was a total blunderer, unsure even of what were the correct utensils to use. That was something else for him to add to his list of things he needed to learn. He'd spent too many years being waited on or eating out. He'd never really had to fend for himself. Now was his chance to do so, though so far Jill had made it very easy for him. He'd done no more than he would have at home. Edward suspected she'd taken him on as some kind of project, though exactly what that project was, it remained uncertain.

Jill headed off a little after two, taking Beti with her. Edward was alone in the shop. They hadn't exactly been inundated with customers, whilst having lunch together. In fact, no one had come in at all. It was the middle of the week. Business really should be picking up by now, Edward thought. If anything, it was tailing off. It was going in the wrong direction. Maybe it would improve in the afternoon. Edward took their dirty crockery up to the kitchen. He also took the opportunity to put his new camera away in his bedroom, before coming straight back down. He would have heard the doorbell ring, if anyone had come in during the few moments he was away from his desk. No one had.

Edward busied himself, as he waited for some customers to appear. He examined the purchases he'd made from the charity shops. He gave them a bit of a dust and straightened a few creased pages. He tried to make the books look as presentable and appealing as he possibly could. He liked them in good condition himself. He assumed others did too. He put prices on the inside covers, perhaps over-optimistic ones, and placed the books in their correct places on the shelves. He also made a note of the various titles on his spreadsheet. He was efficient if nothing else. He realised Jill wouldn't have bothered with any of that. That was one of the reasons the shop wasn't doing quite as well as Edward thought it should be doing.

Edward checked the emails and replied to a couple, enquiring about books he was confident he could get hold of. If he could find them for sale on the internet, he wondered why they couldn't just do it for themselves. He only imagined they were older customers, who weren't especially internet proficient and struggled with such things. He himself hadn't really been part of the web generation. He'd just been forced to acquire the basics as he went along. He'd had no choice. It had been an essential component of his work, even though he'd been no spring chicken when the internet had first become a thing of significance. Over the twenty-five years or so since, he'd achieved a basic competence. He was intent on eventually putting that knowledge to good use, to raise the profile and web presence of the bookshop. In time, he'd even like to design its own basic website. He was still some way off doing that. There were more pressing things that needed doing first.

Whilst Edward waited for the non-existent customers, he continued to sort through the piles of books on the floor. It felt like painting the Forth

Bridge. However many he got through, there seemed to be just as many still to do. He suspected as he cleared some, Jill just brought out more. She probably had them hidden all over the house, he realised, in every nook and cranny. Secretly, she was replenishing supplies when he was out. It didn't really matter. They all had to be done in time. On his next visit to town, he'd look at more storage utilities. He'd order some suitable ones and have them delivered to the shop. He might have to move things round a bit, to make optimum use of the available space.

With only a couple of customers, at least Edward got a lot of other work done. By the end of the afternoon, he could definitely see the fruits of his labours. One or two people had come in, including an elderly couple. He'd enjoyed chatting to them but hadn't managed to sell them anything. Just like Jill, he only sold one book. It was better than nothing. Besides, Edward didn't expect instant success. He was in this for the long haul. There was a certain amount of sorting and reorganising to be done first. Then he'd begin to look at the marketing side. Once he did that, there was a possibility business could suddenly pick up, if not quite boom.

As five o'clock approached, Edward decided it was time to call it a day and knock off a few minutes early. It was highly unlikely anyone was going to come in now. He hadn't seen a single customer in well over an hour. If they came now, they'd be unlucky. They'd have to come back another day. Edward got up from his desk and turned the front door latch, so it was now locked. He flipped the shop sign from open to closed and switched off the lights. He'd already shut down the computer, in readiness for his departure, and unplugged the kettle in the back office. He'd also removed the small amount of takings from the till. He left the modest float where it was, so it was ready for the next day. Jill kept a weighty, metal strongbox under the bed, where she stored cash, before banking it a couple of times a week. She never kept very much on the premises. The bookshop didn't make that much in the first place to keep. Besides, it was all insured, in the unlikely event of theft during a break-in. Edward took the small quantity of cash up to her. He'd heard her come in a few minutes earlier. He knocked on her bedroom door, before entering and passing her the money.

'Another good day I see,' she said, with mock sincerity.

'Business will pick up,' Edward assured her. 'I just need to get the sorting done, then I'll go to work on the marketing side. It will make a difference then.'

'We're not going to get very fat on that. It will be a meagre dinner tonight,' Jill jested.

'We're not eating in tonight. We're going out,' Edward suddenly announced.

'What do you mean, going out?' Jill asked, looking a little confused and vaguely dumbfounded.

'Exactly what I say. We're eating out, my treat. That is if you want to,' Edward said.

'What's the occasion? It's not your birthday or something and you didn't tell me?' Jill wondered.

'Nothing liked that. It's not my birthday. I suppose you could say it's just a small thank you for taking me in and looking after me,' Edward said.

'You weren't exactly on the street,' Jill quipped.

'Perhaps metaphorically I was,' Edward replied. 'Anyway, I've taken the liberty of booking a table for seven-thirty. Perhaps we can head out around seven? That is of course if you want to come. No worries if not. I can always dine alone.'

Booking a table for two was one of the things Edward had done during a sluggish afternoon.

'Of course, I want to come,' Jill told him. 'I'll just need to find something to wear.'

'You'll have plenty of time to do that. I've got a few things to do in my bedroom first anyway,' Edward said.

'Where are we going out of interest?' Jill asked.

'It's a surprise, but hopefully somewhere nice,' Edward said, with a slightly mysterious and mischievous air.

He had it all planned out. Where they were going would at least make sense to him, if not perhaps to Jill. Hopefully, she'd understand once he explained it to her. Edward made a cup of coffee, to take up to his room. He made Jill one too, even though he hadn't asked her if she wanted one. She could always leave it if she didn't. He made sure to put oat milk in hers. He put cow's milk in his own. It would be the last carton of dairy he'd buy, he decided. In future, they might just as well share the same. He'd also make do with vegan cheese, even though to him it was a poor substitute for the taste of the real thing. It would just make things easier than having to buy two of everything. When he was out, he might still have some meat and cheese. On that matter, he was yet to make his mind up. Jill seemed pleased when he handed her a coffee, before going up.

'I hope you don't mind, it's decaffeinated,' he told her. 'It's better for me.'

'That's OK. I often have decaffeinated myself and like it just as much as ordinary,' Jill replied.

In his bedroom, Edward got out sketchbook, pencils, crayons, watercolours, and brushes, and laid them on the bed. He surveyed his purchases from the previous day. Now, he had a top of the range camera to add to them. He lay on the bed and opened the sketchbook. He took out a pencil and began to sketch. Gradually, the rough outline of a woman began to take form. She had no face. There was a window behind her. Light was pouring through. Slowly, it dawned on Edward it was Jill, sitting at her desk. He tried to give her facial features a little more definition, as much as he could remember them. He'd have to get her to sit for him another time. Bit by bit, the drawing began to resemble something more whole and complete. Perhaps he'd add watercolours over the top. It could serve to bring the work to life.

Edward put the drawing down. He sat back to admire his handiwork. It wasn't bad. It wasn't great, but he possessed a modicum of artistic talent, it seemed. He could see that much. Given time, there was a hint of ability that could be developed. He'd finish the drawing another night, he decided. It was a start at least. He opened his notebook. He reread the few lines of loose verse he'd idly jotted down in it. He continued to edit and fine-tune them, changing odd words here and there, so they were more to his liking. A few more lines slowly emerged from his pen and began to approximate a poem. He was quite the *Renaissance Man*, he reflected. In fact, he was probably no such thing and just deluding himself. Now was the time to do so if any, he realised. There wouldn't be a better one. He was sixty years old, and it didn't matter what anyone else thought about him, and what he chose to do with his time. It was his to do with as he pleased for once in his life, without judgement and without mockery.

'Where are we going?' Jill asked again, as they headed out just after seven.

She'd put on a nice dress for the occasion. Edward was wearing a shirt and jacket, but no tie. He'd formally abandoned that fine detail, after retiring from his financial work.

'You'll see,' Edward replied, wishing to maintain a small element of surprise to their evening.

'Tell me now,' Jill whined, sounding almost like a child excluded from a secret everyone else had been told.

'Do you really want to know?' Edward enquired, stopping in the street for a moment, to give her a chance to answer. Perhaps he'd gently teased her enough and should finally put her out of her misery.

'I do,' Jill said.

'Well, in my second year at university, I lived in the Uplands. Every time I walked to the city centre, I passed the same row of expensive restaurants, but I could never afford to go in any of them. I'd liked to have gone with my first wife, Angela, but generally we had to find cheaper places to eat when we went out. So, I'm taking you to one of them now, just because I can. I hope that makes sense,' Edward said.

'It does,' Jill replied. 'It's quite a sweet story really.'

'I hope so,' Edward said. 'I've checked they cater for vegans, and they do, so everything should be fine. It should be a bit better than the pub at least.'

'It's very kind of you,' Jill said.

'It's my pleasure,' Edward replied. 'Tomorrow, we'll just have to ensure we make some of the money back,' he pretended, knowing full well it didn't matter a scrap if they did or didn't make enough to cover the cost of the meal.

Jill was quietly thrilled inside. Whilst they'd been to the local hostelry together, it was a long time since she'd been taken to a fancy restaurant, particularly by a man as distinguished as Edward. He really did have hidden depths and a kind of hidden wisdom, she thought. He in turn was greatly looking forward to a couple of hours of her company.

'Afterwards, I thought we might pop to the *Uplands Tavern* for a drink or two for old times' sake, my old times anyway,' Edward added.

'That sounds absolutely perfect,' Jill said, gripping his arm tightly, as they walked.

Edward made no attempt to disengage her arm and was happy to feel her close to him.

Day Eighteen (Thursday)

'Thanks again for a lovely evening,' Jill said to Edward, over breakfast.

'It was nice, wasn't it?' Edward agreed. 'Hopefully we can do it again sometime.'

'If you're paying,' Jill joked. 'I noticed it was quite expensive, and it will be my turn next time, I suppose.'

'If I choose somewhere expensive, I should pay,' Edward insisted. 'You can treat me at the pub sometime if you like. I'm not short of a bob or two. I got quite a hefty golden handshake when I retired.'

It was quite hefty indeed. Jill would probably have been shocked at exactly how much it was. Of course, Edward had earned his company many more times that over the years, as well as making himself a significantly rich man in the process. He'd been told he well and truly deserved it, by his appreciative bosses. It was more money than many would perhaps see in a lifetime. It wasn't as if Edward even needed it. He consoled himself with the thought that in all likelihood half would probably go to Alice. It was also the first small indication he'd given to Jill that he wasn't exactly hard up. Perhaps she was beginning to suspect as much.

'This evening I've got a meeting of the book club I'm a member of,' Jill announced. 'Why don't you join us? You can make a case for George Orwell, JG Ballard or Kurt Vonnegut being the greatest English-speaking writer. We can all tell you you're wrong and it's Dylan Thomas,' Jill laughed.

Now Edward had taken his first few tentative steps towards writing poetry, she could be his Caitlin Thomas and he could be her Dylan. Was there something of the Caitlins in Jill? Like Caitlin, Jill was a bit chaotic, but not as volatile and belligerent as Dylan's wife had a reputation for being. Theirs had been a stormy marriage by all accounts. Edward's relationship with Jill was calmness personified, if indeed it was a relationship. He wasn't truthfully sure exactly what it was. It was a friendship of two mature people, he imagined. That was probably the best way to describe it. He still hadn't got it precisely worked out in his own head. More importantly, he remained unsure where it was going and where it would end up.

'I'd forgotten you were a member of a book club,' Edward remarked. 'Though you did mention it once, come to think of it.'

'It's all very casual. There are only six of us. We take it in turns to meet in each other's houses. They're coming here tonight. They like to meet in the bookshop, as it gives the club more atmosphere and resonance than meeting in someone's kitchen or front room.'

'I can see that. It's the perfect setting for a book club,' Edward observed. 'What book or books are you presently reading?'

'We're discussing Salman Rushdie's latest novel. It's good, but to be honest it's quite long and I'm finding it slightly hard going,' Jill admitted.

'I have a copy of *The Satanic Verses* somewhere at home, I believe, but I'm not really familiar with his work,' Edward confessed.

It was the only book by Salman Rushdie he was sure he had. He'd probably only bought it because of the religious controversy its publication had caused at the time, leading to death threats to its author. Edward had never actually got round to reading the book, however. He made a mental note to do so when he returned to Oxford, or perhaps he might read one of the less controversial ones, the one Jill was reading for example.

'The good thing is we're all allowed to bring something else along that we're reading just for fun, to share with the group,' Jill continued.

'What will you take?' Edward asked.

'I don't know. Something light probably, a *whodunnit* perhaps or something random from the shelves of the shop. I'm actually rereading Jane Austen at present, but they'll all be familiar with that, so there's no real point taking it,' Jill explained.

'I need to start a new book,' Edward said. 'I may take a look at what we've got in the classic literature section. Don't worry, I'll pay for any I take,' Edward assured her.

'You really don't need to. We are business partners, remember,' Jill reminded him.

'I wouldn't want you to be out of pocket,' Edward protested.

'Anyway, are you coming tonight?' Jill asked. 'We'll probably go for a quick drink after.'

'I'd love to, but I can't tonight,' Edward said enthusiastically, whilst keeping some minor reservations about attending to himself. 'I was thinking I should pop in on Alan and Gwen at the guesthouse and see how they're doing. I'll be sure to go next time. How often do you meet?'

'At least once a month, sometimes every fortnight,' Jill answered. 'We'll set a date for the next one at the end of the meeting tonight.'

'Definitely count me in for that,' Edward said.

'I'll warn them to expect you.' Jill said. 'They're a bit of an odd bunch, like me probably, but nice in their own different ways.'

'I look forward to meeting them,' Edward said, graciously.

He spent the rest of the morning beavering away in the bookshop. He checked the emails, answered a couple of phone calls, and even served a few customers. The rest of the time he spent gradually cataloguing and pricing up the unsorted books. He now had many titles on his spreadsheet, all in alphabetical order of course. He was also endeavouring to keep them cross referenced by subject. He wanted to at least have some idea of the stock they carried. At present, they still had little idea what they had on the shelves, except by looking. The customers could do that for themselves.

Jill came down to take over from him at lunchtime. Edward had a few errands to run in town. He offered to take Beti with him, so she'd have her daily walk. Jill readily agreed. It would be good for Beti to get out in the fresh air. Edward stopped at the vegan coffee shop on the way, to pick up a couple of baps. This time, he chose vegan bacon ones, as well as a cake and a takeaway coffee, to have for his lunch on the way. He bought two baps, as he was certain Beti would want some, just as Jill had done. He wondered if the dog would be able to tell the difference between that and real meat. He'd slowly got used to it. He imagined Beti would do. She'd already had a small taste of vegan sausage, he remembered, but no pretend bacon. It would be a first for both of them. So far, Jill had resisted the temptation to feed her dog a vegan diet, at least as far as Edward knew. It was just him she seemed intent on turning into an unlikely vegan.

Edward had intended to pop into the offices of the local evening newspaper, but it appeared the ones he remembered from his days as a student were now closed. He had found another address in the High Street, but it was unclear simply from googling whether they were in fact open. Instead, he found a telephone number to ring, that he hoped would put him directly through to their advertising department. Edward wanted to place an advert. If it was a success, he'd place another one. He was put through to someone and he gave them a rough outline of what he wanted. Regarding presentation and logos etcetera, he explained they didn't really have any and he was happy to be guided by their design team. The person he spoke to promised to put something together and email it over for approval. Hopefully, it would be a pleasant surprise for Jill, not that she was a great reader of the local newspapers. Edward would have to ensure she read that one.

Edward had just about reached the main shops, by the time he finished his telephone conversation. He then headed to a small, local printers. He recalled passing several on the main road that led down from the Uplands into the shopping centre, before joining the Kingsway via a narrow side street. Edward went to the first of those. He hoped they'd be able to do what he was after. It was reassuring to know he at least had a back-up plan and other options, if for some reason they couldn't manage what he needed doing, though he didn't foresee it being a problem. He simply wanted some flyers drawn up, that they could distribute to local libraries, tourist information centres, the museums and art gallery, anywhere that would have them really. He was thinking of having a thousand printed, although he realised this might be too many. The additional cost compared to five hundred wasn't really that much. He might just as well keep it at a round thousand. The person he spoke to at the printers was accommodating and agreed to design a simple flyer for his perusal and consideration. Edward left his contact details, so they could continue to liaise on the matter.

His final port of call was a discount furniture shop, where he ordered some basic units, suitable for the storage of books. He arranged to have them delivered. If nothing else, they'd be a small gift from himself to Jill. He also ordered one slightly grander bookcase. In his mind, he pictured it housing those few rarities and special editions they had, which over time he planned to add to. One of the things he'd kept an eye open for in the charity shops were interesting first editions. He knew if he could find the right ones, their value over time would only increase. Customers paid a fortune for scarce books by certain exclusive authors, he'd observed.

As Edward completed his various tasks, Beti dutifully trotted along at his side. She was never any trouble. Mostly, she followed him into shops without anyone even being aware of her presence. Edward was reluctant to leave her tied up outside. He knew not all shops welcomed dogs, but Edward possessed a presence and an air of authority that meant he could go about his business virtually unchallenged, in almost anything he did. He had a look of natural correctness and superiority about him, even if he didn't intend to. It seemed to give him permission to do almost as he wished. Righteousness was on his side. As a result, even in premises that weren't keen on dogs, Edward was never once asked to take Beti out. He himself recognised the unjustness of the situation. He was aware that if a homeless person entered the same shops, with some flea-bitten mutt, they'd almost certainly be asked to leave.

Edward took the bay road back, past the council offices and prison and the Oystermouth Road guesthouse that had been his home and which he planned to return to later that evening. He didn't stop to warn Alan and Gwen he'd be coming just in case something came up. Perhaps Jill would drag him to the meeting of the book club. He wouldn't have entirely minded. He wouldn't have minded much at all if she'd really wanted him there. He'd definitely go to the next one, assuming he was still in Swansea. He couldn't see any reason why he wouldn't be. When he got back, he sat with Jill in the shop for a few moments. He let her make him a cup of tea. He no longer even bothered to comment about the non-dairy milk substitute, or oat or soya milk, as she called it. His daily latte was now made with it, and he'd got used to the taste.

'So, how did you get on?' she asked.

'Well, I've been quite busy,' Edward said. 'Hopefully, you'll be pleased with what I've done.'

'What's that?' Jill enquired, sounding quite intrigued by the possibilities of what Edward might have taken upon himself next.

'I've arranged to have some flyers printed, for local libraries and places like that,' Edward said.

'That's a good idea,' Jill congratulated him.

'And I'm taking out an advert in the local paper,' Edward continued.

'How can we afford that?' Jill wondered.

'You don't need to worry about that,' Edward said. 'I'm paying for it myself. Remember our deal, a share of any extra profits,' he reminded her.

'Anything else?' Jill asked, assuming there wasn't.

'As a matter of fact, there is,' Edward confirmed. 'You'll be getting a delivery of some new storage units. Hopefully, they'll take most of the books we haven't sorted yet.'

'Have you gone mad?' Jill asked.

'Perhaps,' Edward agreed. 'I'm not a man who does things by halves.'

'You really have been busy,' Jill commented.

'There's one more thing. I enjoyed last night. I wondered if you'd care to join me for lunch tomorrow. I thought we could shut the shop for a bit and have a snack in the vegan coffee shop. What do you say?' Edward asked.

'Is that a date you're asking me on?' Jill laughed, with a cheeky grin on her face and the glimmer of a glint in her eye.

'Call it what you like,' Edward said, noncommittally.

'I have an even better idea,' Jill said. 'We can go for lunch and then take Beti for a walk together after. The weather's meant to be nice tomorrow.

We won't bother reopening the shop. We'll take the afternoon off. I think we both deserve it.'

'I won't argue,' Edward said. 'You're the boss.'

Jill laughed again.

'I don't think I'll ever be that,' she said. 'I wasn't really the boss when it was just myself.'

Around five, they locked up the shop and banked the day's meagre takings. Whilst Jill prepared for the arrival of her eager book club members, Edward retired to his room. For about an hour he quietly continued with his drawing and even started a new one. The one he now presumed to be of Jill, sitting wistfully in thought at her desk, was nearing completion. He laid some light watercolour on top of his rough pencil outlines. He was adequately pleased with the results he was achieving. Not bad for a beginner, he thought to himself, as he worked. It was coming together quite nicely, though the effort and concentration of painting wasn't entirely relaxing. He found it quite exhausting in truth, more so than he expected. He put his sketchbook down and opened his notebook. He continued with the poem he was writing. It now extended to six stanzas. He even had a few random lines left over that he quite liked, but which didn't quite fit. He realised they probably belonged to a different poem; one he hadn't yet started. Wearied by his creative endeavours, he went down to the kitchen, to prepare himself something to eat.

He could hear Jill busying herself in her bedroom too, presumably getting ready for the night that lay ahead. Her guests were arriving around seven. Edward planned to leave just before then. Part of him wanted to attend. Part of him was less keen. He was anxious not to steal her thunder, or worse still be the subject of any gossip. That was the deciding factor. He'd have hated that. There was nothing worse. He imagined there were already enough false rumours circulating back in Oxford over his sudden disappearance. He could imagine if Jill's guests saw him, there would be a host of questions to be answered. Who was he? Why was he staying there? Was he her lover? He would be the sudden subject of intrigue. Edward was a very private man. He couldn't have borne any of that. No, it was better to make his excuses beforehand and make himself scarce. He'd meet them another time on neutral territory. He didn't necessarily want them to assume he was living there, under the same roof as Jill, even if he was. No, it was best all round to give this meeting a miss, on further consideration and reflection.

Edward had a snacky tea and quickly washed up his plates and cutlery. He never left anything out. If it was his mess, he should clear it up. That was his confirmed opinion, one he'd never waver from him. He cleaned his teeth and tidied himself suitably for going out. On his way, he wished Jill a pleasant and successful evening. It was ten to seven. There was no sign of any of her guests yet. Jill promised to text him if they went to the pub. Edward said he might join them there but was careful not to promise. He thought it might be a little early for all that. He didn't really know what the situation between him and Jill was himself.

Jill had laid out chairs in the bookshop for her guests to sit on. There were also nibbles and a number of bottles of wine. It made Edward wonder if the principal purpose of the evening was drinking rather than reading. It was up them. As long as they enjoyed themselves was the main thing. Jill was evidently a good host. She was clearly going to a degree of effort for those shortly to arrive, just as she had for Edward, in welcoming him into her home. After saying his goodbyes, Edward continued on his now familiar way down Francis Street, onto Guildhall Road South, before turning left into Oystermouth Road. The guesthouse came up very quickly. It was barely any distance at all. It was still only seven when he arrived outside. Presumably, the meeting of the book club would just be getting underway back at the bookshop, with Jill as chairperson. Was the host chairperson, Edward wondered, or was it a function performed by someone else? Edward had no idea, but he imagined Jill undertaking the role for the evening. Meanwhile, he rang the front doorbell of the guesthouse. He no longer had a key. He'd handed it in when he left. He hoped Alan or Gwen would get up to answer it. He imagined they would. Alan came to see who was there first.

'I was just passing, so I thought I'd look you up,' Edward said.

It wasn't entirely true. He wasn't passing. He'd gone out of his way to visit them, to see how they were doing.

'What a pleasant surprise,' Alan said. 'Do come in.'

Alan led Edward into the lounge, that in the morning was the breakfast room. As always, Gwen was sitting on one of the comfortable chairs, watching the television. She looked up when Edward entered.

'Look who's come to see us,' Alan said.

'How delightful,' Gwen commented.

There was a look of genuine pleasure on her face. She was evidently pleased he'd taken the trouble to call on them.

'Can I get you a drink?' Alan asked.

'Yes please,' Edward replied.

'Your usual scotch and soda?'

'Indeed,' Edward said, opening his wallet to offer payment.

'I wouldn't hear of it,' Alan said, beckoning Edward to put his wallet away. 'You're not our paying guest now. You're a guest in our home.'

'I'm very happy to pay,' Edward said.

'No, really, it's very nice of you to offer, but we couldn't accept,' Alan said. 'Have a drink with us, as our friend.'

'If you're sure,' Edward agreed, somewhat reluctantly.

He knew Alan and Gwen didn't charge enough for their rooms. He didn't want them being further out of pocket on his account. At least, he could console himself with the thought he'd left them a generous tip when he left.

'So, how's it going?' Gwen asked. 'Have you settled in all right?'

'Yes, thank you very much,' Edward answered. 'I have my own room at the top of the house.'

'Have you started work in the bookshop?' Alan enquired, passing Edward his whisky.

'I have,' Edward said, taking a satisfying sip.

His eyes lit up a little, as he remembered what he'd done in the shop so far.

'It's going quite well,' he continued. 'Business is slightly quiet. It's only to be expected, but I'm optimistic it will pick up. I have some ideas to get a few more customers through the door.'

'So, Edward, is it just a business arrangement or is it more than that?' Gwen asked, with a mischievous look.

Being a woman of a certain age, she was willing to ask the questions Alan was too much of a gentleman or simply too embarrassed to ask.

'I don't fully get your meaning?' Edward responded, appearing a little confused, or just pretending to be.

'Surely, you know what I mean,' Gwen said. 'Is it a romantic thing between you and Jill or are you just good friends?'

'That is a very good question. There's certainly nothing improper going on,' Edward said, giving the matter further consideration for a moment, but not refusing to answer. 'The absolute truth is I'm not quite sure. I think we're just friends at present, but there have been one or two hints we could become more than that. Nothing has been said by either of us, but we have become close, and we get on very well. There's no denying that.'

'How exciting,' Gwen said, clapping her hands. 'I thought as much.'

'Oh, ignore her, she's just a gossip and a would-be matchmaker. Pay no attention to her,' Alan said dismissively, as if Gwen had touched on a subject that she should have been left well alone.

'There's nothing wrong with a bit of gossip and matchmaking,' Gwen laughed.

'More importantly, have you been in touch with your wife?' Alan continued.

'As a matter of fact, I haven't,' Edward answered. 'I keep thinking I should, but I keep putting it off. I can see on my phone she's both texted and rung, but I haven't answered as yet. I've just let her know I'm OK and will be in touch when I'm ready.'

'She's probably wondering when that will be,' Gwen pointed out.

'She probably is,' Edward conceded. 'Of course, I'd argue that she created this situation herself by having an affair. I doubt she's pining after me anyway. She's probably very happy I've gone and there's nothing to get in the way of her and Paul.'

'I expect she misses you really,' Gwen suggested. 'It's probably quite a shock to her you've just upped sticks and left.'

'Maybe, maybe not. I can only imagine it will all sort itself out in the fullness of time,' Edward said.

'Do you miss her?' Gwen asked.

'Yes and no,' Edward said. 'Sometimes I do. Sometimes I miss my life back in Oxford, or parts of it at least. Sometimes I don't miss it at all.'

'That's always the way,' Gwen nodded. 'When you're back in Oxford, you'll probably miss Swansea.'

'I think I will,' Edward agreed. 'That's if I go back,' he added, in a humorous but vaguely ambiguous fashion, almost as an afterthought.

Was it a joke or was he being serious? He wasn't quite sure. Just then, he heard his phone beep. He pulled it out of his pocket. It was a text from Jill. The meeting had finished early, and they'd gone to the pub if he wanted to join them. Evidently, there wasn't that much to discuss about Salman Rushdie. Of course, there was really. Edward was just being flippant to himself. He'd allowed Alan to top up his glass once already and he found himself accepting another whisky. For his own reasons, he didn't want to meet Jill and her friends in the pub on this occasion. He'd decided against it, having initially thought he might wish to go. He'd stay with Alan and Gwen a while longer, before eventually heading back. Edward had consumed his fourth whisky, before he finally left them, promising to look them up again soon.

'I shan't ask if you'll be wanting your usual cooked breakfast in the morning,' Alan joked, as Edward departed.

Edward smiled back.

'Jill's a vegan and wouldn't allow it,' he laughed, as he proceeded from the guesthouse and stepped onto Oystermouth Road.

Edward had texted Jill to say he'd been detained and would see her back at the bookshop. He took his time, choosing the scenic way home, just as it was getting dark. When Edward got in, he found Jill slumped on the sofa in the lounge, watching television. She was hiccupping. She was clearly the worse the wear for drink. Edward wondered how many she'd had.

'Edward, how lovely to see you,' she almost shouted at him, as if she couldn't quite control the volume of her voice. 'Shame you couldn't join us in the pub.'

'Another time,' Edward said. 'And how was your evening?' he asked.

'It was very agreeable, but I may have had a little too much wine,' Jill admitted.

'Just a little,' Edward repeated, smiling at her. 'I thought you didn't really drink. How many did you have exactly?'

'Well, I'm not entirely sure,' Jill said, examining her fingers, as if she planned to attempt to count on them. 'I probably had over half a bottle before we left, maybe more than that. Then someone bought me a large one in the pub, to say thank you for hosting. Then I think someone else got me another one, but I didn't quite finish it, or maybe I did. It's hard to remember to be honest.'

'That is quite a lot, for a non-drinker,' Edward agreed, sitting down beside her.

Jill allowed her drooping head to flop onto Edward's shoulder. The room was spinning a bit. She gripped hold of Edward's hand for support. He made no attempt to stop her.

'Would you like me to make you a coffee?' Edward asked.

'That might help,' Jill said.

She wasn't keen to let him go and seemed intent on holding onto him.

'You look very handsome,' she told him.

'You look very attractive too,' Edward returned the compliment.

'Do you really think so?' Jill asked.

'I do, even if you're drunk, but if you don't let me get up, I can't make you your coffee,' Edward pointed out.

After making her a cup of nearly black coffee, he sat with her a while she sipped it and started to sober up.

'I think we should get you to bed,' Edward announced.

He helped her into her bedroom and into her bed clothes. She still had her underwear on underneath. He didn't see anything too untoward. When she was in bed, Jill gave him a big kiss on his cheek.

'Thanks for everything,' she said. 'You can stay a bit longer if you like,' she added.

Edward suspected she was flirting with him slightly. She was in too much of a drunken state, however, for him to take advantage of her. It was best to leave things as they were, before he allowed them to get more complicated. He hadn't forgotten they already had their coffee shop *date* the following day.

'Very tempting, but I'd better not. You need your beauty sleep,' he told her.

With that, he tucked her in, turned off her light and closed her bedroom door. He then slowly climbed the stairs to his own bed and much-needed rest.

Day Nineteen (Friday)

As always, Edward got up around eight. He went down to the kitchen, pausing briefly at the bathroom on the way to empty his bladder. He had a vague memory of getting up around two and again about five to do the same thing. It was perfectly normal for a man of sixty. He was confident he didn't have prostate cancer or anything like that. His waterworks seemed in pretty good working order, as far as he could tell, for a man of his age. He could still perform in the bedroom on the very odd occasion he was required to do so. It had become increasingly seldom during the last couple of years with Alice. Presumably, she'd no longer had any great need of him in that way, as she had Paul to cater for those particularly needs. There had been a small period of time, before he'd been diagnosed with atrial fibrillation, when it hadn't been quite so easy for him to get an erection. No doubt, Alice had used that fact against him. Since he'd been on the medication to control his heart rate, things had improved, and that particular problem had gone away. Not that Alice would have noticed. She'd lost interest, and it was more convenient to blame him for any decline in levels of activity in that department, rather than take any responsibility herself. Hadn't she given that as one of her excuses for turning to Paul, in the brief conversation they'd had on the matter? Edward still didn't know how long the affair had been going on, and indeed whether it was still continuing. His best guess was that it had been a while. With Edward now away, it was hard to imagine it could have petered out and stopped. They'd probably only been thrust closer together.

When Edward entered the kitchen, he noticed something was different. Jill wasn't up yet, he realised. That was highly unusual in itself. She was always up before he was, sitting alertly at the breakfast table, consuming her fruit or muesli or whatever she had. Beti would usually be enjoying her breakfast too. Not on this particular morning. There was no sign of either of them. Normally, there would be the sound of gentle clatter and activity. On this occasion, there was only silence. Edward couldn't even hear any noise from the road outside. The only noise was the shuffling about that he made in his pyjamas, as he began to prepare his own breakfast. He recalled Jill had been slightly the worse the wear for drink the previous evening. Unusually for her, she'd consumed a fair quantity of wine. Even for him, it would have been quite a lot these days. In the past, it hadn't been unheard of for him to drink two whole bottles at a particularly boozy lunch or dinner. He'd never felt great afterwards. Those days were well and truly gone. He'd put them firmly behind him. He knew his limits now. More than a few drinks agitated his heart condition. He didn't want that. He wondered if he should check on Jill. He could just call out, to see she was all right. Instead, Edward went and knocked on her door.

'Is everything OK?' he asked, in little more than a gentle whisper, so as not to alarm her.

'You can come in,' Jill said. 'I'm just not feeling so good.'

Edward opened the bedroom door and proceeded inside, as invited by Jill. She and Beti were curled up on the bed together. Jill looked a little bleary-eyed, but also quite cute and appealing in her weary but relaxed repose.

'In what way are you feeling unwell?' Edward enquired, although he could fathom a fair guess of his own accord.

'Just the usual when you've drunk too much,' Jill replied. 'Dry throat, bit of a headache, a slight feeling of sickness in the stomach. It's your fault. I'd almost stopped drinking. You've given me a taste for wine again.'

'Sorry about that,' Edward said. 'So, was it a good night?' he asked.

'It was, but perhaps a little too good,' Jill said. 'It was a pity you couldn't make the pub.'

'I had a nice catch-up with Alan and Gwen. I'll definitely come next time,' Edward promised. 'I just thought it might be a bit soon to meet them.'

'That's all right. I can barely remember the end of the evening to be honest. I must have drunk more than I thought. It's no wonder I've got a hangover,' Jill said.

'Sounds like you had the best part of a bottle and a half of wine, from what you told me,' Edward said.

'It certainly feels like it now,' Jill joked.

'Can I get you some tea and toast?' Edward offered.

'Tea would be nice, and some aspirin or paracetamol if you can find some. There should be some in the drawer. I think I might leave the toast for a while, until I've woken up a bit more and feel slightly better,' Jill said.

'I'll see what I can do,' Edward told her. 'You just close your eyes and have a little rest for a moment.'

Edward left her and returned to the kitchen. He put the kettle on to boil and placed two slices of bread in the toaster to brown for himself. As he waited for the water to heat, he found some aspirin in one of the drawers, to take to Jill. When the tea was ready, he poured out a mug of it and dutifully carried it into the bedroom, together with the packet of aspirin. He watched, as Jill washed down two of the small, white tablets with a gulp of hot tea.

'Hopefully, they'll start to work their magic soon,' Jill said. 'I can't lie in bed all day. We have a shop to open.'

'Don't worry about that. I'll look after the shop today. You just worry about getting yourself better. Remember, we have our date at the coffee shop if you're well enough,' Edward reminded her.

'I'll definitely be well enough for that,' Jill insisted.

'May I suggest you have your tea, then go back to sleep for a couple of hours. When you're ready, treat yourself to a nice hot shower or a lazy bath,' Edward proposed. 'That might do the trick.'

'What about you?' Jill asked.

'I'll be in the shop. I'll be fine there. I'm not short of things to get on with,' Edward said.

'Are you sure that's all right?' Jill asked.

'It's absolutely fine,' Edward assured her. 'My only request is you try and get yourself well enough for lunch. If not, we'll just do it another time.'

Edward then left her to finish her tea and get some sleep. He sat down in the kitchen, to eat his modest breakfast. He missed Gwen's sausage, bacon, and eggs. He was practically a vegetarian these days. No such food was even allowed in the house. His tea was still warm, but his toast had gone cold. He wasn't especially bothered. It was a minor inconvenience, for ensuring Jill was comfortable and would be better in time to go to the coffee shop with him at lunchtime. After washing up his breakfast things, Edward had a quick shower. He then returned to his bedroom, to put on his work clothes or what he considered to be his work clothes. In truth, there was very little difference between what he wore in the shop and what he wore casually. He looked at his face in the mirror. It had been a while since he'd shaved. His white stubble would now pass muster as a neat, little beard. He quite liked it. In a way, it suited him. He imagined Alice would have been less impressed. Of course, that added to Edward's sense of minor pleasure at his slightly changed appearance. He'd love her to see him looking quite different and perhaps doing different things when he finally returned home.

'I'm going down to open up,' Edward called out, when at last he was ready.

He spent the morning pottering in the bookshop. He did all the usual things. He checked the emails. There were a couple of general ones, as well as one or two more specific ones, enquiring after particular books. He answered them as best he could, checking where he might be able to source the requested items. The phone rang several times and a couple of customers poked their heads in. A draft of the advert he hoped to place in the local evening paper had been sent for him to check. He hadn't received a draft of the flyer yet. There was no hurry about that. When he wasn't dealing with these things, he continued with the sorting, cataloguing, and pricing of the random, unsorted books. At least the piles had gone down, though there were still a lot of books to get through. Jill had piled dozens behind her desk and in the back office. Edward hadn't even made a start on them yet. All in good time, he told himself.

Around mid-morning, there was a thud on the doormat. Edward looked up. The postman had left a package. He hadn't stopped to speak. He'd continued straight on with his deliveries at the next building. Edward got up. The parcel was addressed to him. It was book shaped. He opened it. It was the book he'd ordered for a customer – *The Great European Treaties of the Nineteenth Century*. He only hoped the customer would return to collect it. It wasn't the end of the world if he didn't. Edward would just put it on the shelves, in the hope of selling it someone else. This was after all just a hobby really, he reminded himself. It didn't really matter to him if it made money. Of course, it mattered to Jill, he assumed. Even that would eventually cease to be the case, Edward was resolved. Whatever happened between them and whether he stayed or went, when he eventually left Swansea, he'd see her all right. He was determined of that. He'd leave her a generous amount, enough to ensure money wasn't a worry for the remainder of her working life. The money was no great use to him. He might as well give some of it to someone for whom it would actually make a difference, he thought. Otherwise, there was no point having it.

Edward barely noticed time pass. He found he quite enjoyed being by himself in the shop, deciding which task he'd do next, not having to worry about anyone else and their demands and priorities. To all intents and purposes, he was his own boss. He'd probably go as far to say that he now took the lead in the informal business partnership he'd established with Jill. She seemed content to leave him to it and let him run the shop in any way he saw fit. That suited Edward. He liked being in control. He liked to be the decisionmaker. Before he knew it, he looked at his watch and it was quarter to one. He thought he heard movement from above. He sensed Jill was coming down. She suddenly presented herself to him. She was clearly revived by her sleep. She'd even put on a different dress. She did a quick twirl for him.

'What do you think?' she asked.

Edward nodded his head approvingly.

'You look lovely,' he told her. 'Are you feeling any better?'

'Much better thanks,' she said.

'Well enough to go for lunch at the coffee shop?' Edward asked.

'Of course,' Jill said. 'I wouldn't want to miss that.'

'Are you ready to leave now?' Edward enquired.

'Absolutely,' Jill answered.

'In which case we'd better lock up,' Edward said. 'I'll just go and get my jacket and wallet.'

'Beti can hold the fort,' Jill commented. 'We can come back later and take her out for her walk.'

They switched off the lights and turned the *open* shop sign to *closed*. They were done for the day. They wouldn't reopen again that afternoon. The coffee shop was just yards away, barely any distance to walk at all. Edward and Jill wandered in. Jill was a regular of long standing. Edward now considered himself a regular too, even if this was still his first week working at the bookshop. He was now just about at the end of it. It hadn't been too bad. He'd rather enjoyed it in fact. Edward and Jill found a table to sit at. There were only a couple to choose from. Most of the customers just stopped for takeaway coffees and sandwiches, to have on the go in their lunch breaks of inadequate length. Edward and Jill were in no hurry. They'd reached a mutual decision to take the rest of the day off and wouldn't be returning to work at the bookshop.

'Tea or coffee or something else?' Edward asked, getting up to place their order.

'Coffee, I think, to wake me up,' Jill replied.

'Is a latte all right?' Edward continued.

'A latte would be perfect,' Jill said.

The coffee shop only had a very limited menu. They did a selection of savoury vegan baps, cookies, and cakes and not that much else. They also had a couple of salads for the healthier, more discerning diet. Everything was plant-based. Edward didn't ask Jill what she wanted. He simply ordered one of everything on the menu. He thought they could mix and match and share however they liked. What they didn't eat now they could save for later. Besides, Edward wanted to treat Jill. He wanted to show she was important to him. What better way than through generous portions of food.

'What are we having to eat?' Jill asked, suddenly aware Edward hadn't actually asked what she wanted.

'You'll have to wait and see,' Edward said.

He liked to gently tease her, as he had about their dinner date earlier in the week.

'I hope it's plenty. I'm actually quite hungry now,' Jill explained.

'That's probably a good thing,' Edward answered. 'As I've ordered everything they have.'

'What do you mean, everything they have?' Jill enquired.

'Exactly that. I've ordered one of everything on the menu,' Edward revealed. 'I want you to have a complete choice. Just tuck in however you feel like doing.'

'You're crazy.' Jill laughed.

'Not really, it's only a little menu, so it probably won't be very much at all,' Edward commented.

'It will be more than enough for me,' Jill said.

'Don't worry. We'll just keep anything we can't manage to eat now, to take home with us,' Edward said.

They proceeded to enjoy a delicious, snacky lunch together, washed down with more than one latte. Edward had been right. It was fun to order a selection and just dip in, Jill decided. When they'd finished, it seemed too soon to go straight back.

'Shall we go for a walk?' Jill suggested.

'Sounds like an excellent idea,' Edward agreed. 'We can walk a bit of our lunch off.'

They dropped off the food they hadn't eaten at the bookshop first. There wasn't actually that much. They'd done a very good job of finishing it. They then proceeded down Francis Street, in the direction of Victoria Park. Jill took Edward's arm. They looked like one of those old-fashioned couples, captured in a black and white photograph taken a century or so earlier, walking out together for the first time. Edward looked quite formal. He was after all something of a traditionalist. Jill was quietly feminist. She was confident she could convert Edward to her ways, given enough time. She too was willing to compromise to a degree. Returning to the joys of wine was her small concession to him.

It was a beautiful day. The sky above was clear and blue. The few white clouds of early morning had slowly dispersed or moved on. Edward and Jill could feel the warm sunlight on their skin. They found a park bench, where they could sit down. It was so quiet and relaxing they both felt their eyes slowly closing. It was the first week of work Edward had done for several months. He'd forgotten what it was like. It was actually fine, at least in this new job, but he felt quite tired all the same. Jill's eyes may have been closed, but it didn't stop her taking Edward's hand in hers. He didn't mind. He made no attempt to stop her. Indeed, it felt quite nice, he realised, with her soft, white flesh against his. Her touch was light at first. Slowly, she gripped him more tightly and snuggled closer into him. Anyone passing would have assumed they were partners or lovers of long standing. In fact, they were neither.

'So, how did you find your first week?' Jill eventually asked, without even opening her eyes.

'It was OK. I actually enjoyed it,' Edward admitted.

'It didn't make you want to go running back to Oxford then?' Jill continued.

'Not at all. I feel at home here, both in the shop and in your house,' Edward assured her.

'You're just being kind, like always,' Jill suggested.

'I promise you I wouldn't be here if I didn't want to be,' Edward insisted.

'That's good,' Jill replied. 'As long as you mean it.'

'I do. Now can I get you an ice cream or something?' Edward asked.

There was a small kiosk in the park, where they sold such things.

'I'm still pretty full after lunch, to be honest,' Jill said. 'But if you're having one, I'll join you, I suppose.'

'In weather like this, I'm definitely having one,' Edward announced.

'Just get me anything vegan. They may have a sorbet. If not, they'll definitely have a lolly,' Jill said.

'I'll get you the nicest thing they have,' Edward said. 'If I can't see anything suitable, I'll just come back,'

Edward eased his hand from Jill's tight grip and wandered over to the park refreshments kiosk. His eye was immediately drawn to a selection of high quality, locally made ice creams, including several flavours of sorbet. He chose the two that sounded the nicest, mango and blood orange. He was fond of both, so would just let Jill choose which she wanted and have the one that was left. That was the gentlemanly thing to do. Of course, he could have had an ice cream, made with rich clotted cream or similar. He could have done but for some reason, almost to his surprise, he was trying to respect Jill's vegan principles as far as he could. He certainly wasn't a vegan himself and would in all likelihood continue to eat meat and dairy products when out by himself. He realised he was much less likely to in Jill's presence. Edward took the two sorbets back to Jill and held them out for her to select the one most to her liking.

'I don't know,' she said. 'It's impossible to choose. I like them both.'

'Take the one you like best,' Edward told her. 'It's the lady's prerogative. I don't mind which I have.'

'OK, I'll have the mango then,' Jill said.

Mango was one of her favourite fruits, as it was his. That left Edward with blood orange, but he liked that just as much.

'Is that all right?' she asked, in a mildly timid voice.

'Of course, it is,' Edward said. 'If I was the tiniest bit bothered, I could get another mango one for myself. Besides, I love blood orange.'

They sat on the bench together and consumed their sorbets in the sunshine. Jill had a broad grin on her face. She felt much better than she had when she'd woken. Her hangover had as good as gone. The food, followed by a refreshing sorbet, had helped to revive her. Eventually, they moved on from the park and wandered across the main road to a spot where the coastal path ran along the top of the beach. They found another bench to sit on. They had views of the entire bay. It stretched out magnificently in front of them. With sunshine and blue sky above, it looked at its glorious best. Port Talbot stood to the east, Mumbles Pier and lighthouse to the west, as always. It was a view Edward had enjoyed many times since his arrival nearly three weeks earlier. He'd now been away that long, and he'd had almost no contact with Alice, except for the simple text he'd sent to tell her he'd be in touch when he was ready. It was something he knew he had to resolve eventually. He just remained in no hurry to do so. Partly because he still didn't know his own mind. He wondered if Jill was moving inexorably to making some kind of decision for him. He just hoped whatever decision he ultimately came to would be the right one.

'I've been as far as Mumbles Lighthouse in that direction,' Edward pointed with his finger. 'One day I'll walk to Port Talbot in the other, or at least as far as I can get to. It will be a nice challenge for an old man like me. My walking has definitely improved since I got here. I think in the last week, I've even started losing a bit of weight, since I stopped having all those cooked breakfasts and morning cakes.'

'You have lost weight,' Jill told him. 'It suits you. You're looking quite trim.'

A compliment from a woman was quite a rarity for Edward these days. He'd make sure to treasure it. He was occasionally told he had a dignified or distinguished manner to his demeanour. He was never complimented on his figure, which he'd rather allowed to spread outwards in the latter days of his financial work in London. He wasn't quite portly, but he was more than a fraction overweight. He was fully aware of that fact. It couldn't be denied. He was now being less sedate in his activities, however. He'd been rushing about, running errands for the bookshop, and taking Beti on her daily walks. It was perhaps starting to pay dividends. He'd noticed his trousers were no longer quite so tight, and he now wore his belt on a notch smaller than when he'd arrived. He'd just never thought anything of it, until Jill remarked as much.

'I don't know about that, but it's very nice of you to say,' Edward responded, looking very slightly embarrassed.

Back at the bookshop, Edward suggested Jill have a bit of time to herself, while he walk Beti round the block. Jill didn't refuse. She said she'd just read a book or watch some television for a bit. When Edward got back, she'd have a little look in the kitchen to see what they might have for their evening meal. Edward said that sounded like a splendid idea. He set off with Beti on what had now become a regular trek, down to the end of King Edward's Road, past St Helen's Rugby and Cricket Ground and car park, and into the bottom entrance of Singleton Park. He led Beti as far as Singleton Abbey and then crossed to where the park came out in Brynmill and the lower end of the Uplands. Edward meandered his ways through the familiar streets, tightly packed with terraced houses, that he'd known so well in his student days. When he reached Rhyddings Park Road, he began his journey back. He didn't immediately return to the bookshop. On his way, he stopped at an off-licence to pick up some wine. He felt sure Jill would want a glass on a Friday night, even if she'd been somewhat over refreshed the previous evening. He knew he would. He was right. After they'd finished eating, she was happy for him to open a bottle.

'Just a small one for me,' she said.

'Have as much or as little as you want,' Edward said. 'I've got another if we need it.'

'I'm still having flashbacks to last night and everything being rather hazy,' Jill laughed.

'You were a tad the worse for wear,' Edward agreed.

'Well, thanks for looking after me,' Jill said.

'I'm sure you'd have done the same for me,' Edward responded.

'You're far too dignified to get drunk,' Jill pointed out.

'I'm not sure about that. I'm just quite good at hiding it, after years of practice,' Edward commented.

They continued drinking and watching television together, until it was time to go to bed. Edward suddenly realised he hadn't done any drawing or writing that day. He was trying to do an hour or so every night. It could wait. He could pick it up over the weekend. It was only a hobby after all. It wasn't something he had to do. He might also get a chance to try out his new camera, if they ended up somewhere nice. Whilst Edward had at least three glasses of wine, Jill struggled to make much impression on her second and eventually conceded defeat and passed it to Edward.

'I'm feeling very sleepy,' she said. 'Can you tuck me in again.'

'If you like,' Edward replied.

Jill got up and led Edward to her bedroom, where she changed into her bed clothes in front of him. When she appeared comfortably settled, Edward started to move towards the door to switch off her light.

'Don't leave me just yet,' Jill interrupted him. 'In fact, you can get in with me if you want.'

She pulled back the clothes, inviting Edward to join her. He looked a bit tentative and unsure.

'What are you waiting for? Don't be scared. I won't bite. We don't have to do anything,' Jill said, looking amused at Edward's apparent unease and uncertainty.

'I suppose I could then,' Edward agreed, slowly taking off his trousers and socks, until he was wearing only his T-shirt and underpants.

He got in beside her. She turned towards him and kissed him on the lips. Their tongues didn't touch. Instead, she cuddled up close to Edward and fell asleep. They lay together all night, but as promised nothing happened. Edward still sensed things would never be quite the same between them again. Their relationship had changed for good. What would Alice have said if she could have seen him, he wondered? It didn't really matter what she would have thought. After all she'd done much worse herself.

Day Twenty (Saturday)

Beti woke them up around seven-thirty in the morning. She then proceeded to make little whimpering noises at the bottom of the bed, to indicate she was hungry. Edward was slightly surprised to find himself in Jill's bed, but he didn't say anything. It was probably best not to draw attention to their new domestic arrangement.

'In a minute, Beti, I'm just waking up,' Jill told her faithful dog. 'So, who's opening the shop today?' she asked, turning to Edward.

'No one,' he announced, cheerfully.

'What do you mean, no one?' Jill repeated, sounding mystified by what Edward had to tell her.

'Exactly what I said. Neither of us. We're having the day off,' Edward said.

'But it's Saturday, our busiest day, and we had yesterday afternoon off,' Jill reminded him.

'I know. Don't worry. We'll leave a sign on the door saying we're on holiday,' Edward explained. 'I've actually been thinking we shouldn't open at weekends. Monday to Friday is plenty for us at our advancing ages. Instead, we'll increase our web presence and concentrate more on the mail order side of the business. Long term, we can sell more books on the internet through specialist bookselling sites than to customers in the flesh. We just don't get enough of them in anyway, to justify being there most of the time. I was also thinking I could set up an *eBay* shop, to boost sales. Eventually, we could just open the shop by appointment only.'

'I'm glad you've got it all worked out. At least one of us has. You're in charge now. Do what you want, dear. And I'm not being sarcastic either. I mean that in a nicest way possible,' Jill told him. 'So, if we're not getting up, I may as well roll over and go back to sleep.'

'You can't do that. I have a busy day planned for us,' Edward said.

'How so?' Jill asked.

'We're going to have a day of culture,' Edward declared.

'Sounds interesting. So, what will that involve?' Jill enquired.

'I thought we could start at the Glynn Vivian Gallery in the morning, get a spot of lunch somewhere, then do the Dylan Thomas Centre and the two museums in the afternoon,' Edward revealed. 'What do you say?'

'I've not been to any of them in a while. That's absolutely fine, as long as I get to choose where we have lunch,' Jill answered.

'Of course, where would you like to go?' Edward wondered.

'There's a little vegan place in the market. It's only small but they do amazing coffee and donuts,' Jill said.

'Do they have anything savoury too?' Edward asked.

'Oh yes, a few things like vegan pies and pasties. But their donuts are simply divine. They make them fresh on the premises every morning,' Jill said.

'A pasty and a donut would suit me perfectly,' Edward said. 'So, shall we get ready? Do you want to shower first, or do you want me to?'

'You go ahead,' Jill said. 'I'd better get Beti something to eat.'

'Don't worry about her walk. I'll take her out when we get back,' Edward promised. 'It will help me walk off any donuts I have,' he laughed.

Edward and Jill set off just after nine-thirty, leaving Beti to mind the bookshop and home. They intended to get to the Glynn Vivian in time for opening at ten. They wanted to beat the crowds, not that they were expecting any. They knew perfectly well they'd probably be browsing the exhibits virtually on their own. That was the best way, without distraction and interference. Edward couldn't think of a better way to spend a Saturday morning than in an art gallery with Jill. He'd value her take on the paintings he'd already seen several times. Would she like the same ones? Would she prefer different ones?

Edward and Jill took their time looking around. They went from room to room, saying what they did and didn't like about each exhibit. They did the rooms on the ground floor first and then proceeded upstairs. They paused longest at the striking images of the rugged, working faces in the depictions of the industrial landscapes and past of Wales, just as Edward had himself when visiting alone. They were still the works Edward liked best and moved him most, even on his third visit. Jill agreed. They left her moved too. Life had certainly been hard for those people not so very long ago in time. It was unlikely they had Saturdays off, to look round galleries and museums. They almost certainly would have had no such thing. They probably worked twelve-hour days during the week, with Saturday afternoon off for sport at best, and Sunday off to attend church. That was their lot. It was indeed a harsh, grim existence, not for the weak or faint-hearted.

Finally, they finished on the top floor with the fine porcelain and ceramics and interactive visual displays. Edward took photographs on his phone of a number of his favourite works. He hoped they might inspire his own humble artistic efforts. He hadn't brought his new camera. He'd bring that into use another day. They didn't stop for a tea or coffee, even though Edward was tempted. He was more tempted by the thought of a donut, so they proceeded straight to Swansea Market and the vegan café Jill knew there. They'd had a light breakfast and decided to opt for an earlyish brunch/lunch.

The café in the market was pleasingly quiet. They had no trouble finding a seat. Edward observed most customers were just after takeaway coffees and donuts, just as they were at the vegan coffee shop round the corner from the bookshop. Edward was instantly struck by the amazing range of vegan donuts on display. They were all kinds of flavours – chocolate, pistachio, lemon, blueberry, strawberry, cherry and more. They looked fabulous. It was almost impossible to choose one. Eventually, Edward ordered a vegan pasty, a chocolate and hazelnut donut, and a latte. Jill ordered a falafel salad, a lemon donut, and a fruit tea. Edward paid, even though he'd paid for lunch the previous day. He insisted Jill put her purse away. The food barely took any time to come out. Edward made quick work of his pasty. He wanted to get straight to his donut, which appeared to be staring appetisingly at him, demanding to be eaten.

'You're right about these donuts. They're absolutely delicious,' Edward said. 'My God, I'll want one every day, until I've tried all the flavours.'

'You won't keep losing weight then,' Jill joked. 'Have another one now if you want just in case you're not back for a day or two.'

'I am tempted,' Edward admitted.

'Go on, you know you want to,' Jill encouraged him.

'OK then,' Edward gave in. 'Do you want one?'

'No thanks, I'm absolutely stuffed,' Jill said.

Edward went back to the counter and bought himself another donut. He was almost apologetic in doing so. He was told they were for sale by the box if he wished to buy that many. He'd better not, he said. Two was probably plenty. This time he chose blueberry. It was looking longingly and temptingly out from behind a glass cabinet, he thought. If anything, it was even nicer than the chocolate one. What had Jill done to him? She should never have brought him here. He'd be back every time he came into the shopping centre in future. He might even have to forsake poor Meredith's coffee shop. He couldn't do that. He'd just have to take it in turns. That was the only fair thing to do from now on. Most mornings, he'd be too busy in the shop for donuts or cakes anyway. All in all, that was probably for the best if he wanted to maintain his slight weight loss.

'I'm surprised you didn't buy a box,' Jill teased, as they left the market.

'I could have been persuaded,' Edward confessed. 'It was probably a good job she didn't press too hard. I might have, except I didn't want to be carrying them around with me.'

Edward and Jill proceeded up Oxford Street, before turning right into Wind Street, after passing Castle Square. It was the first time he'd been into the shopping centre with Jill, he realised. He'd walked the length of Wind Street a number of times by himself. It was better with someone else, particularly a female of comparable age, if a few years younger. They walked hand in hand. Edward had got used to that, even if he didn't know exactly what it meant. Were they girlfriend and boyfriend now, or were they still just good friends? They'd spent the previous night together in the same bed, though nothing sexual had taken place. Even so, did that mean it was definitely over with his wife, Alice? Edward wasn't quite sure. They arrived at the Dylan Thomas Centre and went in. They started looking around. Jill looked enthralled.

'He's my literary hero. I love it here,' she said, as they examined the various exhibits, highlighting the life and work of the late, great Welsh writer.

There was a black and white photograph of Dylan, with his wife Caitlin.

'That could be us,' Edward joked.

'Except they weren't very kind to each other,' Jill pointed out. 'We'd never be like that.'

'Does that mean we're now an item?' Edward asked.

'Figure it out,' Jill replied, and then laughed.

Edward let his question pass. It would become apparent soon enough, he thought.

'He looked much older than his thirty-nine years,' Edward commented, looking at one particularly bloated picture of the poet.

'That's what happens when you drink too much,' Jill observed. 'Besides, everyone looked older then. They all wore the same clothes as their parents. There was no youth fashion.'

'Even in the photographs of Dylan in his twenties, he's basically wearing what I am, and I'm sixty,' Edward pointed out.

'And Caitlin's wearing summer dresses like mine,' Jill noted.

'I guess not everything has changed,' Edward agreed. 'Though the photos do make it look so long ago. I guess it is nearly seventy years now.'

'Dylan will always be thirty-nine. He'll never get any older,' Jill said, with a hint of poignancy in her voice. 'I suppose that's part of the enigma and mystique around him.'

'That and his love of Wales and alcohol,' Edward added.

On the way out, Edward insisted that Jill select a book from the Dylan Thomas bookshop he could buy for her.

'I've probably got most of them,' she said.

'You can't have all of them,' Edward objected.

Eventually, he persuaded her to have one. He was happy now. He liked to be able to treat her. He liked to spend money on her. One day, he'd buy her something really special when he knew her better. They walked slowly along the banks of the River Tawe towards the City Museum.

'It's lovely here,' Jill said. 'I'd walk here more often if I only had the time.'

'You will be able to in the future,' Edward assured her. 'You won't have to work so hard when the mail order really starts to take off. We'll both be able to work part-time.'

'What happens if it doesn't take off?' Jill pressed.

'It will, but if it doesn't, it's not the end of the world,' Edward said.

'It will be if we're penniless,' Jill insisted.

'We'll never be that,' Edward told her.

'How can you be so sure?' Jill asked.

Perhaps it was as good a time as any to tell her, even if it was sooner than he intended. She should know that she'd never be destitute, as long as Edward had a part to play in her life.

'Let's just say I was quite good at my work, and I was quite well off when I retired,' Edward said.

'How well off is well off?' Jill pressed.

'Some might say rich,' Edward replied, remaining a little vague.

'Rich? Does that mean hundreds or thousands in the bank?' Jill wondered.

'Millions if you must know, or a few million at least. I couldn't say for sure without checking,' Edward said.

Jill's face was a picture. She looked quite aghast.

'Well, the house is probably worth between one and two million,' Edward continued. 'Then I have investments and savings. I had a very generous golden handshake when I left. Exactly what it all amounts to is anyone's guess. I'd have to sit down and work it out. Besides, half will probably have to go to Alice in time. Even then, I'll never have to work again if I don't want to. I'll never want for money in any way. I'm a man of fairly simple tastes anyway. Apart from the house, I'm not extravagant. I doubt I'll ever get to spend most of it.'

'Why didn't you tell me?' Jill asked.

She didn't look angry, just curious.

'I didn't want you to treat me or see me any differently,' Edward explained. 'I genuinely want to make the bookshop a success for you. Of course, the money doesn't matter to me. It never has. But I want to show you that it could be a successful business in its own right, with a bit of effort and some better organisation. It's given me a hobby and an interest, something to spend my time on, which I appreciate. Most of all, I just wanted to help you out. It's my way of saying thank you for the friendship you've extended to me.'

'That's very sweet of you,' Jill nodded, seemingly accepting Edward's explanation for not telling her sooner. 'I think I understand why you didn't mention it now.'

'In fairness, I haven't told anybody,' Edward said. 'You're the only one I have told.'

'Now I feel like a gold-digger,' Jill said.

'You're not that and never will be,' Edward protested. 'That's exactly why I didn't tell you before. I thought it best you didn't know.'

'Does that mean we can go on holiday?' Jill asked. 'I haven't had a holiday in years.'

'It means we can do whatever you like,' Edward said.

They continued hand in hand to the City Museum. Edward took one or two photographs as they went. It was a pity there was no one to take one of them together. Perhaps he'd ask someone at some point, he decided. Inside the museum, it was decidedly quiet. It always had been on Edward's many visits as a student. The quietness was one of the things he liked about it. That and the fact it hadn't changed much in forty years. It had remained pretty much as it always had been. Edward suspected one of the upstairs rooms had been refurbished during that time, but he wasn't even certain of that. It could just be a case of his memory letting him down. He was aware it did more and more as the years passed and he got older, and the memories slowly grew fainter.

'We used to come here on school trips, but I haven't been here for years,' Jill remarked. 'It isn't very different to how I remember it. I thought it might have been modernised a bit since then.'

'That's why I like it,' Edward explained. 'I'm a Luddite at heart. I always have been. Change is the Devil's work,' he claimed, but in only semi seriousness.

'That's why you feel so at home here. You could be an exhibit yourself,' Jill laughed.

'I actually wouldn't mind that,' Edward agreed. 'If I wasn't already working with you at the bookshop, I think a little, part-time job here might suit me down to the ground.'

'I do believe you're right,' Jill said, giving his hand an affectionate squeeze.

They browsed in the costume room first, before continuing into Edward's favourite room, which housed the natural history exhibits. He pointed out the taxidermy examples of British wildlife that he liked, including a faded stoat and a polecat, that had seen better days. As a vegan, Jill was less impressed.

'They look a hundred years old and full of moths,' she joked.

They passed the famous wooden carving of the Swansea Devil, and impressive black and white photographs of the West Coast of Wales from the early twentieth century, before continuing into the ceramics room, and then to the palaeontology room. They finished in the upstairs gallery, which celebrated the cultural past and social history of Wales. An impressive penny-farthing bicycle hung on the wall. A gleaming, miniature steam engine sat proudly behind a glass case. Finally, they came to the rural, Welsh, cottage kitchen. The old lady in traditional Welsh costume was still sat at her table, just as she'd been sitting patiently for the last forty years. She hadn't moved once in all that time. It remained Edward's favourite single exhibit in the whole museum, even more than the dusty, stuffed animals, and the one he remembered best. It remained a fitting tribute to the rural, village past of Wales in the pre and early industrial age.

'I like to wonder what she's thinking,' Edward remarked to Jill.

'She has a pretty impressive spread of food laid out in front of her,' Jill observed.

The kitchen table indeed boasted a plentiful supply of bread, meat, eggs, cheese, and vegetables, among other items of farming produce.

'She does, but I doubt it was always like that, except in the years when the harvest was good,' Edward said. 'When it wasn't, they probably had very little to eat and went without.'

'I expect some sadly starved in rural communities back then,' Jill speculated.

'I'm sure they did. It makes us realise how very fortunate we are today. We never go hungry,' Edward said.

'Thank goodness,' Jill agreed, as they made their way back down the stairs to the main entrance and exit.

She found their next destination, the National Waterfront Museum, a little more to her taste and liking. It had the modern feel absent from the City Museum, not that she hadn't enjoyed that, in its own slightly musty way. She had enjoyed it, in Edward's pleasant and informed company. Its dated ambience and atmosphere were still appealing in a fashion, even to Jill.

'The marina looks lovely at this time of year,' she commented, as they examined the historic ships moored to the harbourside. 'The water looks so enticing I could almost get in.'

'I wouldn't do that, but we could go out on a boat one day,' Edward suggested. 'The thought had already crossed my mind.'

'I'll hold you to it,' Jill declared.

Inside the museum, they toured the main upstairs gallery first, celebrating the maritime and cultural history of Wales, before admiring the larger industry-related exhibits on the ground floor. Edward took a selection of photographs on his phone, to add to several he'd taken earlier at the older museum. When they'd finished looking, they stopped at the museum café and shared a well-deserved pot of tea. They took the coastal route home, continuing to the end of the marina and harbour, and then past the prison and civic buildings, before joining Oystermouth Road. A little way further, they passed Alan and Gwen's guesthouse on the other side of the road. They crossed over shortly after and turned right into St Helen's Road. They took a small detour, so Edward could point out the house on the corner of Rodney Street, where he and Angela had shared a house with fellow students in their final year of university.

'I'd like to see a photo of you then,' Jill said.

'I had more hair,' Edward noted. 'I'd kept it quite long in the seventies, but by the early eighties I used to have one of those public schoolboy haircuts. It was short at the back and sides and long on top. It was fashionable in those days, as it is again now, I suppose. In most of my graduation pictures, my fringe is falling into my eyes. I have no idea why I didn't get it cut.'

'I bet you were very cute,' Jill said, giving him a little hug.

'Hmmm, I doubt it,' Edward replied, remaining unconvinced but nonetheless pleased by her unlikely suggestion to the contrary.

They continued back down Victoria Avenue, past the Brangwyn Hall, and then along Francis Street, with Victoria Park on their left, until they arrived back at the bookshop. Edward decided he wouldn't stop and get comfortable. He'd take Beti straight out for her walk. He knew if he sat down, he wouldn't want to get up again, after all the walking they'd already undertaken. It was better to get everything done, and then he could relax with a glass of wine in front of the television with Jill later.

'Are you sure you don't want a cup of tea at least before you go?' Jill asked.

'I'm sure,' Edward said.

'Well, thanks for a lovely day,' Jill said, giving him a light but affectionate kiss on the cheek.

'I hope you enjoyed it,' Edward said.

'I certainly did,' Jill assured him. 'I'll find something for our tea, while you're out.'

Edward was amazed how quickly they'd come to resemble a happily married couple. It had only been a week, but he felt entirely comfortable there in Jill's house with her. Edward led Beti to the end of King Edward's Road, right into Finsbury Terrace and left onto St Alban's Road, where he recalled other friends had once lived. At the end of Park Place, they entered Brynmill Park and did a complete circuit of the woodland and lake, before heading out. They walked up Alexandra Terrace, into Rhyddings Terrace, and eventually back to where they'd started via Rhyddings Park Road. It had been an approximately circular tour.

Edward picked up another bottle of wine on the way, although he knew he had at least one left over from the previous night. With two sharing, it was easy to get through it, he reflected. A bottle was only a couple of generous glasses each, he observed. It wasn't that much, he supposed, though he was aware he tended to have the lion's share of each bottle. Jill wasn't a huge drinker. She sipped, while he quaffed. Perhaps she was just drinking to humour him, though she appeared to quite enjoy a glass of wine. Edward hoped it wasn't doing him any great harm. He wasn't that bothered if it was. He was in that great tradition of educated, middle-class folk, who had a tendency to slightly overindulge in alcohol. Edward had cut back since the diagnosis of a minor heart condition. He doubted that he'd ever stop completely.

Edward spent a little time alone in his bedroom, working casually on his drawing and writing, as Jill prepared their evening meal. Later, he found himself sitting next to her on the couch in front of the television. Edward wasn't really watching what was on. They each had a glass of wine in their hand. Jill snuggled into him. He made no attempt to stop her or move away. It had become the norm in their relationship. He'd allowed that boundary to be crossed and broken. There was no putting it back in place. They'd reached a level of familiarity, that was beyond normal friendship. When it neared midnight and it was time to go to bed, Edward made a move towards his own bedroom. Jill pulled him back.

'No, you don't, not tonight,' she said. 'You can stay in my bed.'

Edward didn't protest, as she led him into her bedroom. She turned the light off.

'Take your clothes off,' she whispered.

Edward did what he was instructed, and Jill did the same. He got in beside her.

'Hold me,' she said, as she turned to face him.

Edward could feel her naked skin next to his. He was naked too. His hands accidentally brushed against her generous breasts. It was enough to arouse him, as he hadn't been aroused in many months with his wife, Alice. Jill kissed him on the lips. This time her tongue entered his mouth. It felt warm and wet and tasted good. Jill pressed into him. He pressed back into her. She lightly touched his penis. He made no attempt to stop her.

'Make love to me, Edward,' she said, guiding him inside her.

It was an unexpected but very pleasant end to their wonderful day together. The genie was now well and truly out of the bottle, Edward realised, and couldn't be put back. Afterwards, neither of them said a word. They just curled up quietly and fell asleep. Edward didn't feel that bad about what had happened, even though it was technically adultery. It was nothing Alice hadn't already done presumably many times over.

Day Twenty-One (Sunday)

It was Sunday morning, and Edward woke early, shortly after seven. Jill was still asleep beside him. Beti hadn't come to disturb them yet. She was in her basket in the kitchen. Edward lay awake thinking. He was suddenly struck by the enormity of what had happened the previous night. Had it really taken place, or had he simply imagined it? He had memories of he and Jill making love. He realised he was still naked, and Jill was naked alongside. So, it had happened. There was no denying it. They had been intimate together. They had consummated their friendship, so it was no longer simply friendship. It was now something more than that. Like it or not, Edward was in a relationship, and not with his wife. He was in a relationship with someone else. He was in a relationship with Jill. Jill was now his girlfriend or his partner. He could call it what he wanted, but it made no real difference. The facts were evident. They'd taken things to another stage; one he'd never really anticipated. Even after he'd moved into her house and started work in the bookshop, he'd kidded himself they were just friends. He was a married man after all. He'd denied his true feelings. There was a line he'd never cross, he thought. Except he had crossed it. They'd crossed it together, and there was no returning to how things were.

Edward could no longer pretend things hadn't changed. Everything had changed, finally and forever. He understood there was no going back, neither literally nor metaphorically. Things had fundamentally altered. The dynamics of his life and relationships had inexorably shifted. Things could never be the same again. In an instant, he understood the decision he'd been putting off, the one for some reason he'd refused to make, had now been made for him. That was it. Everything was now decided. His mind wouldn't be changed. He'd remain here in Swansea with Jill. He wouldn't be returning to Oxford anytime soon. He wouldn't be heading back, to reunite with Alice, in a matter of weeks or even months. That wouldn't happen. He'd stay where he was for the foreseeable future, perhaps now for years or even forever. It was as good as over with Alice. Jill was now his new partner. He'd reside with her permanently or for as long as she wanted him to.

It made perfect sense to him now. He realised it was what he'd wanted all along but had been too scared to admit. He'd liked Jill from day one and perhaps she'd liked him too. He'd been in denial. Perhaps because he was married, she'd been in denial also. They were no longer in denial. It was out in the open. The cards were on the table. Passions had been aroused. Intimacy had taken place. There was no longer room in Edward's life for Alice. She'd been unfaithful to him with Paul. She'd chosen to wreck their marriage. Edward considered he'd always been a good husband to her, or an adequate one at least. She'd never gone without. She'd never wanted for anything. She'd repaid his generosity and decency by having an affair.

That wasn't gratitude, as far as Edward was concerned. He'd given her a lavish home and a very comfortable lifestyle; one she'd never have enjoyed otherwise. She'd chosen to throw it in his face and humiliate him. It was true she was a very glamorous and attractive woman but looks didn't mean everything. At the end of the day, they counted for little or nothing. What he had, with a decent, honest person like Jill, meant so much more to him. The last few weeks had taught him he didn't actually need the grand life he'd enjoyed back in Oxford. He was better suited to a simple, more mundane existence. Now he'd found that, he had no intention of letting it go. He had no intention of letting Jill go either. He hoped Alice would be understanding of that and happy with her own choice in Paul. Edward wished her no harm. Now he'd found happiness, he only hoped for the best for her too.

Edward was a kind and honourable man. He was determined to still do the right thing by Alice. He'd make all the necessary arrangements, to ensure her financial security and future were looked after. He'd allow her to remain in the house. She could stay there for the duration of her lifetime, until it eventually passed to Victoria and Henry to share the proceeds equally between them. Edward and Alice had never had children together, even if Edward had wanted to add to his brood. He'd give her a fair and considerate divorce settlement, such that she'd have no reason to try and drag him through the courts to get more. He'd save them both that particular embarrassment. Once he'd collected the things he needed, he'd rarely return to Oxford. He'd begin a new life here in South Wales. He'd invite Victoria and Henry to stay whenever they wanted. He'd slowly pass on more of his considerable wealth to them, his daughter and son. It might enable Victoria to work a little less hard and Henry to eventually settle down.

Edward resolved to ring Alice in the week, to tell her what he'd decided. He'd make his announcement over the phone. He'd inform her of the decision he'd finally reached. He hoped she'd accept it. He imagined she would. It would be better if it fitted in with her plans too, and she was as content to be with Paul, as Edward was to be with Jill. When he'd made his indecently hurried exit from Oxford, he'd have earnestly wished for nothing more than to learn Alice's relationship with Paul had hit the buffers or was on the rocks. Now, he hoped for the opposite. He trusted it hadn't cooled since Edward's hasty departure. It was better for all concerned if they both had new partners that they were happy with.

Edward was no longer jealous. Naturally, he had been at first, at the thought of another man with his wife. He'd now got over that. He had Jill. What Alice did with Paul was her business. He didn't really want to know, even if he eventually returned to collect his things to find Paul living in the big house. It wouldn't have surprised Edward. In fact, it would have been entirely natural. Why would they wish to live elsewhere? It was one of the best residences in the area. Who wouldn't have taken it with open arms given the opportunity?

Of course, Edward knew a phone call alone wouldn't be enough. He'd have to return at some point, to face Alice in the flesh and thrash out all the fine details person to person. Now, it was Edward hoping there wouldn't be a scene. He knew he didn't have to tell her about Jill, but not to do so would be dishonest. Alice had told him about Paul. Edward would do the same. He had nothing to hide or be ashamed of. He'd gone away because of his wife's infidelity, where he'd happened to meet someone else. That was the long and short of it. Nothing was planned. He hadn't gone away with that on his mind, far from it. If anything, the opposite was true. Edward had planned to spend the time alone. By chance, he'd met someone else, who he happened to get on with.

When Jill eventually woke up, they made love again. This time Edward took the opportunity to explore her body much more fully than the first time and she his in return. He could no longer argue it had been a one-off or a mistake or an accident. It had gone beyond that. It had been none of those things. It had been a very deliberate act on both of their parts.

It had been a calculated expression of their growing affection. They wished to be intimate and be together. Edward was determined nothing would part them now. Jill felt the same. Their union had been confirmed both physically and emotionally. It was funny, Edward reflected. In many ways, Jill wasn't his usual type. It just showed true love didn't have types. Such ideas were outdated. Jill was now his type by default, or perhaps he simply no longer had a type. He only knew what he liked, and that person seemed to like him back. Maybe his type had just changed, and he hadn't realised that fact. One thing was certain. His type, if he still had one, was now Jill not Alice.

As Jill set about preparing breakfast, Edward went out to buy Sunday papers. He took Beti with him. The dog had remained remarkably well behaved, as Edward had frolicked with her mistress. Of course, Edward didn't like to think of it like that. That made it sound improper and indecent. Edward like to think of sex as a correct and natural expression of his love. He'd never indulged in it casually. It had always had to mean something, with someone he had serious intentions towards. Anything less was unacceptable to him and seemed a trifle sordid. His intentions towards Jill were entirely honourable. He could envisage marriage in the fullness of time if Jill wanted that formality. Somehow, he suspected she wouldn't be bothered with a piece of paper and that just being together would be commitment enough for her. He was content to be guided by her in that department. After breakfast, they sat at the kitchen table, discussing possible plans for the day. Only a week earlier, Edward had been moving his things in. That had been on a Sunday. A lot had happened in the week since. It almost shocked him to think about it, but in a good way. He was very happy how things had worked out.

'I know a nice little vegan café in The Mumbles which is open on a Sunday. How about I take you there? We can go in my car if you like,' Jill suggested.

'It might make a pleasant change from walking or taking the bus,' Edward agreed, realising it would be the first time he'd driven with Jill.

'We can stop at Clyne Gardens, to walk off our lunch, on the way back,' she continued.

'I used to go to Clyne Gardens on a Sunday sometimes with my first wife, Angela. It will be quite nostalgic and poignant for me to do the same with you,' Edward said.

'Sounds like that's decided then,' Jill announced. 'We'll bring Beti with us. I think they take dogs in the café. If not, we can always sit outside.'

Edward put down the newspaper he was reading, *The Observer*, and went to have a shower and get ready. As he was getting dressed, he made a mental note to take his new camera with him. He could take some pictures of views of both Mumbles and Clyne Gardens, in the late spring, early summer sunshine. The weather had turned pleasanter towards the end of the week. It had been quite wet the previous weekend and at the start of the week. It hadn't rained now for several days, even if Edward had spent most of his time working inside in the bookshop and out of the sun. It looked like the fine weather would continue for a few more days at least. It was up to Edward and Jill to make the most of it. Edward fully intended to do that, although it would be back to work for the pair of them the following day. They could always finish early again and do something afterwards if the mood took them. Business wasn't exactly thriving that it would matter all that much.

They went out shortly after eleven. Jill led Edward to where her car was parked. It was a small, blue *Fiat*. It had a slight dent down one side. Edward resolved to get it fixed for her. Perhaps it would be easier just to buy her a new car, however. He still had one back in Oxford, which was bigger and newer. She could just have that. He might collect it when he finally returned. Jill's car was a little messy on the inside, for Edward's personal taste. Whilst she'd tidied the house in readiness for his arrival, she'd clearly forgotten to tidy the car. As they got in, she muttered some apology about its state, promising to sort it soon.

'Don't worry, I'll clean it for you tomorrow, if you let me,' Edward said. 'I'll give it a full valet. It will be as good as new,' Edward promised.

'You can if you want to, but you really don't have to,' Jill responded, happily.

Edward did want to. It went against his natural sense of order, to allow it to remain in the state it was in, although it would do for now. He was slowly learning to be more relaxed about such things. It wouldn't have done for Alice, it amused Edward to think. She'd have refused to get in. It might have spoiled an expensive, designer dress she was wearing. That would never have done. She'd have insisted on ordering a taxi instead or perhaps a limousine.

As Jill drove, Edward enjoyed the familiar views of Swansea Bay. He could tell Jill wasn't a natural driver and didn't drive all that often. A couple of times she slipped gear and she stalled once at traffic lights. It didn't matter. Edward was content just to be driven by her, as they passed all the sights and landmarks he knew so well. They'd come back vividly to the forefront of his mind since his return to the city of his degree. His memory had been jogged. Each one was now engrained there, as if he'd never been away - St Helen's Rugby and Cricket Ground, Swansea University campus, Singleton Park Boating Lake, Blackpill Lido, West Cross and finally The Mumbles itself.

Jill found somewhere to park. They then proceeded to the café she recommended. She'd only been once before, but she said it was nice. Edward was happy to be guided by her. He couldn't quite believe that in a week he'd gone from eating sausage and bacon to practically being a vegan. Even after moving in, he'd initially continued to eat eggs and dairy products. Now, he was barely doing that. It was easier just to eat whatever Jill had, for convenience if nothing else. He'd made no conscious decision to become a vegan. It was just simpler to eat the same things. It was also partly out of respect for Jill's principles, he realised. He had no wish to offend her. He liked animals himself. Perhaps it was time he stopped eating them. Edward had a feeling that whilst he'd steadfastly maintain he was still a carnivore and no vegetarian or vegan or anything like it, in reality he would be as good as one. He'd be a vegan in everything but name. Remarkably, the thought didn't actually bother him too much.

When Edward arrived in Swansea, the thought of giving up meat and cheese would have been abhorrent to him. It no longer felt like a consideration or a sacrifice even, as he'd just eat whatever Jill ate and drink the same too. As it happened, what she ate was plant-based, so by default he'd be a plant-based eater also. It wasn't as hard as he expected. In fact, it felt entirely natural to him, just as making love to her the previous night and in the morning had felt.

The café was in a road parallel to the main Mumbles shopping street. It wasn't one Edward knew well. It was unlikely he'd have been passed it by accident. He'd have needed to know it was there and consciously sought it out. They found a table to sit at. Beti was so well behaved no one seemed to notice her presence. She sat quietly under the table, whilst Edward and Jill perused the menu. Edward ordered deep-fried tofu, whilst Jill ordered one of their health bowls, packed with nutritious vegetable and salad goodies.

'At least, you'll have room for a cake afterwards,' Edward remarked. 'They look delicious.'

They did indeed, and Edward liked a cake. He'd certainly make sure he had room for one himself and he'd try and persuade Jill to have one at the same time. After they finished eating, they did the customary Mumbles walk down to the pier and lighthouse. They did it at a leisurely pace. Edward took the opportunity to try out his new camera, pausing occasionally to take a couple of photographs. The bay cycle path was busy with other Sunday afternoon strollers and cyclists. Edward and Jill held hands as they walked. They felt very happy in each other's company. Oxford and thoughts of Alice now felt worlds away. Edward was no longer concerned what she might or might not be doing with Paul. It didn't matter to him anymore. He had what he wanted right there in front of him. Alice was his past. Jill was his future. He knew that now. He'd always known it in fact since he first met Jill. That was why things had progressed as they had. That was why he'd gone back to the shop after his first visit. That was why he'd offered to take her dog, Beti, for walks. That was why he'd agreed to move out of the guesthouse and in with her. That was why he'd taken a job in the bookshop. It all fitted neatly into its proper place in the scheme of things. He'd done it all for a reason, so they could be together, even if he hadn't known it at the time. He knew it now. It made perfect, logical sense to him.

When they returned to the car, they continued their journey back round the bay, stopping off at Clyne Gardens roughly halfway along Mumbles Road. There was a car park signposted for Clyne Valley Country Park, where they pulled in and parked. They just had a short distance to walk back, past the pub where the week before Edward and Beti had enjoyed lunch, to reach the gardens. Edward had still been a meat eater then. He couldn't really say that anymore. Jill had accidentally converted him, or maybe it had been deliberate on her part. Maybe she'd had everything planned all along. Women could be quite devious like that. Maybe one day she'd tell him how clever and calculating she'd been. Edward didn't mind if that was the case. He'd been a more than willing co-conspirator in their mutual game. He'd been very happy to go along with it at every stage. It had been his choice too, and his choice was turning out to be a good one. He was confident he'd finally made the right decision.

They took the same route through Clyne Gardens as Edward had alone with Beti, following the watercourse up through the ornamental and bog gardens, until they eventually reached the Japanese Bridge, where Edward stopped to take pictures. Jill didn't remark on his new camera. Now she was aware of his considerable wealth, nothing he had with him or purchased would surprise her. They proceeded back through the Bluebell Wood and Heather Beds, as Edward had the week before, until they reached the Italian Bridge and Clyne Castle, where they stopped on a bench to admire the view. Jill cuddled into Edward's shoulder. He placed his arm round her, pulling her body closely to him. Beti sat obediently at their feet. Jill turned to kiss Edward on the cheek.

'It's lovely here,' she said. 'We should come again.'

'We must,' Edward agreed. 'We can come as often as you like, through all the changing seasons.'

They sat for a while, happy just to enjoy the warmth of the sunshine and gentle, cooling, sea breeze on their skin. The combined distance of their two walks was several miles, Edward estimated. Their legs felt pleasantly weary, but they weren't exhausted. They let some time pass, until they felt sufficiently revived to continue their way down the sloping grass lawns and flower beds towards where they'd started out. At the bottom of the estate, they passed a mobile coffee van, where Edward bought himself and Jill an ice lolly each. The chill of the frozen fruit juice made their tongues tingle. It was a pleasingly invigorating experience, a small pleasure to be savoured, before slowly making their way back to the car.

Jill found a space near the bookshop to park. It was late afternoon, but it still felt warm. It could be June or July not late May. It felt like the height of summer. Edward had been away for exactly three weeks. In that time, he'd done many things and visited many places that were intricately tied to his past and his youth, his days as a student, and his early life with

Angela. Every day had brought something new to delight and excite him. He'd experienced fine days and wet ones. He'd reacquainted himself with the attractions Swansea had to offer, the museums and galleries, the parks and gardens, the shops, cafés and restaurants, the historic landmarks, the famous market. Many he'd come to take for granted forty years ago as an undergraduate. Familiarity hadn't exactly bred contempt but perhaps a sense of complacency on Edward's part. Now he approached everything again with fresh eyes and a new perspective, a new appreciation. He'd known the Swansea of forty years ago. Now he knew the Swansea of the modern day, a more multicultural, metropolitan city. It no longer had the feeling of a provincial town. It was an urban conurbation and would only continue growing and developing.

As good as it had been to revisit his memories of Swansea and familiarise himself with the city in the twenty-first century, it was the people he'd met along the way who'd really made his visit. He'd come on his own but hadn't felt alone. He'd been made to feel welcome everywhere he went. Friendship had been warmly extended to him, by Alan and Gwen at the guesthouse and by Meredith at the coffee shop, and most of all of course by Jill at the bookshop, who was now his new life partner, although they were yet to put an exact label on what they were to each other. Edward hadn't expected any of that. He'd fully anticipated spending his entire time away by himself, deep in his own thoughts, in his own little bubble of quiet reflection and contemplation, wondering what to do about Alice. In the event, he hadn't had to find an answer. An answer had duly become apparent. He'd just continued to happily muddle along, until a clear way forward had presented itself. Eventually it had.

When they got in, they sat down quietly in the lounge and shared a refreshing pot of tea together. Whilst Jill watched television and stroked Beti's thick coat, Edward retired to the peace of his bedroom for a little bit. He sat at his desk and opened his sketchbook. He began a new drawing. He realised he was drawing the small stretch of Swansea Bay that continued from Mumbles Beach to Mumbles Pier. He was doing it more or less from memory. It was a view he'd stared at many times over recent weeks. It remained engrained in recollections from the distant past, that his stay in Swansea had gently revived and brought back. He'd taken a few photographs earlier that day, to help jog his memory too. Gradually, the picture started to take form and shape, as he gave it more detail. He included a minute couple, walking a dog along the cycle path, as well as other tiny people. It was of course himself, Beti and Jill. They were so small, as to be barely visible. It didn't matter. Edward knew who they were. Once he'd finished the outline, Edward sat back to admire his handiwork.

He then put down his sketchbook and opened his notebook. He jotted down a few thoughts and observations from the day's walk along Mumbles seafront. He tried to express what he'd seen in words, the café-bars and restaurants, the ice-cream parlours, pier, amusement arcade, beach, sand, cyclists, dogs, walkers, locals, and holidaymakers, all merged together, walking en masse either in one direction or the opposite one. Some had been heading to the end. Others were on their way back, having already reached it. It was both a relaxed scene and a hectic one at the same time. It was a mix of contrasts, as perhaps the whole of Wales was itself, of urbanisation and stunning countryside.

Life too was a mix of contrasts, of ups and downs, Edward reflected. He'd had a happy childhood and adolescence in the Home Counties. He'd spent his formative years in Swansea, where he'd met Angela and formed his first serious relationship. He'd returned to Oxford, where Angela had launched a successful career in accountancy. Edward had commuted into London, where he'd become a high-flying financier and investment banker. For a while, everything he touched seemed to turn to gold. He'd become rich and it had enabled them to buy a big house in a village just outside Oxford. Eventually, they'd had children, a girl and a boy, Victoria and Henry. Happiness for the family hadn't lasted. Their world had fallen apart at Angela's cancer diagnosis and eventual premature death at only forty-five. Edward had been left to bring up his teenage children alone. He hadn't done a bad job. Eventually, he'd met Alice and in time they'd got married. Now he realised she'd been little more than a trophy wife. They'd been content for a while, until shortly after retirement he'd lost her to a younger man. Now, he in turn had found happiness again with Jill.

In truth, he'd had more ups than downs in his life. Angela's death had been the hardest to thing for him to deal with and recover from. Eventually, he had, although a small part of him had never quite come to terms with her death. At least he had twenty-five years or more of precious memories of them being together to look back on. He also had two offspring to remind him of her. He was determined he would see more of Victoria and Henry in the future. He'd do whatever it took to achieve that aim. He knew Jill would be welcoming, just as he would be with her daughter, Megan. He was happy to move on from Alice, with no hard feelings. He wished her only happiness in her life with Paul. A small part of him was happy for her. It made it easier for him to start afresh with Jill, with no sense of guilt or regret.

Edward jotted down some more thoughts. phrases and reflections in his notebook. They were beginning to form loose poems. A thought occurred to him. He could use the words to illustrate his drawings. It could make a little book in time. Some lines were short, some were long. One simply read: *The tide comes in.* It was coming in now for him, in a good way, he thought. This was what Sunday afternoons in retirement were about, he considered. It was as he'd always imagined them during his last few working years. Of course, technically he was no longer retired. He had a bookshop to run and manage. He'd continue to do so, whilst it amused him to and whilst Jill wanted to keep it going. He'd try to make it a success perhaps for a year or two, just to realise some of the potential he genuinely believed it had. Once Jill was satisfied that they'd taken it as far as they could, they'd close the shop and turn it into another room or even two perhaps. After that, they'd hopefully live out their retirement years happily together.

Edward had a feeling they wouldn't even bother to move, even though he could have bought a much bigger house for them. They were perfectly content where they were. It was near the shops, and it suited their modest needs. Perhaps in time, they'd look at that house in West Cross or Mumbles, overlooking the bay, he'd always dreamed of, but only if Jill wanted that too. He wouldn't press her if she preferred to remain in their present home.

Edward put down his pens and paper. He was already looking forward to a quiet evening in front of the television with Jill, probably with a glass of wine. His time away had been very good to him. Only three weeks earlier he'd set out in a hurry from Oxford, with no idea what the future held in store. Somehow, it had all worked out well. After many years away, he'd finally returned to Swansea and fallen in love with the city all over again. He knew he'd probably remain there now for the rest of his lifetime. Not only had he renewed his love affair with the city, by chance he'd also met and fallen in love with a new woman in his life.

Edward knew Angela would have approved of what he was doing and the fact that he was staying in Swansea with Jill. She'd have been happy with the decision he'd finally reached. He felt certain she'd have been pleased for him. Edward had always suspected she wouldn't have liked Alice too much. Angela would have found her a little cold and aloof. That wasn't the case with Jill, who was the exact opposite in temperament. Edward felt he and Jill were ideally suited.

Just then Edward's phone beeped. He looked at the screen. It wasn't Alice as he feared. Perhaps she'd given up trying to contact him. It was a text from Jill. It read simply: *I love you and thank you.* Edward typed *Thank you and I love you too*, and pressed send. He hoped if Angela was looking down on them, she'd have given them her blessing.

Printed in Great Britain
by Amazon

60896230R00147